## PRAISE FOR
## THE LOVE CODE

"This is a paradigm shift breakthrough, turns most conventional wisdom about how to achieve success on its head, and explains why so many things that have sounded good have failed to produce results over the last fifty years. I, for one, am 'all in'! I plan to live by and teach *The Love Code* from now on."
—Janet Attwood, *New York Times* bestselling author of *The Passion Test*

"*The Love Code* is a *game changer*! It's rare for a book to come along that's not only a great read, but that also fundamentally changes our perspective. The information and tools in these pages will radically transform your ability to create success in your life."
—Marci Shimoff, #1 *New York Times* bestselling author of
*Happy for No Reason, Love for No Reason,* and *Chicken Soup
for the Woman's Soul*

"Forget everything you thought you knew about creating success, and then buckle your seat belt and read this."
—Christopher Hegarty, DSc, paid consultant to more than 400 Fortune
500 companies, including Apple, CBS, and AT&T

"Valuable information for everyone to access. This book is in perfect harmony with ageless wisdom: In all ways, to thine own self be true. Seek your answers to life's questions from within, rather than from the world without."
—William A. Tiller, PhD, professor emeritus, Stanford University

"There is a constant global demand to find ways to better resolve universal success and health issues, especially if the answers are fast, easy, effective, and inexpensive. This book can help many who have a wide range of challenging personal success, health, interpersonal, and emotional issues. Sometimes the help will take only a few seconds. You doubt it? Just try it."
—Doris J. Rapp, MD, *New York Times* bestselling author of *Is This Your
Child?* and world renowned pioneer of environmental medicine

# THE
# LOVE CODE

# THE
# LOVE CODE

The Secret Principle *to*
Achieving Success *in* Life,
Love, *and* Happiness

Previously Published as *Beyond Willpower*

## ALEXANDER LOYD, PhD, ND

**HARMONY**
BOOKS · NEW YORK

*The Love Code teaches you certain spiritual and mental techniques, including hand positions, guided meditations, and affirmations, to support achieving abundance in your life. The program is not financial advice or financial education, nor does Dr. Alexander Loyd provide recommendations for specific financial decisions.*

Harmony Books is a registered trademark, and the Circle colophon is a trademark of Penguin Random House LLC.

Originally published in slightly different form in hardcover in the United States as *Beyond Willpower* by Harmony Books, an imprint of the Crown Publishing Group, a division of Penguin Random House LLC, New York, in 2015.

Grateful acknowledgment is made to *The Dallas Morning News* for permission to reprint an excerpt from "A Cell Forgets" by Sue Goetinck Ambrose (*The Dallas Morning News*, Oct. 20, 2004). Reprint by permission of *The Dallas Morning News*.

Library of Congress Cataloging-in-Publication Data is available upon request.

ISBN 978-1-101-90283-7
eBook ISBN 978-0-451-49603-4

Printed in the United States of America

Book design by LaTricia Watford
Cover design by Jenny Carrow

First Paperback Edition

To Hope!
Most of the beautiful things in my life
have bloomed through you, including the
information in this book. What began with so much
pain and heartache has now transformed my life
into "hope fulfilled," and beyond. If anyone benefits
from these pages, it would never have happened
without you. Thank you for putting up with me. I know
that's a full-time job.
I LOVE YOU!

# CONTENTS

## ACKNOWLEDGMENTS

A special thank you to Kathleen Hagerty—you helped me get this from my head and heart to the page and made it a BLAST! To Amanda Rooker—you took a very rough manuscript and created sense out of it; I couldn't have done this without you. To Harry, Hope, and George— thanks for putting up with all the note-taking and writing at weird times, and loving me through it all. To my agent, Bonnie Solow—all I can say is that you saved this book, and I will be forever grateful. You are the best! To Diana Baroni and the Random House team—thank you for all your wonderful work, and for giving me a vibrant, warm, and caring home. And to God, for giving me something to write about—I am yours!

# THE
# LOVE CODE

# THE GREATEST PRINCIPLE IN THE WORLD THAT ALMOST NOBODY KNOWS

I've been waiting twenty-five years to share this information with you. In my last book, *The Healing Code*, I shared the key to healing the source of almost any health issue. I believe that in these pages, you will find the key to happiness and success in every area of your life. I know that's a bold claim—hold me to it! In my experience, it's not a matter of whether this process will work for you; the only question is whether you will do it. If you do it, *it always works*. In fact, once you understand how it works, it's nearly impossible for it not to work.

Before we go any further, I'd like to ask you a question: What is your biggest problem or unrealized potential? What are you searching for? What is the number one thing in your life that needs to be pulled out of the pit, kicked off the couch, or have a magic wand waved over it? I would ask you not to read any farther until you have at least one thing in mind from your life that needs fixing—even if you've tried everything to fix it and nothing has ever worked. One thing that needs to be rescued from failure or mediocrity to roaring success.

I believe the Love Code is that magic wand you need. I know this claim sounds presumptuous, but I'm only saying it because I have watched it happen virtually 100 percent of the time with my private clients over the last twenty-five years. I believe you can apply the process outlined in this book to any aspect of your life and see it transform from a caterpillar to a butterfly.

Let me guess what's going through your mind right now: you're thinking, *I've heard that before.* In fact, you've heard it a hundred times, and for some of you, you've heard it so many times that you can't even believe that what I'm telling you is possible. *Yeah right, another magic bullet that cons me out of twenty-five bucks and leaves me right back where I started.* If that's what went through your head, I get it. I've been there myself. But I need to let you in on a secret about the success/self-help industry: it has a 97 percent failure rate.

## THE 97 PERCENT SELF-HELP FAILURE RATE

Most of us have read or have figured out on our own that the vast majority of success and self-help programs fail. If they worked, we wouldn't keep looking for a new one every year, would we? And this so-called industry (worth $10 billion annually in the United States alone)[1] would dry up, because if there were one program that really worked for everyone, we'd all be living happy, healthy, and fulfilled lives. For example, one of the top-selling nonfiction categories of books is weight loss. Now, who do you think buys the weight-loss books this year? Answer: The same people who bought them last year—because last year's books didn't work! But the secret isn't that most success and self-help programs fail—it's that *the success industry experts already know this*. And the failure rate is far worse than we thought.

According to industry insiders, the failure rate in the success industry (which includes books, lectures, workshops, programs, and more) is approximately 97 percent. Yes, you read that right—97 percent. My colleague and friend Ken Johnston ran the largest personal development seminar company in North America and has openly lectured for years about what most industry insiders will only whisper behind locked doors: that the average success rate is about 3 percent. From that successful 3 percent, they get enough testimonials for their marketing to portray a success machine that works for anyone and everyone. But *according to their own experience*, that isn't so.

What's even more interesting is that the vast majority of these programs follow the same basic blueprint:

1. Focus on what you want.

2. Figure out a plan to get there.

3. Put the plan into action.

That's it. Pick your program, book, doctor, or mentor, and chances are he or she will teach some version of that template. In fact, you can trace it back to the seminal self-help book *Think and Grow Rich* by Napoleon Hill, published in 1937, and it's been popularized by other books and programs for at least the past sixty-five years. Focus on the result you want, make a plan, and use your willpower to put that plan into action.

The formula makes sense, right? Of course it makes sense. It's what we've heard all our lives. Problem is, it won't work. According to the latest research out of Harvard and Stanford, which we'll cover in detail in chapter 1, this paradigm is not only ineffective, but for 97 percent of us it is a veritable blueprint for failure.

Why? The typical three-step self-help blueprint—determine what you want, make a plan, and work that plan until you achieve what you want—relies on two components: expecting an external end result (steps 1 and 2), and relying on the tool of willpower (step 3). As we'll learn in chapter 1, expectations inherently cause chronic stress until the end result is achieved or not—and medical science has proven repeatedly that stress is the clinical source of virtually every problem we can have in life and essentially guarantees failure. Depending on willpower (step 3) also virtually guarantees failure, because willpower depends on the power of the conscious mind. As we'll also discover in chapter 1, our subconscious and unconscious attitudes are literally a *million times* stronger than our conscious mind, so if our subconscious and unconscious directly oppose our conscious willpower for any reason, our conscious mind will lose every time. Furthermore, trying to "force" a certain result with willpower that our unconscious is blocking spikes your stress level—again, activating the cause of virtually every problem you can have in your life.

In other words, the reason why there has been a 97 percent failure rate for the past sixty-five years is that the accepted blueprint literally teaches failure. The students who used that process had simply learned what they were taught. Here's the clincher: if expectations inherently put us under stress, and using our willpower to achieve happiness and success is a million-to-one shot (and will result in even more stress), then this blueprint not only guarantees we won't have happiness and success long term, but also means that following it will make things *even worse* than if we had never tried it in the first place.

You may be wondering, *If this blueprint is a blueprint for failure, then why does it seem so right and natural to me?* There are three reasons:

1. **It's how you're wired.** Focusing on the end result comes from your hardwired programming, otherwise known as your

stimulus/response or seek pleasure/avoid pain programming.
It's part of your survival instinct, and it's what you used
almost exclusively during the first six or eight years of your
life: want ice cream cone, plan to get ice cream cone, go get ice
cream cone. That's why it feels so natural. The big problem is
that as adults, we're not supposed to live this way unless our
life is in immediate danger. After around ages six to eight,
we're supposed to start living according to what we know is
right and good, by and large regardless of the pain or pleasure
involved. (I'll explain more about this in chapter 1 as well.) So
in essence, if we live by this blueprint as adults, we are acting
like five-year-olds and don't even know it.

2. **It's what you see everyone else doing.** In other words, this
blueprint is what you've seen modeled as the right approach in
almost every context: you see something you want, you figure
out how to get it, and you use your willpower to go get it. It's
modeled for you by your peers, your teachers, and your parents.

3. **It's what the experts have been teaching for the last sixty-five
years.** As I mentioned previously, this blueprint has formed
the basis of virtually every self-help bestseller or program for
nearly seven decades.

The typical methodology of today's self-help and success programs
is not only outdated, it was defective to begin with. But I don't really
need statistics or studies to tell me pursuing an end result with my
willpower is a blueprint for failure. I know it from experience.

About twenty-five years ago, I was working as a counselor for
teenagers and their families to help them stay on the right path
and become successful in life. I was trained in this typical self-help

blueprint, and I had been following it for years in every aspect of my life. Nevertheless, I found myself failing in my work with teenagers. Even more, I was failing in my finances, to the point of financial bankruptcy. Even though I was painting on a happy face, I was miserable inside. I had been searching for the answers to how to help people—particularly myself—become successful in life for years: through religion, self-help, psychology, medicine, and advice from people I respected. Nothing worked. And, of course, I blamed myself, not the teachings. *I'm just not trying hard enough, or doing it right!* I told myself.

I was at the point of throwing everything overboard because I felt I couldn't live my life this way anymore. I remember thinking, *How did I screw everything up so fast?* I was only in my twenties, and I felt like I was failing in every single area of life. Well, apparently I wasn't quite done yet.

One stormy Sunday night in 1988, after three years of marriage, my wife, Hope, said she "needed to talk to me." Even though she'd said that thousands of times before, she'd never said it like this. I knew in my bones that something was up, and it wasn't good. She had a hard time looking me in the eye. Her voice was trembling, but I could tell she was also trying to keep it steady. "Alex, I need you to move out of the house. I can't stand to live with you anymore."

Now, I grew up in an Italian-like family. We argued and debated incessantly about everything, from politics, to religion, to what we were going to do on the weekends. But I didn't have one word of rebuttal in this single most important moment in my life. All I could come up with was . . . "Okay."

So I left. I numbly packed my little bag with a few essentials and quietly left without saying another word. I went to my parents' house and spent all night in the backyard praying, searching, crying—feeling like I was dying inside.

What I didn't know at the time was that this was the best thing that could have ever happened to me. Over the next six weeks, I would experience the most positive turning point in my life. I had just been inducted into a sort of "spiritual school" where I would learn the key to all things: what I often call the Greatest Principle in the World That Almost Nobody Knows.

But that night, it felt like my life was over. I kept asking, over and over again, "Why is this happening?" It was a fair question, because if there was anything I should have succeeded at, it was marriage. When Hope and I got married, we were more prepared for marriage than anyone we knew. On our very first date, we went to the park, laid a blanket out on the grass on a beautiful starry fall night, and we *talked*. And talked. And talked. And talked. That's it. For six hours straight, we talked. You name it; we talked about it. And that was just the first date.

When we ran out of things to talk about, we read books together. We would get the same book—one about relationships or something we were both interested in—and read it on our own, underlining and taking notes. Then, on our dates, we would compare notes and discuss what we'd read. We did premarital counseling *voluntarily*. We took personality tests and compared them and talked to counselors about our possible issues and their resolutions. When the day of our wedding came on May 24, 1986, we were ready.

Well, we *thought* we were ready. Now, less than three years later, she couldn't stand the sight of me, and I was very unhappy as well. Why?

That night in my parents' backyard was when my real education started. I heard a voice in my head that I believed to be God's. The voice told me something that I didn't want to hear—something that offended me, in fact. Then the voice asked me three questions that shook me to my core and over the next six weeks deprogrammed and reprogrammed me to the very source of my being—and I would never be the same. Those three questions would become the beginning of the Love Code, the process you'll find in this book. It happened to me in an instant, but it would take me the next twenty-five years to work out exactly how to do it on demand for anyone. In fact, as it exists today, you might say it's the exact opposite of the typical three-step self-help blueprint. And it also has the exact opposite effect: a 97+ percent success rate or higher, based on my experience, versus the 97 percent failure rate of the typical self-help blueprint over the past sixty-five years.

After about six weeks of separation, Hope reluctantly agreed to go on a date with me again. She would tell me later that the first time she looked in my eyes that day, she knew I was not the same man. She was right. Even though I looked the same on the outside, I had transformed into a completely different person on the inside. Because of her past pain, she wouldn't tell me that or let down her guard for quite some time. But the result was inevitable and inescapable.

Even though we later had struggles related to Hope's health and with finances,[2] the most important things in our lives were never the same again. I had been, and was being, transformed by the Love Code. And Hope was starting to be transformed, too.

From that day on, I began teaching the Love Code to everyone I could, including the teenagers and parents with whom I was working at that time. No matter what they thought their problem was, no matter what they thought they needed to be saved from, what they really needed to know was the Love Code. Here it is in a nutshell:

*Virtually every problem or lack of happiness and success comes from an internal state of fear in some form—even physical problems. And every internal state of fear results from a deficit of love in relation to that particular issue.*

Another name for the fear response is the stress response. If fear is the problem, then love, its opposite, is the antidote. In the presence of real love, there can be no fear (except in a life-threatening emergency). This may sound very theoretical. Fortunately, in the last few years, research has been done to back this up scientifically (which we will discuss throughout this book). Everything, even your success issues and external circumstances, boils down to whether you are in an internal state of fear or an internal state of love.

When I began my counseling practice, this is what I began teaching every single client in therapy: no matter what their presenting problem was—health, relationships, success, anger, anxiety—I believed the underlying source was always a love/fear problem. If love could replace fear, I believed their symptoms would get better in a way that may never happen otherwise.

But I soon discovered a problem: just telling people to "love" didn't work. Having them read, study, and meditate on ancient manuscripts and principles rarely worked. I tried to teach them to "just do" what I had been transformed to naturally do, but virtually none of them could. Guess what: I was teaching them the three-step failure blueprint, and I didn't even know it! I was telling them to change their conscious fear-based thinking to love-based thinking, change their fear-based emotions to love-based emotions, and change their fear-based behavior to love-based behavior. In other words, I was telling them to focus on expectations of external end results using their willpower! Several said, "Yeah, thanks a lot for the advice." Another told me sarcastically, "Yeah, I'll just start that right after lunch—no problem." I later figured out why they were so cynical: they had already tried to live this way and couldn't, just like I had tried countless times in my life before that night at my parents' house, and hadn't been able to either.

Something real and transformative happened to me that night and over the next six weeks that I have come to call a "transformational *aha*." It wasn't that I just "decided" to love that night and started doing it with my willpower. Something happened in an instant that replaced my internal fear state with a love state and made me naturally love in a way I simply couldn't before, without having to exert willpower. I saw the truth in a way I had never seen it before, and I deeply understood and "felt" what love was and knew it to be true. I instantly started thinking, feeling, believing, and acting in love rather than fear, peace rather than anxiety; light flooded into my darkness, and I started effortlessly doing things I could hardly force myself to do before.

If you think of your brain as a computer hard drive, it was like my brain was instantly deprogrammed and reprogrammed about the issues of love and fear. It was like exchanging one software package for another. To be honest, this transformational *aha* was like a type of vision in which I glimpsed the truth about love in a single moment and held on to it. In fact, Einstein wrote about a similar experience regarding his theory of relativity. He saw himself, in his mind, riding a beam of light, and he credits that vision as the beginning of his famous theory ($E = mc^2$). The whole truth was revealed to him in an instant—but it took him twelve years to come up with the math to prove it.

I soon learned that you can't have a transformational *aha* just because you want to. I realized I hadn't yet "come up with the math," so to speak. I needed practical tools and specific instructions I could teach that anyone and everyone could apply to any situation that would deprogram their fear and reprogram them in love—at the deepest level, to actually *live* in love. Tools that would really address the source of whatever issue they had, just like my transformational *aha* had done for me.

Over the next twenty-four years, that's exactly what I did. As I worked with clients, I eventually discovered the Three Tools (which you'll learn about in Part II) that helped them go directly to the subconscious source, deprogram fear, and change their default programming to love. Not only did I discover the Three Tools, I also discovered the futility of the typical three-step self-help blueprint. In this book, I'll teach you how to finally achieve happiness and success in all areas of your life using these Three Tools—naturally, organically, and *not* based on trying harder with your willpower.

When I first got my master's in counseling, I hung out my shingle before I was even licensed—when I was still under the supervision of a psychologist. Then I did something that either really irked, or became the source of jokes of, my more experienced colleagues in Nashville, Tennessee: I charged the full psychologist rate of $120 for 50 minutes (and this was twenty-plus years ago). Nobody does that with a master's in counseling! But I knew that, based on my experience, I would usually only see my clients for one to ten sessions, typically over the course of six months, until their problems were resolved and they wouldn't need me anymore. Other psychologists typically saw their clients once a week for one to three years. (Perhaps you're seeing some of those psychologists now.) Also, while other psychologists primarily taught clients coping mechanisms to deal with issues that would likely remain problems for the rest of their lives, I was consistently seeing full resolution of issues with my clients. I simply taught them what you will find in this book.

Six months after starting my practice in this very unorthodox way, I had a six-month waiting list. I also had a line of colleagues knocking on my door and calling me, either cursing me or sweetly asking me out to lunch to find out what the heck I was doing over here, because their clients were coming to me.

The Love Code changed not only my life, but also the lives of countless others in my private practice. And I believe it will change yours, too. You'll experience a level of happiness and success not possible any other way. Now, I don't mean that you have to use this book. You might have a grandmother or a neighbor who are already experiencing maximum happiness and success. But if they are, it's because they're following the same basic principles the Love Code is based on. There isn't any other way.

## THE 97 PERCENT SUCCESS RATE

The Love Code is in perfect harmony with ancient spiritual wisdom and the very latest clinical research and methodology—and it provides the solution that willpower can't. According to research we'll discuss in chapters 1 and 8, the typical three-step self-help blueprint literally turns on the mechanism in the brain that

- dumbs us down;
- makes us sick;
- drains our energy;
- suppresses our immune system;
- increases our pain;
- raises our blood pressure;
- closes our cells;
- destroys relationships;
- causes fear, anger, depression, confusion, shame, and worth and identity issues; and
- causes us to do everything we do from a negative perspective, even if we paint on a happy face.

In contrast, not only can the Love Code turn *off* the mechanism above, it can literally turn *on* another mechanism in the brain that, according to clinical research,

- enhances relationships;
- increases parental bonding;

- results in love, joy, and peace;

- increases immune function;

- reduces stress;

- lowers blood pressure;

- counteracts addiction and withdrawal;

- stimulates human growth hormone;

- increases trust and wise judgment;

- modulates appetite, healthy digestion, and metabolism;

- promotes healing;

- stimulates relaxation;

- stimulates nonstress energy;

- stimulates higher neurological activity; and

- opens cells to healing and regeneration.[3]

What exactly are these mechanisms? The first is the stress response, which results from internal *fear*. The stress response causes the release of cortisol, which results in all the symptoms in the first list. The second mechanism is activated by the absence of internal fear, which is internal *love*. The experience of internal love releases oxytocin (commonly known as the "love hormone") and other peptides in the brain and hormonal system, which results in all the positive symptoms in the second list.

To give you a sense of the depth of clinical research behind these lists, George Vaillant recently published the findings of Harvard University's Grant Study of Human Development, the "longest-running longitudinal studies of human development in history." Beginning in 1938, the study followed 268 undergraduate males well into their nineties to determine the factors that contributed to human happiness and success. Here's how Vaillant, who directed the study for over thirty years, sums up the findings: "The seventy-five years and twenty million dollars expended on the Grant Study points to a straightforward five-word conclusion: Happiness is love. Full stop."[4]

Hopefully now you can see how our success and failure depend upon our internal state and whether it is based in love or fear. If the first mechanism, the stress response, is operating in your life—and in my experience, it is for the vast majority of people—*you are going to fail*, or at the very least fall short of your perfect success. You can only push against that immovable rock for so long until you give out. Conversely, if the second mechanism, internal love, is operating in your life, *you will become successful*—and not because you're trying harder. You are simply "programmed" to succeed.

My friend and medical doctor Dr. Ben Johnson says that if we could ever create a pill that would activate this second mechanism in the brain and cause the natural release of oxytocin, it would immediately be the top-selling drug of all time. It would not just be the wonder pill. It would be the "100 percent happy and healthy all the time" pill! How would you like a prescription for that? Well, this book is your prescription.

## ALIGNING TRUE SCIENCE WITH TRUE SPIRITUALITY

Now I can explain more about what I learned during those six weeks in "spiritual school," after Hope kicked me out of the house twenty-five years ago. It began when I realized that not only had I not truly loved Hope, I didn't even know what love was. Even more, I realized that no one else I knew understood what love really was either.

In other words, my marriage hadn't been based on my love for Hope in the context of an intimate relationship; it had been based on a negotiation and a business deal. That business deal was my safety net: if you do this for me, I'll do that for you. If not, well . . . it would be fair for me to withhold something until I got what I bargained for, right? If Hope hadn't done what I wanted and acted in the ways I wanted when we were dating, I knew I would have never asked her to marry me. Even now that we were married, I still expected Hope to do what I wanted her to do and not do what I didn't want her to do as an unspoken condition of my love. While I never would have said those words, I did live them. When she didn't do what I wanted, I felt irritated and angry—and the same was true for her.

This business-deal kind of love is what almost everyone means when they use the word *love*. But a more accurate name for it would be WIIFM (What's In It For Me) love! WIIFM has been the credo of almost every business negotiation and business deal for decades. In the 1970s, bestselling books began to teach us to overlay this paradigm onto our relationships and other areas of our life. I'll do this, if you will do that. And we bought it—and have applied it to our lives ever since. Then we wonder why we are failing! WIIFM love is the exact opposite of love. WIIFM love is fear based, is based on instant gratification (which we'll talk more about in chapter 4), and inevitably leads to greater long-term failure and pain.

Loving truly, on the other hand, has nothing to do with the other person's response. If you truly love someone, you're all in: no safety net, no plan B, nothing held back. Loving truly means giving up WIIFM love so that all involved parties can win, even if you have to sacrifice for it. Loving truly may lead to delaying momentary pleasure now, but it always leads to long-term success, and the kind of pleasure that is beyond words and that no amount of money can buy.

Scholars throughout history have distinguished between these two kinds of love with the terms *agape* and *eros*. Agape is the spontaneous and unconditional love whose source is the divine. With agape, the person loves simply because it is in his or her nature to love, not because of any external conditions, circumstances, or qualities of the other. In fact, agape creates value in the other as a result of the unconditional love. *Eros*, or WIIFM love, is the opposite: it uses the object of love to manage personal pain or pleasure, and then moves on to the next object. Eros depends on the external qualities of the other, and payoff from the other. In contrast, agape has nothing to do with the external payoff from the other.[5]

This realization hit me like a sledgehammer, and I began weeping. Then I was faced with a question: Now that I knew what love really was—no safety net, no plan B, nothing held back—would I choose to love Hope now, even if nothing in our relationship changed? I didn't answer right away. But finally, after a few days of thinking and praying, I was able to decide, yes, I would love Hope in that way. All in, and no strings attached. And that's when I received my transformational *aha*. Not only did I understand in an instant what love truly meant, I was able to do it. The change happened not in my conscious mind, but at the place where true science and true spirituality meet: what some people call our subconscious or unconscious mind, and what I call our spiritual heart.

Earlier I called this principle a magic wand. Historically we tend to call things "magic" when we don't understand how they work or how they happened. But when we understand the mechanism behind how something works and can replicate it, we call it technology.

When you get home in the evening, do you go around the house with a box of matches, lighting your oil lamps? When you want to go somewhere, do you go out twenty minutes early to hitch the horses up to the wagon? When you want to eat, do you start building the fire in the stove? If I had asked all those same questions a century or so ago, people would have looked at me like I was nuts. "Of course we do; everybody does." So why don't you do those things today? Because we have new technology!

Newer technology doesn't necessarily mean that the principles are new; surely you've heard the expression "There is nothing new under the sun." When the lightbulb, the automobile, and electricity were invented, principles were used that had been around since the dawn of time. Those inventions had always been possible, but it took many centuries for us to put all the building blocks together. I believe the process I'm sharing with you is a new technology for overcoming our physical, emotional, and spiritual problems—one that is forged from ancient principles that have been true all along.

Please understand that I do *not* mean anything religious by the term "spiritual." I run from religion. In fact, it took me decades to recover from my religious upbringing. I believe that much of religion is fear based and therefore does more harm than good more often than not. However, I try very hard to be a spiritual person, prioritizing love, joy, peace, forgiveness, kindness, and belief. These are spiritual issues, and as you will learn from this book, they are the controlling issues of your life.

Although science has only recently discovered that love is the key to happiness and success, all the great spiritual teachers throughout history have been teaching this idea for millennia, even though we may not have had the methodology or the technology to consistently put it into practice.

For example:

> "*Being deeply loved by someone gives you strength,
> while loving someone deeply gives you courage.*"
> **Lao Tzu**

> "*One word / Frees us of all the weight and pain of life: /
> That word is love.*"
> **Sophocles**

*"If I have prophetic powers, and understand all mysteries
and all knowledge, and if I have all faith, so as to remove
mountains, but have not love, I am nothing."*
**The Apostle Paul**

*"Until he has unconditional and unbiased love for all beings,
man will not find peace."*
**Buddha**

*"When I despair, I remember that all through history, the way
of truth and love has always won. There have been tyrants and
murderers, and for a time, they can seem invincible, but in the
end, they always fall. Think of it—always."*
**Mahatma Gandhi**

*"If you want others to be happy, practice compassion.
If you want to be happy, practice compassion."*
**The Dalai Lama**

*"Darkness cannot drive out darkness: Only light can do that.
Hate cannot drive out hate: Only love can do that."*
**Martin Luther King Jr.**

*"Learning how to love is the goal and the purpose of spiritual
life—not learning how to develop psychic powers, not learning
how to bow, chant, do yoga, or even meditate, but learning to
love. Love is the truth. Love is the light."*
**Lama Surya Das**

One of the most exciting breakthroughs in our time is the fact that
science is now starting to quantify these ancient spiritual principles and

verify not only the existence of our "spiritual heart," but how it is the source of everything that happens in our lives, both good and bad. True spirituality has always been aligned with true science, and we're seeing more and more evidence of that today.

Because this process is the alignment of true science and true spirituality, your success with it does not depend on your worldview, your demographic, or whether you even believe the Love Code itself. You just have to *do* it. In the twenty-five years I've been teaching it privately, I've seen it work virtually every time for people of every worldview and any and all demographics you can imagine. My practice is one of the largest in the world now; we're in all 50 states, as well as 158 countries and counting. Out of all these clients, I can count on my two hands the number of clients I have personally worked with who have not had their perfect success created for them through this process. Among those five to ten clients, there are two groups: (1) those who just wouldn't do the process (for whatever reason), and (2) those who never tried the process because they disagreed with its philosophical principles. Everyone else I know of has been successful.

One of the most popular ideas right now is that you have to "believe it to achieve it." That's not true here. You don't have to believe it works or believe anything I say. But if it is *done* exactly the way I show and teach you, it will transform personal relationships, the source of physical and emotional health symptoms, and yes, material wealth and circumstances.

## THE RIGHT TOOLS FOR THE JOB

True happiness and success mean living in love internally and externally in the present moment, regardless of your current circumstances. If you can do that, everything will get better—inside and out. Of course, most *can't* do this through willpower alone, any more than you can get your computer to do something that it's not programmed to do.

Your spiritual heart, or your subconscious and unconscious mind, works very much the way a computer does. In fact, your very cells are made of a silicon-like substance, just like a computer chip. (Remember, computers were modeled *after* the way you work, not the other way around.) For example, if you have a computer virus or if you've loaded some software that keeps crashing your computer, you could be the best-intentioned, most determined person in the world, but if you don't have the right tools or the right knowledge, you are never going to erase that virus or uninstall that software. On the other hand, if you have the right process and the right tools, it's surprisingly easy. In fact, you almost can't stop it from working, even if you wanted to—because that's what it's programmed to do.

The tools you need to be successful in your life must address the subconscious and unconscious mind, not the conscious mind (as willpower alone does). This is the location of our spiritual heart and cellular memories, and the source of all our issues in life. I've developed and tested Three Tools over the last twenty-four years that can deprogram the fear-based, human hard-drive viruses keeping you in destructive cycles in your life, and reprogram you at the subconscious and unconscious level to live in truth and love from the inside out— without relying on willpower, and without end result expectations. After deprogramming and reprogramming, living in love in the present (internally and externally) will be your default programming.

So in *The Love Code* you will find not only the principles that will show you how to create happiness and success in every life area, but the process and the tools to make the Love Code work for you. You will find the perfect, complete process first written about thousands of years ago and now confirmed by new research and doctors from our best universities—but with all the pieces put together in practical, step-by-step instructions.

In Part I, we'll identify your ultimate success goal, or that one thing you truly want more than anything else—an important concept that will form the foundation for putting the Love Code into practice. Then we'll learn more about some scientific and spiritual principles to help you understand why the Love Code works the way it does.

In Part II, you're going to learn how to put the Love Code into action for your own happiness and success. First you'll learn how to use the Three Tools that will deprogram and reprogram your success issues at their source—tools you won't find anywhere else. Then I'll show you how to run some Basic Diagnostics with those Three Tools to identify the source of your success issues. At this point, you will have everything you need to put the Love Code into practice, but for those of you who prefer a more detailed plan, in the last chapter you'll find the Love Code Success Blueprint, a step-by-step, forty-day process for creating and achieving the success you want in any specific area, based on all the concepts you've learned thus far.

The Love Code does more than just rescue you from failure. It can transform you into an overachiever, even if you are already extraordinarily gifted and talented. While the three-step self-help failure blueprint will often cause you to fail "worse" than you would have if left to your own devices, the Love Code will empower you to reach a level of peak performance not just beyond your willpower, but beyond your expectations and even your hopes and dreams.

Just as the earth was always round even when everyone thought it was flat, the Love Code has always been true. Only in the last few years have we had the science to prove it. And, for the first time, you have in your hands the complete program and tools to create your perfect happiness and success.

*part I*

# THE FOUNDATIONS
## *of the*
# LOVE CODE

## chapter 1

# DETERMINE YOUR
# ULTIMATE SUCCESS GOAL

———————

Let me start this chapter with a question. If you can't answer it correctly, there's very little chance you will ever get what you want most in your lifetime. You'll likely become locked in a vicious cycle for years, decades, or maybe even the rest of your life. As critical as it is, in my experience very few people know the correct answer to this question. So here it is.

What do you want more than anything else right now?

To help you come up with the correct answer, I have just one rule: no filtering. What do I mean by that? Most people, when they hear this question, have a superfast, gut-level answer flash into their mind. The problem is that many times, they will immediately try to convince themselves that this should not be their answer. They'll start building a case for another answer that is more socially acceptable, more in line with their upbringing, less in line with their upbringing, more religious, less religious—you name it. I've heard it all. Don't do that!

This book is about helping you get what you *really* want. Answering this question honestly is the first step, because if you don't know what you really want—or don't admit the truth about what you really want—you'll almost certainly not get it. So I want your honest, from-the-gut response. If what naturally comes up for you is a million dollars, terrific, go with that. If it's a health issue you want to heal, fantastic, that'll work. If it's a relationship you want to improve, wonderful. Whatever comes up for you, naturally and spontaneously, is your answer.

## THE GENIE EXERCISE

To help you answer this question without filtering, let's walk through an exercise right now. Do you remember the story of Aladdin and his magic lamp? This was one of my favorite stories as a child; I don't know how many times I imagined, while walking around in the backyard, what I would choose with my three wishes, and then what might happen as a result. I was a sports nut as a kid, so I'd usually wish to be the next Jimmy Connors, or if it was baseball season, to be the game-winning pitcher in game 7 of the World Series for the St. Louis Cardinals—and then I would go outside and pretend to pitch the whole game.

   Close your eyes and imagine that Aladdin's genie is standing right in front of you, right now. There's no one else around, just you and the genie. Here's what he tells you: "I'm going to give you one wish. You can wish for anything you want, with only two limitations: You can't wish for more wishes, and you can't receive a wish that will take away someone else's free will. But wish for basically anything else, and you will get it. If you wish for ten million dollars—done! An 'uncurable' health issue healed—you got it! A big achievement goal accomplished—victory! You get the idea. No one will ever know how you got it; they will think it just happened naturally through the course of life's circumstances. Also, you can never have another wish in your lifetime, and if you don't tell me your wish in ten seconds, you lose it."

Okay, this is it; the moment of truth. Treat this as if it were really happening to you right now. No filtering; you've got ten seconds. Close your eyes—go.

What did you tell the genie your wish was? Write it down.

Guess what? I tricked you. Sorry about that—I had to do it, and maybe you'll thank me later. This is the only way I've been able to figure out how to help you identify what you really want most in your life. You see, your answer above is actually the number one goal of your life right now. But if I'd asked it that way, chances are you would have said something different. Most likely, something *very* different—an answer that won't help us in our quest to get you what you really want most.

So why do I want to know the number one goal of your life? Because it's why you do almost everything that you do. It's why you have the thoughts that you have. It's what you really believe in the most, no matter what you might say. And it betrays your underlying programming. Everything you do, everything you've ever done, and everything you will ever do is because of a *goal* you've set at some point in your life, even if you've long forgotten what it was. You don't get up in the morning unless at some point you have that as a goal, consciously or unconsciously. The same is true for brushing your teeth, getting dressed, hailing a cab, getting married, getting divorced, having children, using the restroom—you get the idea. Identifying the number one goal in your life is the first step to making any real change.

## THE WRONG ANSWER

I've been asking people this question for twenty-five years, both one at a time and thousands at a time. The last live group I did this with had over sixteen hundred people. Only six gave the right answer.

If the only rule was to give an honest answer, how could they have given a wrong answer? Well, I know they've given me the wrong answer because after I ask them two more questions, they tell me that they had the wrong answer. I'll ask you those two questions a little later. But I'll give you a hint: the right answer is always an *inward state* (such as love, joy, peace, etc.). The wrong answer is an *external circumstance* (money, health, achievement, a relationship based on what someone else does or feels, etc.). It is the wrong answer because it's self-defeating: it will take you away from the happiness and success that you long for and literally create failure (or more failure) in your life.

Why? Let's return to the typical three-step "blueprint for failure" we mentioned in the introduction. Remember, this model, which is used by most in the self-help industry, has a 97 percent failure rate:

1. Focus on what you want.

2. Figure out a plan to get there.

3. Put the plan into action.

Steps 1 and 2 involve focusing on the end result to achieve success. Dr. Dan Gilbert, Harvard psychology professor and bestselling author of *Stumbling on Happiness*, describes the conclusion of his research at Harvard like this: "Expectations are a happiness killer."[1] He did original research on this issue for years.[2] If you read his research, you'll see that when he says "expectations," he is referring specifically to particular life circumstances in connection to some future event (in other words, an end result). He also has a wonderful video on the Internet that describes how this phenomenon works inside every one of us, without us being aware.[3]

But expectations of end results not only kill your happiness, they also kill your health and your likelihood of success at almost anything. Why? Expecting a future end result instantly puts you into a chronic state of stress until you either get that result or don't. If you have been alive on this planet during the past thirty years, you probably already know that virtually every medical school and medical doctor says that up to 95 percent of all illness and disease comes from stress. But here's what most people don't realize: even beyond health problems, stress is also the source of just about any and every other problem you could have in your life as well.

From a clinical perspective, virtually every problem in your life comes from stress. In other words, stress creates failure. How?

1. Stress makes you sick. Up to 95 percent of all illness and disease are related to stress, according to virtually every medical school and medical doctor on the planet. This is old news.

2. Stress dumbs you down. It shunts blood flow away from your higher intellectual centers and kills creativity, problem-solving skills, and all the things you need for happiness and success.

3. Stress drains your energy. After an initial energy spike from cortisol, you experience an adrenaline overdose and your energy crashes. This is because you're not supposed to go into stress unless your life is in danger and you need to fight or flee (which will burn up all the cortisol). But the number one complaint I hear from people, "I'm tired all the time," comes from chronic or constant stress.

4. Stress makes you approach everything with negativity. "I can't do it. It's not going to work. I'm not good enough. I'm not talented enough. I'm not attractive enough. The economy's too bad." When a person thinks these things, he or she believes them to be an honest evaluation of the circumstances. But they're not; they're the stress talking. Fix the stress, and the distorted thoughts, feelings, beliefs, and actions will automatically become positive. If you don't fix the stress, you

can try to change these with your willpower "till the cows come home," and it will almost never work.

5. Stress makes you fail at almost any task. This is the only logical conclusion of numbers 1 to 4. How do you think it's going to go, trying to succeed at something when you're sick, dumbed down, tired, and have a negative attitude? You may be able to push that rock uphill for a while, but usually it rolls back down and crushes you. Now, you may still achieve your desired end results if you're particularly gifted in that area, such as in sports, science, finance, or sales. But you will not be happy, fulfilled, and content in the long term. These feelings are a crucial part of my definition of success, at least: achieving your desired end result *and* being happy, fulfilled, and content in the process. You should settle for nothing less.

Step 3, putting the plan into action, relies upon our willpower, which is just as ineffective as external expectations. Science has finally verified what our personal experience has proven over the years: we can't get what we want through willpower alone. Dr. Bruce Lipton, former cell biologist at Stanford Medical School and now a bestselling author, states that trying to create the life, health, and success that you want through willpower (if you have not deprogrammed and reprogrammed your subconscious first) is a million-to-one long shot.[4] That's because, according to Dr. Lipton, the subconscious mind (i.e., where our programming resides) is one million times more powerful than the conscious mind (i.e., where our willpower resides).

Dr. William Tiller, my friend and Stanford physicist who also starred in the film *What the Bleep Do We Know?*, has told me in our personal conversations, "Everywhere you go today, you hear about conscious intention. But what you don't hear is that we also have an unconscious intention. When the conscious mind is pitted against the subconscious mind, the subconscious will win every time." The great majority of the time we're not even aware that our unconscious disagrees with our conscious intention. We think we simply decide to do whatever it is we do: make that call, sit on the couch, or spend another three hours looking at something online we shouldn't. But the whole time it's our subconscious making that decision, not our conscious mind. (We'll talk more about this in chapter 2.)

Let's return to the problem of setting goals based on expectations and external circumstances (steps 1 and 2). If the number one goal in your life is an external circumstance, it will instantaneously put you into a chronic state of stress until you either get that thing that you want, or not. That means the goal itself may actually be the cause of your life problems—not the lack of a goal in your life or even the visible symptoms of the stress. I've seen this happen over and over with my clients. When the number one goal of their lives is an external circumstance, they invariably experience one of three possible outcomes:

**1. If they achieve that external circumstance or goal they always wanted, they are absolutely overjoyed—temporarily.** After a day or week or month, they move right on to pursuing the next thing in their life that they don't have and decide they want most—and they enter right back into the chronic cycle of stress, elation, and stress again. So many people repeat this cycle over and over and over for decades, and then get to the end of their life and think, *What was that all about?*

I have a dear friend whose dream for decades had been to write a *New York Times*–bestselling book. Every time I talked to him, he was either thinking about it or working on it. Finally, after twenty-five years, he did it! He was over the moon when his book hit the list—I got four text messages, three phone calls, and several e-mails from him. I celebrated with him, but because I knew these principles, I also knew what was coming next.

Two and a half weeks later, he finally confided, "This didn't do what

I thought it would do." In fact, he went into a fairly deep depression and developed some health problems—even though he had realized his lifelong goal and was more financially prosperous. Why? Before he achieved his goal, he had a hope that this one thing, writing a *New York Times*-bestselling book, would cause a particular set of problems to disappear and a particular set of dreams to come true. When those things didn't happen, he felt an emptiness that he didn't have before, and it replaced the hope he had experienced for years of writing the bestseller. That's a bad trade, emptiness for hope. In other words, achieving this external-circumstance goal eventually made him feel *worse* than if he had never achieved it at all. However, before long he had put it behind him, and he was on to the next external thing that he thought would bring him happiness—which put him right back into the cycle of stress again.

**2. If they achieve it, they immediately end up feeling like their ladder is against the wrong building.** In other words, sometimes they don't experience the elation part of the cycle. Rather than simply bouncing back and chasing the next thing, they feel disillusioned and disoriented. I once saw a documentary on television about a world-famous band, in which the group talked about their very first hit record. When the interviewer asked one of the band members, "How did it feel when the thing you'd worked toward for so long finally happened?," I was struck, but not surprised, by the band member's response: "Is this all there is? I thought it would be different—this isn't what I expected."

I work with a number of musical entertainers, professional athletes, actors, and actresses who are multimillionaires. One in twenty will be both wealthy and famous, and truly healthy, happy, and content. The other nineteen are stressed to the max, feverishly working toward their next platinum album, paranoid that their voice is going to give out or that they won't be able to write any more hit songs. It's truly unbelievable the things they find to be stressed about, when, to outsiders, they seem to be on top of the world.

When I come across those rare individuals who are wealthy and famous as well as happy and content, they'll tell me clearly that they're not happy and content because of the money and fame. It's because they know these principles: that internal love and truth are more important than any end result or external circumstance. And they usually discovered them the hard way—often through alcoholism, drug abuse, and other addictions. Finally, somehow, they realized money and fame wouldn't truly satisfy. At that point, whenever tempted to focus on the external circumstance, they run in the opposite direction: "I'm not even going to think about the money and the fame, because they almost killed me."

Both numbers 1 and 2 happen if individuals achieve their number one goal. But they are likely pursuing this external circumstance based on willpower alone, and we know how effective that is. So what happens if they never achieve their goal, after years, decades, or maybe even their whole life?

**3. If they don't achieve it, they often go into full-blown hopelessness and despair and never recover.** I've seen this happen over and over again. One of the saddest things in my life has been counseling elderly people who realize these principles late in life. Some are in pain because of health, financial issues, or not being on good terms with people close to them. But by far the most crushing issue I've helped people deal with, even and perhaps especially if they were famous, was regret—for the life they did not lead. I've had elderly country music stars point to walls of awards. They curse them and say, "I'd give every bit of it to live in love and joy and peace, to have prioritized my family and spent time with them and the people I love." Universally, when people become older, they begin to inherently understand that living in love is the greatest principle of all.

Occasionally I'll deal with elderly individuals who still haven't gotten it. They are still living in internal fear focused on external circumstances. They're probably hanging on by their fingernails to those trophies and accomplishments. In every circumstance, they were unhappy, bitter, anxious, unhealthy, and estranged in their relationships. They may be filthy rich and a living legend. It doesn't matter. If you visited them with me, you would walk away feeling sad for them. You might use the word *pitiful* and be determined that you will *not* end up like that. If they come to see me, I help them live in love, joy, peace, and right relationships, in this moment—and it's amazing how they can heal, even if they don't have much time left. But that doesn't mean they wouldn't change past choices in their life. That's exactly why I'm writing this book: so you don't end up in the same place at the end of your life. You can get to a place of true success—being happy and content *and* achieving at your highest and best level—usually just forty days after you start the process in this book.

These are the reasons why an external circumstance is always the wrong answer to the question "What do you want right now more than anything else?" Being truly happy and fulfilled while pursuing an external circumstance as your ultimate goal—according to the ancient manuscripts and the latest scientific research—is simply not in the realm of possibility.

## HOW TO FIND THE RIGHT ANSWER

If you are one of the 99 percent who answered that first question with the wrong answer, these next two questions are going to help you figure out the right answer. If you recall, question 1 was: What do you want right now more than anything else? Here are the next two:

> **2.** If you got what you most wanted in question 1, what would that do for you and what would it change in your life?

**3.** If you got the things that were your answers to both questions 1 and 2, how would you feel?

Your answer to question 3 is actually the right answer to the original question, "What do you want right now more than anything else?" That's what you *really* want more than anything, and it is always an inward state; it is never an external material circumstance.[5] This internal state is what we're going to call your *ultimate success goal*, because that's exactly what it is. But if this inward state is really your ultimate success goal, then why didn't you naturally answer that way to begin with?

Here's why: almost everyone answers question 1 with an external circumstance because they believe that circumstance will purchase for them the inward state of how they answered question 3.

Let me give you an example. A few months ago I was doing a live event in Los Angeles. I was taking the audience through this exercise to help people find their ultimate goal. A dear, sweet lady volunteered to come up on stage and share her answers. She had had a rough few years, like so many have in the recent economy. Her answer to question 1 was "a million dollars." When she said it, the look in her eyes was the same as if she were talking about the love of her life, her favorite food, or a decadent chocolate dessert. Her answer to question 2 was what you would probably expect: "I could pay off my bills, have a little breathing room, go on a much-needed vacation, and have less pressure on my life." Her answer to question 3 was "peace." She thought that in order to have peace, she had to have money. In her situation, she thought money would literally purchase peace for her.

I explained how all this works, and then asked her: "Is it possible that what you 'really' want more than anything is peace, but you think that money is the *only* way to get that peace for you internally?" Her jaw dropped, she covered her face, and she started weeping right there on the stage in front of many people—gasping-for-air weeping. When she calmed down, she shared with the audience that until that moment, she had never known what she really wanted in her life. For decades she thought it was money, focused incessantly on that, pursued that, and just became more and more stressed, unhappy, and filled with anxiety. The next thing that occurred to her was that what she really wanted most, she could have right now. It didn't require money; in fact, it didn't require any external circumstance in her life to change at all. Then she started laughing and became extremely joyful and started hugging me. Her entire countenance changed, right there onstage in front of the audience.

So many of us pursue some end result—whether it's a career, a possession, an achievement, or a relationship—because we think that this external circumstance will purchase the internal state we really want most in our lives. In fact, we probably believe that achieving the external circumstance is the *only* way we can have the inward states of love, joy, and peace. But this is never true. In fact, it's one of the greatest lies on the planet—and the biggest reason for the self-help industry's 97 percent failure rate over the last sixty-five years! According to Dr. William Tiller, "The unseen is always the parent of the seen." And the opposite is never true: the seen (or the external circumstance) is *never* the parent of the unseen (the inward state of love/joy/peace, long term). It just doesn't work that way—in nature, or in us.

Here's a common example that proves the point. Let's say you have two people in Los Angeles's rush-hour traffic, side by side—and the traffic is as bad as it gets. One has gone into road rage—his veins are popping out, his face is getting red, and he's gripping the steering wheel, yelling at people next to him. But the person next to him is as cool as a cucumber. He's talking to his friends in the car, singing to the radio, laughing. I know you've seen this before—if not in traffic, then waiting in line at the grocery store, experiencing poor service at a restaurant, or waiting for a delayed flight. Two people in the same external circumstance have very different reactions. The external circumstances can't be the cause of their internal state, because the circumstances of the two are the same!

That doesn't mean that external circumstances won't affect you internally—for instance, if you tragically lose your spouse in an accident. But in times of true danger or significant loss, our stress response, or fight-or-flight response, is supposed to kick in. If we experience the internal states of love, joy, and peace under normal circumstances, we will go through predictable stages of grief for a while, but after about a year, we'll bounce back and we'll be fine. But if you experience an internal state of fear under normal circumstances, that's when you don't bounce back, and an external stressor can put you down for the count. However, the true cause of the stress is not really the event—it's your internal programming.

The external is never capable of producing the internal; the internal is always what creates the external. Ultimate success in your external circumstances depends completely upon your internal state of love, joy, and peace. These qualities are the necessary prerequisites for achieving health, wealth, creativity, happiness, and success in every area. In the same way, the internal states of fear, depression, and anger will produce external circumstances that are the opposite of success: health problems, financial difficulty, a feeling of stuckness, unhappiness, and failure in every area. (Chapters 2 and 3 will explain more about how this actually happens.) Now we are right back at our original point: stress is the cause not only of the vast majority of our health problems, but also of virtually any other problem we have in life.

Now, if you are gifted in a particular area, such as athletics, finances, engineering, or writing, your number one goal may be an external circumstance, and you may still make a lot of money or reach a tremendous level of achievement. But you will not be able to make a lot of money *and* be happy, fulfilled, and content long term. In other words, you will not "have it all," which is my definition of "true" success.

Let's return to my earlier point that you can't do anything unless you have an internal goal to do it. The lady who wanted a million dollars had an internal goal related to wanting that million dollars. The question is, what was it, and why did she have that particular goal? The reason is her *pain/pleasure programming*.

## OUR PAIN/PLEASURE PROGRAMMING

One of our most basic, hardwired instincts as humans is to seek pleasure and avoid pain. This programming is part of our survival instinct: we had it as a fetus, and we will have it until the day we die. In fact, it drives our primary reality from birth to age six, and for good reason. During our first six years, when we're at our most vulnerable, our survival instinct is on high alert to figure out as quickly as possible what's safe and what's not. We develop a "stimulus/response" belief system that basically says pain = bad and pleasure = good. Other names for the stimulus/response concept include cause/effect and action/reaction. This programming is in accordance with one of the natural laws of the universe, specifically Newton's third law of motion, which says that every action has an equal and opposite reaction.

In this context, I call it our pain/pleasure programming. In other words, if it causes pleasure, it's safe and therefore good and desirable. If it causes pain, it's not safe, and therefore our brain tells us to fight, freeze, or get away fast. From a survival standpoint, this stimulus/response belief system is very effective for our first six years of life—it probably saved our lives a number of times as children! If a two-year-old touches a hot stove, she pulls her hand away instantly—no one taught her to do that, and after experiencing it once she will never do it again.

And when our pain/pleasure (i.e., fight/flight) programming kicks in as adults when we're truly in danger, it can save our lives as well.

A few years ago, after receiving a speeding ticket, I was given the option to go to driving school instead of paying a fine. The state trooper in charge of the class was absolutely brilliant. He told us that we could be driving in normal conditions on a clear day, following a car in front of us at the appropriate distance, but if the driver in front of us slammed on his brakes, it would be impossible to avoid a wreck if we had to think fast enough with our *conscious* mind. It would go something like, *Oh, look. The driver in front of me just slammed on his brakes. I need to take my foot off the gas and put it on the brake and mash it down as hard as I can, or I will run into the back of him.* You don't have enough time to do that—you would be in a wreck every single time.

The trooper went on: fortunately, we have a mechanism built into our brain that will *prevent* us from having a wreck every single time (if we're following at the appropriate distance). As soon as our eyes see the brake lights, our unconscious mind literally bypasses our conscious thinking and causes us to take our foot off the gas and apply the brake before we have time to think about it consciously. Before we even realize what's happening, we're already stopped—all thanks to our fight/flight instinct.

Our pain/pleasure programming is not bad, in and of itself. It's directly linked to our survival instinct and our stress response and was designed to play a dominant role in our lives up to about age six, and after age six, kicking in only in life-threatening circumstances. Our pain/pleasure programming is awesome when it keeps my car insurance from going up, but it is a major bummer when it blocks me from happiness, health, and success in my life. What do I mean? If my life is not in imminent mortal danger, then I'm not supposed to be living, believing, feeling, or acting out that mechanism that state trooper was talking about.

Of course, the pain/pleasure mechanism is exactly what is behind the typical three-step success blueprint in self-help over the last sixty-five years. The one with the 97 percent failure rate.

In fact, as children, we are wired to follow this exact blueprint, and it's how most kids try to get what they want. For example, if a five-year-old wants an ice cream cone, he would first think, *I want an ice cream cone* (step 1). Then he would make a plan: go ask Mom (step 2). Finally, he would put the plan into action and ask Mom for an ice cream cone (step 3). But what if Mom says no? He would likely revise his previous plan in step 2 from "go ask Mom" to "bargain with Mom." Then he would follow step 3 again, asking Mom, "If I clean my room first, then can I have an ice cream cone?" This time she says yes. Success!

But for adult success, this blueprint takes us *away* from what we really want precisely because it keeps us focused on a "pain equals bad and pleasure equals good" mentality. As adults, we should think of this blueprint as our "training wheels" belief system and learn to choose to live in love and truth, regardless of pain and pleasure. As adults we all understand that sometimes pleasure is unhealthy and sometimes the painful choice is best. Unfortunately, few adults ever discard their training wheels belief system; most still seek pleasure and avoid pain at all costs, even if it costs them love and truth and the inward state of peace. In essence, most of us are still living as five-year-olds.

You see, when we live according to our pain/pleasure programming and go into fight or flight, it is a state akin to shock. You may have experienced shock if you've been in a car accident or another kind of sudden trauma. When someone is in shock, the unconscious mind disconnects the conscious mind. It wants to get the conscious thinking out of the way and save your life. (It also dumbs you down, suppresses your immune system, and does all the other things stress does that we mentioned earlier.)

Let's say a married man has a one-night affair in the heat of passion. After the fact, he feels terrible; he goes home and, in a terrified outburst of pain and guilt, calls his best friend and tells him what happened. His friend is shocked; the man has never done anything like this before. Finally, the man's friend talks him down and they both decide that the man needs to tell his wife. In agony, after dinner that night, he sits down with his wife and tells her he's had an affair. His wife is devastated—and they both endure a terrible hour of painful questions and answers. The husband is racked with guilt but still maintains he didn't mean to do it and will never do it again. The wife is confused and heartbroken and feels as if she doesn't even know the man she's been married to for years.

If you asked the man directly, "Did you really want to have an affair?," he would usually say, "No! I love my wife; it was just the heat of the moment." I know this; I have counseled hundreds of men in this exact situation. But if you asked me what I thought, I'd respond, "If he did not want to have an affair, he would not have had an affair." As you might imagine, when I've counseled people who have had affairs and told them that, they got hopping mad at me! So why in the world would I say that? Am I trying to make people mad? Absolutely not. Behind every action is an internal goal. And behind every internal goal is a belief. No matter what our beliefs are, we always do what we believe, 100 percent of the time.

In order to have an affair, the man had to believe before he did it that having an affair was the best thing for him at the time: *This will give me enormous pleasure that I need and want right now. My wife hasn't been responsive lately, so I'm justified. I'm only going to do this one time—I'll repent and never do it again.* At the same time, he very likely also had a belief that he did *not* want to have an affair. When you have two beliefs that conflict, what you do in the moment comes down to which belief you're focused on, and thinking and feeling more strongly, in that moment. One belief was rooted in his pain/pleasure programming (his five-year-old thinking), and one was rooted in love and truth (his adult thinking).

In that situation, maybe the man started taking little baby steps toward a compromising situation and really didn't mean to do anything for a period of time. Maybe he and this other woman were having a perfectly casual conversation after an evening meeting at work. Maybe one of them invited the other out somewhere, and the other justified the action and said yes, thinking continuing the conversation would be harmless. But at some point the man crossed a line, and because somewhere deep down he had a belief that an affair is good because it is pleasurable, following through on the affair became inevitable.

At the moment of decision, this man is in fight or flight—he's thinking, *This is one of the worst things I'll ever do.* He may even get close to shock, where his conscious rational thinking is so turned down that he doesn't have the ability to resist. He gets to a place where he is almost like an animal, just "feeling," and then acting on those feelings. When he gets to that line, his conscious mind is so turned off he almost can't turn back. He can barely access his rational mind anymore. When the affair is over, his rational, adult thinking returns—and he feels lower than dirt. *Why did I do that? I knew I shouldn't have done that!* He did it because of his pain/pleasure programming. He was acting and thinking like a five-year-old, and his wife agrees.

If you've been on the wife's side of this kind of behavior, the "I didn't mean to do it" can sound quite hollow. Pain/pleasure programming doesn't excuse anyone's behavior, but hopefully it helps explain it. Yes, the husband chose to do it, but in a way, it wasn't him who chose it. His decision was caused by destructive, unconscious programming based on the pain/pleasure response. So when someone says, "I won't do it again," typically the only way for this to be true is to heal those wrong beliefs. The only way is to fix their programming.

This doesn't just apply to affairs; your pain/pleasure programming also explains why you yell at your kids, why you can't resist cookies-and-cream ice cream when you're trying to lose weight—almost any circumstance in which you do what you don't want to do. Your willpower simply doesn't stand much of a chance.

The presence of our pain/pleasure programming not only explains why willpower is so ineffective, but it also explains why pursuing an external circumstance should never be our primary goal if we're seeking success in our lives.

When we are honest with ourselves, as I hope you were in answering my questions earlier, and realize that what we think we want most is an external circumstance—particularly if it's not a winning situation for all parties involved (such as our spouses, our families, or our business partners)—our wanting an external circumstance above all is a sure sign it's a goal rooted in our fear-based survival instinct. For some reason, we believe this circumstance is going to either bring us pleasure or protect us from pain, and we need it to survive. Somewhere along the way, something happened, probably early in life, that taught us achieving this circumstance was a matter of survival, or of "being okay" in life. We tend to revert back to our pain/pleasure programming to quiet and soothe the place inside us that feels unsettled or lacking.

I had a client one time who was a multi-multimillionaire. It would have been very difficult for him to ever spend all the money he had. However, he was also one of the most miserable people I have encountered. He was always stressed, hard-driving, and irritated or angry. You know the type (or maybe you are the type). With just a tiny bit of digging we found the source: this gentleman had grown up on the "wrong side of the tracks"—poor, ridiculed for his old, worn clothes, and ashamed. So the individual made a "vow," much like Scarlett O'Hara did in the movie *Gone with the Wind*: "With God as my witness, I will never be hungry again." This man vowed that he would never be poor again, and it became a matter of life and death.

He thought money would purchase for him the internal states of love, joy, and peace. *If I can just get X amount of dollars, clothes, cars, and possessions, then I will be okay.* But we know now that this never works, and it certainly didn't with him.

So although we may think an external circumstance is what we want most, the majority of us have made at least two hidden assumptions that are simply wrong—that an external circumstance will make us happy and fulfilled long term, and that an external circumstance will purchase an internal state for us right now (love, joy, peace, etc.). The greatest teachers of all time have always taught that success in life does not come from seeking pleasure and avoiding pain at all costs. Success comes from living in truth and love at all times, and whatever circumstances come from that are the best ones for us, even if there is pain involved.

## WHY THE INTERNAL STATE IS THE RIGHT ANSWER

Let's review just a bit. If the number one goal in your life is an external circumstance, you will most likely not achieve it, because the stress it inherently causes sabotages your best efforts. And even if you do achieve it, it will not satisfy and fulfill you long term. On the other hand, if the number one goal in your life is an internal state, your outcomes change quite a bit.

1. **You will almost always achieve it.** Nothing external has to change, and the only thing internally that has to change are energy patterns, which can change very easily with the right tools. As I said, I've rarely seen this *not* work for any of my clients, around the globe and in any imaginable circumstance. You'll see many of their stories throughout the book.

2. **Once you achieve it, no one can take it away from you.** This is what Victor Frankl discovered during the Holocaust. He called it the last of the human freedoms: the right to choose your internal state or attitude, regardless of your external circumstances. After he was out of the prison camps, he wrote the classic *Man's Search for Meaning* and helped millions to focus on their internal attitude (inward state) rather than the external circumstances of their lives.[6]

3. **Once you achieve it, you are guaranteed that it will completely satisfy and fulfill you, because it's what you really wanted all along, but probably just never knew it.**

4. **If your number one goal is the internal state, you almost always get the external circumstances you desire as a free bonus.** Here's the true magic: once you create the internal state of love, joy, or peace, or whatever you answered number 3 with, you have created the internal power source that creates the external circumstances of your life that you desire. But without that positive internal state, it's like vacuuming your rug without the cord being plugged in.

## HOW THE LOVE CODE WILL HELP YOU GET WHAT YOU REALLY WANT

Most people live their whole lives believing some external result is what they really want. Many people go after a dozen or two in their lifetime, thinking each time that "this one will do it for me." Realizing that you've spent the best resources of your life on a lie can be a shocking and even devastating experience. You may have given up your youth, your money, your relationships, your energy, and your health to pursue "the thing" you thought you wanted most—only to discover not only that it isn't what you really want most, but that it actually led you *away* from what you did want most. Perhaps you've discovered that you have believed the lie the vast majority of our culture also believes: external circumstances purchase the internal state of love and peace.

On the other hand, if you are among the small segment that answered question number 1 with an inward state, let me be the first to congratulate you. You are truly in the top percentile of what I believe is the most important metric for success. However, that doesn't mean you have *achieved* the internal state. You don't tend to want something you already have. If you already had the inward state of love and peace, you probably would have answered the genie question with something like, "I don't wish for anything. I have everything I need and want. Maybe more love and peace."

Whether you've just discovered that the internal state is your ultimate success goal or whether you've known it for a long time, the tools and process of the Love Code are how you're going to get it. As a concept, the Love Code is actually very simple: it means doing the opposite of what ignites your stress response. Specifically, you need to give up your expectation of a specific and future end result attained by willpower, and instead focus on creating the internal state that is the power source for your external circumstances. Here's another way to put it in more practical terms:

*Do whatever you do from an inward state of love, focusing on the present moment.*

That's it. That's the Love Code. I know, this is only chapter 1. But now I've walked you through all the background information you will need to fully understand why the typical success blueprint doesn't work, and why this theory and application does. Living in love while focusing on the present moment is all you have to do to achieve the most success imaginable, in every life area—the *perfect* success for you.

If you answered the three questions in this chapter honestly, you should have discovered what you really want in life, and you know the basic theory behind how to get it.

If I could give you one gift for your life, it would be your answer to question 3: the inward state of love. But I can't give that to you. You can get it for yourself, through the process you'll learn in the following chapters. It is what you want and need most, and what will truly satisfy, fulfill, and create your perfect success! But to get it, you have to give up the external end result that you thought you wanted most. This step of faith will open the door to the results you want most!

Before we go any further, I'd like you to give yourself the opportunity to receive the same kind of transformational *aha* experience I had twenty-five years ago, after Hope kicked me out of the house, that changed my heart in an instant and made me capable of living out the Love Code right away. The transformational *aha* is akin to a near-death experience, where someone—even his or her personality—is forever changed in ways that likely never could have happened through willpower. The person may have even tried to make such changes before unsuccessfully. But the heart and mind control the body. When the programming changes, everything can change, and often on a dime. When this happens, you can't mistake it!

We can't control whether or not we receive this transformational *aha*, but it's such an incredible gift, I want to be sure you give yourself every opportunity to receive it. All you have to do now is pray[7] and meditate on this idea of the Love Code, being open to the possibility of receiving this experience. Specifically, I'd like you to meditate over each of the following points, one at a time and in this order:

1. It's not *ever* your fault.

   Note: Ancient manuscripts put it this way: "When I do what I don't want to do, it's not me doing it." Your actions are the result of fear-based programming, which is a million times more powerful than your conscious ability to choose. I hope and pray that this helps you with any guilt and self-worth issues, as it did me. If you consistently make the wrong choice, you simply have the human version of a computer hard-drive virus.

2. The internal always creates the external—never the other way around.

3. What you really want most is never an external circumstance—it's always the internal state of love, joy, and peace.

4. WIIFM love (which is what most people call, and believe is, real love) often looks like love on the outside, but it is really an unhealthy attempt to control others and circumstances to get the external circumstances that you think will make you happy—but they never will, long term!

5. Your willpower, fueled by fear and faulty programming, has a one-in-a-million shot at making you happy and successful. Ninety-nine percent of the time, it will leave you stressed and frustrated.

6. The internal state of love, joy, and peace is a miraculous/divine power source for life and success that virtually always works.

7. Living in love for the next thirty minutes as best you can, giving up external and physical results and circumstances, will produce success and happiness beyond your wildest dreams—no matter what!

I recommend this approach first for every one of my private clients, and about two-thirds of them experience the transformational *aha*. Here's what I tell them: pray and meditate on these principles for an hour, or a week, or as long as it takes for them to really saturate your mind and heart. You don't necessarily have to memorize them. Just keep praying and meditating on these principles until you find that you not only believe them, but you have made the *commitment* to follow this path of living in love in the present moment, no matter what—not using willpower and expectations, but doing the best you can, with the support you need, moment by moment.

I've found that about half my clients get to this point gradually, and about half get to this point all of a sudden, like an epiphany. But whether it happens gradually or quickly, one day they discover themselves believing. They can see how their problem is not their fault, they can see how the external never creates the internal—and they know it deep in their heart.

We'll talk more about belief in a later chapter, but I should warn you that even trying to believe can become a matter of willpower and expectations. Ladies and gentlemen, it is not our job to believe. Trying to believe blocks true belief, because that means we've turned it into an expectation we have to achieve with willpower. Don't try to believe, and don't put a timetable on it. If you do, you'll be blocking your ability to experience true belief, because you'll be working against yourself.

It takes most people three weeks or less to get to this point of belief and commitment. But however long it takes, if you can give up willpower and expectations, one day you will discover yourself believing these principles and committing to living them.

Once you do, my advice is to exclusively pray and meditate on principle number seven *only*. Maybe read through the first six principles once a week to review. Focus intensely on the seventh principle for a period of time (remember, don't put a timeline on this process!). That's when the transformational *aha* typically happens for my clients. Give yourself the opportunity to receive that transformational *aha* that can deprogram you and reprogram you in an instant. You can also pray and meditate on these principles daily as you use the tools over time. If you do receive the transformational *aha* and find yourself instantly better able to love everyone and everything in whatever you do, unhampered by any expectation for the future, then you may not even need the remainder of this book, but I still suggest you read it to understand more about the mechanisms behind what has changed in you—or to work on a new success issue. Or share the book with someone else who does need it.

I am often asked, "How will I know if I have one of these reprogramming, transformational *aha*s?" *You will know!* It's like love (the real thing): it transcends words. You will know and feel that something deep inside of you has changed and you will never be the same. You may feel warmth, excitement, peace, a sense of well-being beyond the physical, a lightness, an absence of fear or worry, or a feeling of love. Your thoughts, beliefs, and actions will spontaneously change. Trust me: you will know!

But please don't worry if this transformational *aha* doesn't happen. It doesn't mean you've done anything wrong. It may happen later, or it may be that your best path forward is to use the tools set forth here to deprogram and reprogram, which cause the transformation mechanically and automatically.

If you don't receive the *aha*, whatever you do, *don't stop here.* Remember, that's what most books do: they take two hundred pages or more to explain the principles, and then stop, assuming that once you know what to do, you can simply use your willpower to do it. It may feel like it's enough to know what to do. You may want to try it right away and test it out for yourself. So I also want you to feel completely free to close this book and commit to living out the Love Code by willpower alone. You may do a pretty good job of loving everyone and living in the present moment for the first day or two, but I'm afraid you'll find out that it rarely lasts. In fact, it almost can't last.

Your internal hardware and software have you programmed against it. Almost no one I've seen has been able to do it with willpower alone—including me. Merely understanding the concept and using your willpower to live it out just won't work in the long term.

On the other hand, you might still be having trouble understanding the concept itself. So many of my clients I've worked with one-on-one couldn't understand the principles at first, because they're so upside down to how we are innately programmed and to what almost everyone teaches. It was almost like I was telling them that the world really is flat, or I was speaking a different language. They just couldn't conceive that they could achieve their end result by giving it up, and that they could achieve what they have never been able to achieve by not trying as hard!

In cases like this, I would simply repeat the principles over and over, which would result in an intensely confused look on their face. Finally, inevitably, they would get it. Every time, an excited smile would come over their face, their entire body language would ignite, and they would say something like "Ohhh . . ." or "Wow . . ." or "I see . . ." The light had come on; they now understood. So if the light has not yet come on for you, that is the norm. Keep praying and meditating on the principles, and it will happen. When it does, it will be as if you found a secret door to happiness in your life that you never knew existed.

Either way, the good news is that your success depends neither on willpower nor on intellectual understanding alone. The rest of the book will explain the tools and the process to put it into practice successfully.

But before we get into the tools and the process themselves, we're first going to learn about two important concepts: cellular memory and what I call Spiritual Physics.

## chapter 2

# CELLULAR MEMORY

It's usually pretty easy to know when something's not working in our lives; the symptoms of pain or anxiety are hard to miss. You might have a toothache, or be up late at night worrying over your teenage son's whereabouts. What's not so easy is discovering the true source of those problems, and actually healing the source rather than simply managing its symptoms. We have a natural tendency to think the problem is our current circumstance, but this is often inaccurate. If we invest our energy in changing our circumstances as the source of our problems when our circumstances are *not* the source of the problem, we simply create more stress!

Over the last fifty years and especially the last fifteen, experts have verified that the source of your symptoms of pain and anxiety is usually not located in your body or even in your environment. The source is located in the unseen issues of your unconscious and subconscious mind, or what science calls "cellular memories."

So what exactly do we mean when we say "cellular memories"? Really, we are simply talking about your *memories*. Researchers began adding the word *cellular* because we used to believe that all memories were stored in the brain—until over many years with lots of patients, surgeons removed every part of the brain and found the memories were always still there. The experiences of organ transplant recipients also support this idea. Now we know that memories are stored in cells all over the body, but they're still just what we would call our "memories," which is how I'll refer to them throughout the rest of this book. Also, out of the various terms writers and researchers have used for cellular memories, I've come to prefer the term that King Solomon used, particularly since he was the earliest source I found for this concept: the issues of the heart. But to distinguish this concept from our cardiovascular heart, I call it the "spiritual heart." So when I refer to the *spiritual heart* throughout the rest of the book, you can just as easily substitute *cellular memories* or *the subconscious or unconscious mind*. I simply mean the place where our good and bad memories, the source of all our life issues and problems, reside.

On September 12, 2004, the *Dallas Morning News* ran a story, "Medical School Breakthrough," about a new research study that had just been completed at Southwestern University Medical Center in Dallas, Texas. Scientists had discovered that our experiences do not just reside in our brains but are recorded at the cellular level throughout our bodies, and they believed these *cellular memories* were the true source of illness and disease. They interviewed Eric Nestler, an MD from Harvard, who said,

> Scientists believe these cellular memories might mean the difference between a healthy life, and death. . . . Cancer can be the result of a bad cellular memory replacing a good one. . . . This may provide one of the most powerful ways of curing illness.[1]

This article was reprinted all over the world. If you read the fine print about what Southwestern is calling cellular memories, and what Solomon is calling the issues of the heart, they are talking about the same thing.

In October 2004, the *Dallas Morning News* ran a follow-up article to the one cited earlier: "A Cell Forgets." It's a long excerpt, but worth seeing at length:

Throughout the natural world, scientists are finding, cells and organisms record their experiences, all without the benefit of a brain. Scientists believe these cellular memories might mean the difference between a healthy life and death.

Cancer can be a result of bad cellular memories replacing good ones. Psychological trauma, addiction and depression may all be furthered by abnormal memories inside cells. Diseases that turn up later in life, scientists suspect, may be due to errant memories programmed into cells as people age. Even real memory, the kind that requires a brain, also seems to rely on memories locked in cells.

Now scientists are striving to understand how cells acquire these memories and perhaps treat disease at its roots by adjusting them.

"This may provide one of the most powerful ways of curing illness," said Dr. Eric Nestler, chairman of the psychiatry department at the University of Texas Southwestern Medical Center at Dallas.

For many diseases, he says, treatments today aren't much better than Band-Aids. They address a disease's symptoms, but not its cause. "Harnessing this knowledge," Nestler said, "offers the potential of really correcting the abnormality."[2]

The article goes on to explain that Dr. Nestler and other cellular biologists, such as Dr. Susan Lindquist and Nobel laureate Dr. Eric Kandel, have discovered specific chemical markers on our cells that seem to signal whether to use a certain gene or not. In fact, Dr. Nestler published research in the *Journal of Neuroscience* that shows how electric shocks can change the markers on brain genes in mice.[3]

However, research has revealed that something else besides electric shock can change these markers of cellular memory: a mother's love. Through lab experiments with rats, the researchers found that a mother rat licking her pups literally changes the chemical markers attached to the gene that governs their experience of fear, resulting in the pups displaying less fear throughout their lifetime and indicating that a mother's love can "program their brains for life."[4]

In other words, these researchers have verified that love is an antidote to fear, and both love and fear can be measured on the cellular level. They are also discovering that outside influences can "brainwash" an otherwise "peaceful cell" to become an invasive cancer cell, and you can see that in these markers as well. "The peaceful cell is *reprogrammed* [emphasis mine] with strategically placed gene markers that cause it to grow out of control."[5]

This research is from 2004. Today scientists are still putting their best efforts into studying the specific markers of cellular memory and understanding how to manipulate them in the laboratory. In fact, you may have already heard about the power of cellular memory through the stories of organ transplant patients. One famous example is Claire Sylvia, who wrote about her experience in the book *A Change of Heart*. After her heart and lung transplant at Yale–New Haven Hospital in 1988, she noticed significant personality changes: she experienced strong cravings for Kentucky Fried Chicken, which as a health-conscious dancer and choreographer she would have never eaten before; she suddenly liked blues and greens rather than the bright reds and oranges she typically wore; and she became aggressive in her behavior, which was even more out of character. After some investigation, she discovered that all these new personality traits were characteristic of her donor. Dozens of similar experiences by other organ transplant donors have been reported as well. The explanation is cellular memory.[6]

As a research scientist at the University of Wisconsin, Dr. Bruce Lipton was cloning human muscle cells, trying to determine why they atrophied. He discovered that individual muscle cells react and change based on their "perception" of their environment, not necessarily the "actual" environment. Further research led him to discover that the same is true for human beings as a whole: we react and change based on our perceptions of our environment (*not* our environment as it really is). Another word for these perceptions are our beliefs.[7] Dr. Lipton says that virtually every health problem originates from a wrong belief in the subconscious mind. After reading the fine print in their supporting research, I believe what Dr. Lipton calls the beliefs of the subconscious mind are exactly what Dr. Nestler and his colleagues call cellular memory, and what Solomon called the spiritual heart. And as we said in the last chapter, because the subconscious mind is literally one million times more powerful than the conscious mind, the odds of having the life you want without changing those beliefs is a million-to-one shot.[8]

The phenomenon of cellular memory applies to every person on the planet, not just the sick or underachieving. Our cellular memories (or subconscious beliefs, or issues in your spiritual heart) will catch up with you sooner or later—just as they did in our example of the husband who had an affair in the last chapter. Like a virus on your computer, you can't just ignore them and hope they'll miraculously disappear; it simply won't happen.

Dr. John Sarno of the NYU School of Medicine has done groundbreaking work in psychosomatic illnesses and the mind-body connection, specifically with back pain.[9] Dr. Sarno agrees with Dr. Lipton and Dr. Nestler and says that adult chronic pain and illness originate from destructive cellular memories. If you heal the memory, the chronic pain and illness go away.

In fact, holistic practitioner Dr. Andrew Weil says in his bestselling book *Health and Healing*, "All illness is psychosomatic."[10] He doesn't mean it's not real (and neither does Dr. Sarno); he means it does not originate from a physical source—thus also agreeing with the aforementioned experts.

Dr. Doris Rapp, a world-renowned pediatric allergist, is a dear friend of mine and one of my heroes. Many years ago Dr. Rapp was willing to go outside the box of standard medicine in order to help children. She has taken criticism from her peers for doing so but has stayed the course. Today, there are thousands and thousands of people around the world who point to Dr. Rapp as their turning point, and she has received a list of humanitarian honors as long as your arm.

In her bestselling book *Is This Your Child?*, she talks about the "barrel effect."[11] In fact, her book was the first place I'd ever seen it discussed, and it made a big impact on me many years ago. According to the barrel effect, we can think of all the stress in our life as being in one big internal barrel. As long as the barrel is not full, our body can deal with new stress. Somebody might get angry at us, something might not go our way, or we might be exposed to a toxin, and we would still feel okay; our body and mind can deal with it. Once our barrel is full, however, the tiniest little thing will get us. So the concept of the straw that broke the camel's back is fairly scientifically accurate.

For example, let's say yesterday you ate some peanuts and you felt fine. But today you eat one peanut and have an allergic reaction. It makes absolutely no sense—it can't be the peanuts, right? You ate some yesterday, and you were fine. What's different about today? The truth is, it was the peanuts, and it wasn't the peanuts. Yes, eating that peanut triggered a negative physical reaction. But the peanut would not have triggered the reaction if your stress barrel had not been full. The real cause was not the peanut, it was the stress (or, more accurately, the internal "source" of the stress). Your stress level was the only differentiating factor.

This theory proves true both physically and nonphysically. If you're a parent, you've probably seen it with your kids. When you tell your two-year-old it's time to go home from the playground, on Wednesday he might trot along obediently. But on Sunday, when you tell him the same thing, at the same time of day, and at the same park, he may go ballistic and shoot off a geyser of adrenaline in the worst temper tantrum he's ever had. His reaction each time depended on how full his stress barrel was. Once his stress barrel was overflowing, his unconscious treats having to leave the playground as a life-threatening emergency. (Externally, it simply appears as if he overreacted.) You can see from this that we are not designed to live life with a full stress barrel. Living out of balance in this way leads us to "malfunction" physically and nonphysically.

But the number one job of our stress response is to protect us, not to make us happy. Whether physically or nonphysically, our stress response would much rather overreact than underreact, and it will often set off the fight-or-flight reaction "just in case." If it underreacts, we could be dead, and it will have failed at its most important job. Also, the amount of adrenaline released at the time of the event, based on how stressful the situation feels in the moment, determines the strength of that memory in our spiritual heart throughout our lives. Our mind will always prioritize experiences that it believes will keep us safe and out of danger, and it determines this based on our memories— specifically, fear-based memories. You can see why all of us have unhelpful programming in our spiritual hearts—a stressful memory wreaking havoc in our life right now might be because we had a bad day at the park when we were two!

Our stress barrel even includes generational memories. You could have had an idyllic childhood and a trauma-free life, but for some reason still have significant confidence issues, depression issues, health issues, or addictions. I've worked with many people who fit into that category, who later learn that a significant trauma occurred generations back—for example, a child was hit by a train and died—and no one in the family was ever the same again. These memories, which are powerful human hard-drive viruses, are passed down like DNA. The more adrenaline released when the event happens, the stronger the memory is, the more it affects you, and the more likely it is to be passed on to future generations. So the memories affecting you may not even be yours. Generational memories can explain the existence of what we started calling "the cycle" and "breaking the cycle" a few decades back, or the behavior, thought, and feeling patterns that keep repeating in certain families. If you can remove the stress from the person who has the problem now (even if it is genetic and many generations removed from the origin), even the genetic problem will usually heal.

One of my clients finally figured out that the source of her current symptoms went back over a hundred years. After doing some poking around in her family history, she discovered that during the Civil War, her great-great-grandmother witnessed her husband and three sons killed by the enemy in their home and her entire house was burned to the ground. We can only imagine how that event affected that woman's stress, her health, and the circumstances of her whole life. She passed those stress memories (and their symptoms) down to her descendants, even those so far removed from the situation that they didn't even know about it—including my client. But such stresses don't mean there is no hope of healing them. Once we identified this memory from past generations, we could address the source of my client's problems and she was able to heal. You'll learn how to do that for yourself in Part II.

If you compare the details of the research of all the experts mentioned, they say the same thing: the source of every problem can be linked to our subconscious mind, otherwise known as our cellular memories, or spiritual heart. The trigger is something in our current circumstances related to the past memory, and the symptom is the stress response.

## HOW CELLULAR MEMORIES CAUSE THE NEGATIVE SYMPTOMS IN OUR LIVES

Here's what all this really means. Your body is made up of 7,000,000, 000,000,000,000,000,000,000 (7 octillion) atoms. Every single one of those atoms is influenced by your thoughts. Every time you have a new thought, you are creating new connections or neural pathways in your brain. When you have the same thoughts or emotions automatically triggered by a certain event, this emotion or thought comes from a neural network that was wired when you experienced an event for the first time. These neural networks are your cellular memories. Every time you experience a similar event, the same memory is triggered, and you are usually not consciously aware of where it comes from or why you feel that way.

The challenge is that most of your responses happen on autopilot, based on these memories of previous experiences. If you grew up with great role models and an empowering life, then you may be one of the lucky ones who have a pretty great life today. But if you had traumas in your past that you haven't yet healed, whether in your own life or the lives of your predecessors, then your life is likely to be filled with similar experiences that keep coming up again and again based on your cellular memories.

Your cellular memories are the reference points your brain uses to decide how to respond in the here and now. It's the reason so many of us role-play our parents in our relationships as adults, for better or for worse—even when we know better and try our best not to act that way.

So if you have a memory with anger in it, or fear, or low self-esteem, or hundreds of other similarly negative feelings, that memory can make you sick, lead to failure, and destroy your most important relationships. When you encounter any situation in your life, you may think you're approaching this situation completely anew as a rational logical adult, and making new conscious decisions about how you're going to react in the present moment. In actuality, your spiritual heart is searching for a memory that best matches the sensory input it's receiving. According to research, our sensory perception (a sight, smell, feeling, etc.) is gone after one second. So however we respond after one second has nothing to do with our senses, it has to do with our memory banks.[12] "We don't see things as they are. We see them as *we* are."[13] Recall the example we used earlier about two people side by side in rush-hour traffic. One goes into road rage; the other is cool as a cucumber. They are in the exact same external circumstance. The difference can't be the circumstance. It has to be something internal, and it is.

If your spiritual heart finds a happy memory, you tend to react positively. If it finds a painful memory, you tend to react in fear or anger. That fear-based memory will produce negative symptoms in your physiology, thoughts, beliefs, emotions, and behaviors. A memory functions a lot like a cell phone, broadcasting and receiving constantly. That memory broadcasts a "fear signal" to surrounding cells, as well as to the hypothalamus in your brain, which governs the stress response. When the cells receive that signal, they close and go into death and disease mode; they don't eliminate toxins or take in needed oxygen, nutrition, hydration, and ions. If the cell remains in this closed state long enough, the odds skyrocket that it will unmask a disease gene. In fact, Dr. Bruce Lipton says that this is the *only* way you can have a disease manifest in your life. If this doesn't happen, you literally can't get sick, because your immune and healing systems will always be working at optimum levels.

When the hypothalamus receives the fear signal from the memory, it turns on the stress response. Bingo—that's where every problem begins. Our fight-or-flight reaction is triggered, our hypothalamus floods our body with stress hormones such as cortisol, and we shift into pain/pleasure programming so that we must seek relief from this pain or fear at all costs. Now we want to either run from that thing or destroy it. Our brain has disconnected or turned down our rational conscious thinking *except* to rationalize fight or flight. That stress makes us sick, tired, dumb, negative, and a failure—producing virtually every kind of negative symptom possible. See the connection?

This concept has very important implications for the role of our conscious mind in decision making and action. Dr. William Tiller told me the following about conscious and unconscious intention: "If they conflict, the unconscious wins every time." When we act on something, one second before we consciously decide to do it, there's a chemical spike in the brain, mandating what our decision will be and already mobilizing the body to do that action—all just a second before our conscious mind decides what we're going to do. So our conscious choice is actually mandated by our programming if we have a fear memory related to the situation (which you are frequently unaware of): we're only coming up with a logical explanation for what our unconscious/ subconscious has already decided. *National Geographic* refers to this as "the illusion of intention."[14]

You've seen many examples of it in your own life. In America, some farmer families have driven nothing but a Chevy for generations ("It's a family thing—we drive Chevys"). Even if Chevy is ranked number 47 in quality, drivers in these families will come up with every possible rationalization or explanation why there's a conspiracy at work here and why Chevy *should* be ranked number one, but somehow isn't. Of course, these arguments aren't based on the true quality of the vehicle, but on the programming they've received from their parents and grandparents, and their surroundings. If Chevy is number one, then their conscious and unconscious mind are in harmony. If not, they're wondering why people are writing all these lies about Chevy, and they're constantly in stress—which, as seemingly unimportant as the surface issue sounds, is still adding to their stress barrel and possibly causing a variety of symptoms in their lives they can't find the cause for. Why do they keep doing this? Why can't they see what they are doing and just start believing the truth? Because their unconscious is "mandating" that they buy Chevy, and the conscious mind has an innate "need" to make sense of circumstances and why you think, feel, believe, and do what you do. So they do what they are "compelled" to do, not knowing why, and rationalize why, because they don't really know.

A more serious example would be our religious upbringing. As for me, I was raised in a very strict religious household, which resulted in something like a schizophrenic conflict inside me: I was taught that God is love, but that he was also just waiting for me to put a toe out of line to smack me down. As a young adult I threw this concept of God overboard because it made no sense to me. Or at least my conscious mind threw it overboard, because it was causing me so much pain. It literally took decades for my spiritual heart to follow. But starting at that moment, I went on a search. Over time my beliefs healed and changed, and today, I have chosen not to be part of any religion (i.e., regularly visiting a certain building by a certain name and with a certain set of rules to follow to be a "good member"). I have found good and bad in all of them.

However, in no way do I intend to imply that I think less of, or look down on, people who believe and live religion. I don't. I am simply relaying my own beliefs and my own path. Today, I consider myself to be a follower of Jesus—period—nothing more or less. Jesus taught that if you love, you have done it all; if you don't live in love, you have missed the mark. I believe my job, with every person and in any and every situation, is to love with no agenda and no strings attached—whether they like me, are nice to me, or the opposite. My job is not to judge, just love. I believe this is "spiritual," not religious, living.

But here's my question: What is inside of you? Is it Ford or Chevy? Religious or not? Big government or antigovernment? Is there any sense of comparison or competition where whatever you believe in has to come out on top? Or are you continually seeking and open to the whole truth, no matter what? America is one of the richest and blessed nations on the planet. Yet so many Americans are incredibly stressed about finances because they're comparing their situation to someone else whom they think has it better. Whenever someone comes into my office stressed about finances, I ask them: "Do you have a home? Do you have food on the table? Do you have electricity?" Ruefully they usually answer, "Yes." They're typically worried about something that will never happen—and even if they have lost something big, somehow they will still have a roof over their head and food to eat. But the source of their stress is the internal fear programming causing them to compare themselves with others, not because their true safety or survival was threatened.

I once saw an online poll that asked, "If you could pull up your home, possessions, and wherever you're living right now and put it all in the poorest part of Ethiopia, would you feel any different?" The typical reaction has fascinated me. Most people said yes, they would feel differently—but not because they'd feel more content and compassionate. They'd feel anxious because now they'd need to protect their stuff from everyone else who has it so much worse than they do! This kind of unconscious intention is why we have to deprogram and reprogram the memories in our spiritual heart. Otherwise, we'll be a puppet to subconscious or unconscious issues that not only don't help or serve us, they might not even be true in the first place.

Let's see what unconscious intention looks like in action. A man approaches a line of traffic at a red light, and he becomes angry. Anger is a fear-based emotion, so if he is experiencing fear in a situation that is not life-threatening, this is a sign that he has a human hard-drive virus, which simply means something in his survival mechanism is malfunctioning. That is to say, he has memories in his spiritual heart (or subconscious mind) that are telling him this is a life-threatening situation, whether it's from his upbringing, past experience, or even generational experience he may or may not know about. Let's also say he's read the introduction to this book, so his conscious mind knows what he's supposed to do: sit in his car patiently and love the driver in front of him. Good luck with that, right?

You can already see the problem: conscious insight doesn't stand a chance. When his brain and body chemistry are telling him to fight, the last thing he wants to do, or can do, is sit in love. That's the last thing any of us would want to do! Few are capable of resisting our pain/pleasure programming when our bodies are in an active state of fight or flight. Willpower just won't work, because the trigger is pulled before we even realize what's happening. In fact, whatever willpower individuals can muster in fight or flight is usually just enough to get them to the car horn, or whatever they can get their hands on the fastest that will allow them to "blow off steam" or bring them some instant relief from the pain they're feeling. It is usually not enough to get them to do what they believe is right.

## THERE IS NO TRUE HEALING WITHOUT THE HEALING OF YOUR MEMORIES

So there is no true healing without healing your memories—physically or nonphysically! If there's something you don't like about your current experience, you can take this to the bank: you have memories that contain similar negative experiences, and specific programming for what you are experiencing. In other words, you're reliving and reproducing your fear-based memories over and over. If you find yourself in any kind of cycle in your life, those memories are the source of the cycle. In fact, everything—your physiology, your thoughts, your beliefs, your emotions, and your behaviors—are all manifestations of your memories and the beliefs that come from them. Your fear-based programming is mandating your current situation.

I hope you're seeing more clearly now why willpower and most therapy don't work: they don't get to the source of the real problem. Even therapies such as conscious desensitization that *seem* to get at the memories themselves do not usually provide lasting healing. Why? They tend to program our unconscious to *repress* those memories and thus disconnect our emotional responses from them. This is coping, not true healing. Also, even repressed, these memories fill up our stress barrel. In other words, they effectively place us in a constant state of internal unconscious stress. Even if those memories don't actively bother you anymore emotionally, they may still be causing more problems than ever in a variety of symptoms you can't seem to get rid of. Repression plus coping is the *opposite* of healing. Many people simply end up feeling numb, rather than experiencing the positive results of love, joy, or peace. Repression plus coping still equals stress.

Over the years, many times someone would come to me to deal with a particular problem, but then offhandedly mention another more traumatic incident that happened long ago. They'd believe they had dealt with that incident because they had done therapy for thirty years for it. I would say, "That's great," but also know that issue would probably come up again in my work with them. Most likely it had just been repressed, or they had learned coping mechanisms—it hadn't been healed.

Hypnosis is another technique that attempts to go in and heal issues in our unconscious. But I would never allow even the person I trusted most in the world to do hypnosis on me. I'm not saying it can't work. As well-meaning and as experienced as the therapist may be, a hypnotist can very easily disturb something in our unconscious without meaning to, or leave an unintentional posthypnotic suggestion that could make things potentially far worse than they were before. And no one—not even the hypnotist—would know why.

I've witnessed this happen more than once. I'll never forget seeing this during one of my doctoral practicums. The guy doing the hypnosis was a genius—according to me, at least. He was the head of the department at a top academic university, and he was extremely experienced and respected as a practitioner. I was observing him working with a person using hypnosis, when I faintly heard someone else talking outside through a closed window. The person outside had no idea a hypnosis was going on inside the building; she was just having a conversation. But through the closed window, I heard this very faint "never going to be able to do it." I had no idea what they were talking about. An assignment, a relationship, a new blouse? But when I heard the comment, I had what seemed to be a random thought: *I wonder if that person in hypnosis heard that.* The look on the hypnotized person's face made me believe that he had heard it, and if he did, that phrase "never going to be able to do it" instantly became a hypnotic suggestion that went straight to his unconscious. Whatever solution the hypnotist was suggesting, the person's unconscious was telling him he would never be able to do it. About six months later, I found out that the person's problems had increased tenfold after hypnosis and no one knew why. When I heard this, I approached the hypnotist and told him what I had heard and seen and asked if this might be why things had gotten worse. Based on the look on his face, I could tell that he knew it could very well be the reason. However, he said, "I doubt that has anything to do with it." But he didn't really know, and there was nothing he thought he could do about it anyway. To further complicate matters, the unconscious mind can interpret the hypnotist's words in a different way than they are meant, based on previous fear memory programming.

Please note that this is just my opinion. I have seen some good things come out of hypnosis, such as quitting smoking, but personally I would never do it based on the potential for things to go wrong.

Typical therapy can go on for years and fail to have a lasting impact because it's either focused completely on the conscious mind ("let's talk about your mother"), or it's stumbling around in the depths of your unconscious without a flashlight, and without the proper tools for the job. Instead, we need to target and heal the source, which is the original memory that's triggering this reaction in the first place. More specifically, we need to identify the human hard-drive virus, deprogram that memory so it no longer sends that fear signal that is turning off our immune system and our best resources, and then reprogram it so that it can operate in truth and love, producing all the positive symptoms our bodies were designed to produce naturally. For that we need concrete tools that are designed, tested, and capable of deprogramming and reprogramming, not just willpower or words.[15]

## HEALING SOURCE MEMORIES

Even though scientists are still learning about how to manipulate the markers on our cells in a laboratory environment, I am happy to tell you that you don't need to wait for a laboratory breakthrough to deprogram and reprogram your memories. It is possible to do now.

Wait a minute: How can it be possible to heal something that happened in the past—particularly if it didn't even happen to you, as in generational memories? For the spiritual heart (or subconscious/ unconscious mind)—where all the programming for these issues resides—there is no past or future, only the present. Everything is immediate, 360-degree, surround-sound raw experience happening now, in the moment. Even though we think of memories as being in our past, they are very much in our present to the unconscious mind, and we can access them right now. In fact, you're going to learn exactly how to identify and heal your source memories in Part II, but we're just going to cover the general concepts here. You'll need to understand these before we put them into practice later.

The first step to healing our memories is to understand the whole truth about the incident that created the memory. Whenever a painful memory is created, we typically simultaneously create an incorrect belief (a lie, or a misinterpretation of the event), and it is actually this incorrect belief, or our *interpretation* of this event, that causes us to react in fear, not the event itself.

In fact, a memory that triggers fear *always* goes back to a wrong interpretation of the original event. The true source of my fear and stress is not the fact that Mom died; it's my belief that because Mom died, I'll never be okay again. It's not the diagnosis of cancer; it's my belief that because I've been diagnosed with cancer, my life is over. It's not the unkind thing someone did to me in and of itself; it's my belief that this unkind thing means that I am a person of inferior worth and value.

By the way, the original incident may or may not have been what a psychologist (or anyone else) would call traumatic. The incident may have happened during our first six years of life, when we had a temper tantrum for whatever reason, and it was programmed as a trauma. I have had many clients whose success issues go back to these kinds of seemingly minor incidents, and I often call them "Popsicle memories," after a client who discovered that her success issues went back to when she was five years old and had a tantrum over not receiving a Popsicle.[16]

Whether we would define our past experiences as "traumatic" today makes no difference to our subconscious and unconscious mind. What's important is to heal the memory and fear signal it's transmitting. We must identify and remove the lie created from the past painful memory and replace it with the truth. Just like you would pull out a splinter, you can pull out the lie that's causing your pain and causing you to see the world through dark-colored glasses.

To be clear, when I say "understand the whole truth" about the incident, I mean as much of the truth as we can find—we don't necessarily need all the historical details about a situation. Even so, most people are unable to search for the whole truth about an event, because fight/flight/shock prevents them from it; it's simply too painful. In fact, we cannot find most of our memories because they are in our unconscious. Don't worry, I will show you how to heal these as well. This is yet another reason why willpower won't work: we need subconscious tools that can go straight to the source and heal it, which we'll learn more about in Part II.

How do you know when your memories have been fully healed and that you've broken the cycle—without willpower? The next time you're under external pressure, you feel peace and joy (the by-products of love), rather than anxiety and stress (the by-products of fear).

My wife, Hope, was depressed for a number of years earlier in our marriage. During that time, one day a big package came to the house by UPS. This was back when our sons, Harry and George, were little, and everyone was excited to see what was inside this gigantic box. As it turns out, it was something small, but very fragile, so the box was filled mostly with those Styrofoam peanuts. The day went back to normal until about three hours later, when I heard the most horrible commotion upstairs. I rushed up to see what it was, only to find George crying, Hope furious, and the little white peanuts strewn all over the freshly cleaned house. Needless to say, a trauma situation was created in our home for the next twenty-four hours or so.

Two years later, after Hope's depression had been healed, you guessed it: UPS delivered another big box, also full of Styrofoam peanuts. Once again, all was well until about three hours later, when

I heard a terrible commotion upstairs again. On the way upstairs to put out the fire, I was experiencing déjà vu. But when I got to the top of the stairs, I was shocked. I saw my beautiful wife laughing like a ten-year-old schoolgirl, throwing handfuls of peanuts up in the air, pretending they were snowflakes. Harry and George, following suit, were frolicking, rolling, singing, and having the time of their lives. This event also affected our home for the next twenty-four hours, but in a very different way. I would give a million dollars today for a video of those five minutes.

So what in the world happened in those two years that changed Hope's reaction so dramatically? Hope had been reprogrammed. When the first event occurred, Hope was looking at the situation through lenses of pain and fear. Two years later, that programming was gone, which changed how she saw the situation, and now her natural instinct was *fun*. No one suggested it; there were no "shoulds." Her natural, immediate response had been completely reversed. That, my friends, is what "breaking the cycle" looks like.

Note: I need to add a word about addictions here. I have never met anyone with significant problems in their life who did not also have an addiction or unhealthy habit. I've been a supporter of Alcoholics Anonymous (AA) and Narcotics Anonymous (NA) for as long as I can remember, and I have known more than a few people whose lives were saved by these and other similar programs.

The overall relapse rate for most addictions is over 90 percent. AA reports its relapse rate to be approximately 50 percent, although other experts in the field say it's significantly higher. Wouldn't it be fabulous if we could cut that relapse rate by another 25, 35, or 45 percent—so the success rate of AA and similar programs could be 75 percent or higher? I believe we can, if we can address the subconscious source of our programming, in accordance with the latest research.

## chapter 3

# THE SPIRITUAL PHYSICS
# OF TRUTH AND LOVE

As we learned in the last chapter, both new scientific research and ancient spiritual wisdom have shown that your memories are the source of virtually every physical, emotional, and spiritual symptom you have, and that they reside in the information field of every cell in your body. There's an important implication here. The source of all the symptoms you experience in your life, even the undeniably physical ones, is not tangible. It is not bone, blood, or tissue; rather, it is made of *energy*. That everything is energy shouldn't be a surprise to us, as Einstein's equation $E = mc^2$ shows us that everything boils down to an energy pattern. As researcher William Collinge wrote, "Einstein showed through physics what the sages have taught for thousands of years: Everything in our material world—animate and inanimate—is made of energy, and everything radiates energy."[1] Yet we have not yet systematically applied this idea that everything is energy to our own life issues, particularly to our most pervasive struggles.

## THE KEY TO HEALTH AND SUCCESS IS SPIRITUAL, NOT PHYSICAL

Let's start with the big picture. If you're keeping up with the news, you probably already know that, even though we are living longer, our society's health has been getting worse. In 1971, Richard Nixon declared war on cancer, back when it was the eighth-leading cause of death in the United States. Today, more than forty years later, it is the number one cause of death worldwide—and it's increasing to epidemic proportions. In 2014, the World Health Organization stated that cancer cases were expected to increase 50 percent over the next ten years.[2]

It's not just cancer. The number of almost every other diagnosis has skyrocketed, too—as has the amount of money spent on managing diseases' symptoms and researching their potential treatments and cures. In some cases, the side effects of traditional treatments and medications are worse than the symptoms of a disease itself. We spend billions of dollars on pharmaceuticals and testing—and in many cases the results show that the placebo is as effective as the treatments they are testing, or even more so.

This is true for both standard Western medicine and alternative medicine. Yes, I believe in natural health. For years I took supplements every day. My wife and I also took homeopathy for years. I meditate. I pray. I exercise and drink clean water. But if we're going to be honest, we have to admit that despite the natural health tidal wave over the past twenty to thirty years, our health has *still* been getting worse. I've thought and meditated about this a lot. How can this be? How can we be making medical discoveries *and* relying more on natural health therapies, while our health continues to free-fall? The only thing I can come up with is that *we've got to be looking in the wrong place for the solution*. We've been thinking solely in terms of traditional versus alternative medicine. But the source of healing is not found in traditional medicine *or* alternative medicine. It's not in the physical world at all. It's in the spiritual world—the world of energy.

After I discovered the power of the Love Code back in 1988 and then the Three Tools to deprogram and reprogram over the next twenty years, I did a lot of research to try to figure out how it really worked, both in scientific studies and in ancient spiritual manuscripts. I found the first building blocks in an ancient manuscript written more than three thousand years ago by King Solomon, a king of Israel famed for his wisdom even beyond the borders of his tiny country. In it he wrote, "Above all, guard your heart, for from it flows all the issues of life." Even though he didn't completely explain what he meant by "guarding your heart," we at least know that whatever King Solomon meant by "heart," it was not the heart that pumps your blood throughout your body. It was the spiritual, "I love you with all my heart" heart. It was the source of all the issues we experience in life.

In another ancient manuscript written about two thousand years ago, the Apostle Paul explained this concept of "guarding your heart" a little bit more. He said if you have love, you have everything; if you don't have love, you have nothing. And if you do things in love, they will create success in your life; if you don't do them in love, they will profit you nothing.[3] In the twentieth century, Mahatma Gandhi described the same truth from a different angle: "When I despair, I remember that all through history the way of truth and love has always won. There have been tyrants and murderers, and for a time, they can seem invincible, but in the end, they always fall. Think of it—always."[4]

If Solomon is right and every issue we have comes from the spiritual heart, that means if I get cancer, it's got to come from a spiritual heart issue—whether we experience love or fear, forgiveness or unforgiveness, joy or sadness, peace or anxiety, self-worth or self-rejection. The same is true for diabetes, multiple sclerosis, and any other health problem. Now, I'm not saying there isn't a genetics piece

or a nutrition piece that affects how that disease takes hold of us. But
the linchpin, the yes-or-no switch, is in the spiritual heart. Clearly our
collective spiritual life as a society is far from where it needs to be—and
it's why our stress is out of control, too. Our spiritual reality is the most
powerful reality of our lives, yet we tend to focus the lion's share of our
time and attention on the physical and external circumstances.

If it is, in a way, that's good news. We've been focused on standard
and complementary medicine, but we haven't yet focused on the
spiritual. Or if we have, we've been looking at it in the wrong way.

## WHY MOST AFFIRMATIONS DON'T WORK

One way many people have incorporated spirituality into achieving
external results is through the use of affirmations. We've already
mentioned Dr. Bruce Lipton's work establishing that our beliefs are
the source of almost every symptom and problem we have. Because
physical and nonphysical results come through the door of belief, it has
become very popular over the last fifty years to try to "manufacture"
belief through affirmations. This approach is like trying to pick up a
very heavy rock—you might be able to do it through great stress and
strain, but you might also hurt something in the process.

About ten or twelve years ago, I felt as if affirmations were coming
at me from all sides. A number of bestselling books on affirmations
came out at that time, and people were telling me about them at every
turn. It seemed to be the "hot" thing of the day in the self-help world.
One day I was with this guy who had a stomach problem. Everywhere
we went he was saying, "My stomach problem is already healed. My
stomach problem is healing completely right now. My stomach problem
is already healed. My stomach problem is healing completely right
now." I watched him for a while. Finally I said, "Is that helping?" He

said, "Yeah. I really think it is." Well, three months later, I was still hearing him say, "My stomach problem is already healed. . . ." Of course, people don't use affirmations just for health problems. In the success field, you often hear people saying, "A million dollars is on the way. A million dollars is coming to me right now."

Several years ago, the first university double-blind study I've ever seen on this subject came out from the University of Waterloo. It was headline news all over the world. CNN, ABC, NBC, Fox, and newspapers everywhere were talking about it. The study found that the people who already had strong self-esteem felt even better about themselves after repeating positive affirmations. But those who did not already have strong self-esteem (the great majority of people in the study) and repeated the same positive affirmations felt even *worse*.[5]

Why is that? The two most important ingredients for achieving results through belief are *truth* and *love*. First, we need to believe the real truth to produce long-term, sustainable results. Just like there are different kinds of love (agape and eros, for instance), there are different kinds of belief. I distinguish them as "placebo," "nocebo," and "defacto." A placebo belief is believing a positive untruth, which creates a temporary positive effect (as we see in the example of pharmaceuticals). The average effect, according to studies, is that a placebo works around 32 percent of the time, and temporarily.[6]

A nocebo belief is believing a negative untruth, which prevents a positive effect from happening. Nocebo beliefs are the misinterpretations, or "splinters," from our internal programming that we discussed in chapter 2, and they block the healing and success that could be yours. For example, let's say you visited the doctor and you were diagnosed with breast cancer. They completed a biopsy, measured your white blood cells, and completed your treatment, whether conventional or alternative. You return for the results of the follow-up tests and the doctor says he has good news: there's no evidence of cancer. As far as he's concerned, you look great. But you go home and don't believe the truth of what the doctor told you. You worry, *What if he missed something? What if it comes back?* This is nocebo belief. It can literally block whatever healing is possible or is happening already, or it can create new health problems. Nocebo results can produce external results, according to research, also around 30 to 40 percent of the time.

Ben Johnson, a dear friend of mine and the only medical doctor in the movie *The Secret,* told me about a patient of his whose father, grandfather, and great-grandfather had all died of a heart attack at age forty—quite an unusual situation. Even though the patient had no heart problems, he was totally convinced, and terrified, that he would die at age forty, and no one could convince him otherwise. Sure enough, he turns forty and falls over dead. The thing is, when they did an autopsy, there was absolutely no reason for the young man to die. No heart problems or heart attack, no health problems of any kind. He had literally noceboed himself into dying.

A defacto belief is believing the whole truth, or objective reality. This works 100 percent of the time, if you believe it and act on it. It is worth noting that nocebo and placebo beliefs are both fear based, while defacto beliefs are love based.

We live in interesting times. A great many people and books these days would have us believe that there is no objective reality, that perception is the only reality. If this is true, it would have to mean that every belief is a defacto belief—even if you hold conflicting beliefs. If there is no objective reality, why try to be healthy and eat right or exercise, if it's all just perception? Just placebo or nocebo yourself, depending on the effect you're trying to achieve. Of course, we don't live this way because we inherently know that there *is* an objective reality about most things.

Many affirmations don't work because not only are they often not true, they're often not done in love. If your affirmation is repeated from a place of fear-based self-interest alone, it is likely not being done in love. Let's take the earlier affirmation, "My stomach problem is already healed," as an example. First of all, did the man repeating it believe it was true? No! Did he hope it would be true? Certainly—but as we said before, this kind of belief does not yield lasting results. Second, was this affirmation done in love? We can't be sure—but it was almost certainly done in fear, which is the opposite of love, the parent of selfishness, and the instant trigger of stress, which is how he got the stomach problem in the first place. You may be able to rationalize that your affirmations are done in truth and love, but only by honestly examining your own heart and intentions will you know for sure.

For about a year and a half I tested affirmations such as this one in my practice with the heart rate variability test (the medical test for stress). What I found was that when people said affirmations that they did not believe, their stress level spiked. Well, stress is how they got the problem in the first place. So, in reality, they were trying to solve their stress problem with something that was causing more stress.

In addition to being true and being in love, in order to be effective the person has to *believe* the affirmation. There's a difference between a belief that's more like a hope or a pipe dream, and a belief I tend to call "I know that I know that I know." The latter is the effective kind of belief that gets results. Over the last seventy-five years or so, throughout the history of the faith healing movement, a number of extremely popular faith healers have been found to be frauds. News organizations have done exposés that revealed clearly incriminating evidence: the healers were using "spies" planted in the audience, eavesdropping on conversations and sharing information with the so-called healers so they could know things they would otherwise not have known. At the same time, without a doubt, some people have been miraculously physically healed. Now, here's the interesting thing: some of these healings happened *with* the frauds! How can this be? It all has to do with belief. Their healing was always possible, with or without the healer. Their bodies could do it, they believed it was possible, and so it happened. Plus, from my perspective, God's not going to penalize *you* if the guy onstage is a fraud. The converse is also true, though: just because you know somebody who received a million dollars in a short period of time after reciting certain affirmations doesn't mean it's going to happen to you. For you, it may not be true, it may not be in love, or you may not truly believe it.

More recently, other studies have come out that have documented positive effects from certain "affirmations" that are true statements the subjects already believe.[7] The important point is whether the statements meet all three criteria—they are based in love, are based in truth, and are believed—not whether they are called "affirmations."

True belief is not manufactured. It's less like solving an algebra problem and more like finding a twenty-dollar bill on the ground. As you pour the whole truth into your heart and mind (which may take some time and searching to discover) and apply love to it, trying not to be biased because of the result you are trying to obtain, you will eventually discover yourself believing! You see it, feel it, taste it— you *know* it! The reason why you must remove your subconscious viruses is that they are lies keeping you from understanding the whole truth. Once you remove them, you have built-in mechanisms that will recognize and integrate the truth naturally, otherwise known as your conscience (or what I call your "love compass"), which is located in the spiritual heart. Your conscience is preprogrammed and constantly updated to respond to the whole, real truth—and to love.

Certain affirmations can actually be harmful if they are trying to program a new "truth" in, which may not be the truth at all and is fear based, not love based. They may also be in opposition to your own truth/love conscience, and these affirmations attempt to change your conscience without removing the viruses. As a result, you will now either have two internal viruses about that issue, or the truth competing with a lie, which causes internal confusion and more stress. Neither is effective for achieving what you really want.

So how do we cross over from ineffective belief to effective belief, from placebo and nocebo to defacto, where we no longer desperately hope for something deep down we fear will never happen and we can say in peace and love "I know that I know that I know"? It's actually very simple: we need *understanding*. The difference among placebo, nocebo, and defacto beliefs (aside from being love based or fear based) depends on whether you understand the whole truth or misunderstand it. I've seen this misunderstanding at work over and over with my clients. If someone claims to believe the truth but nothing in their life is changing for the better, it's almost always because they have a wrong interpretation or misunderstanding of the truth.

An example of this can be found in the way men's and women's brains are wired differently. In the early years of our marriage, I would always drive when Hope and I went somewhere. Every single time we went anywhere, I would stop in plenty of time behind a car, but Hope would become tense, physically push on the dashboard with her hands, and shout "ALEX!" I started to get irritated at this regularly recurring emergency that wasn't really an emergency, and it became a point of contention and argument between us. Not a big deal, but like an emotional thorn in our side. Then I read research that said that men's and women's depth perceptions are physically and genetically different, and the example the author used in the book was the driving and stopping example—exactly what was happening with Hope and me. As soon as Hope and I read that, we "understood," and it became a total nonissue from then on.

When you finally understand that missing piece and "see" the whole truth, you instantly and effortlessly believe the truth in a profound new way—and that creates results not possible before. When this would happen with my clients concerning their life issues, I might hear them say, "Oh, I see," or "Now I've got it." They will almost always take a very deep breath and a glowing smile will come across their face. They now truly "believe"—defacto.

Most of us already know that whatever we do needs to be done in truth and love. We inherently know that it is right to be honest, and wrong not to be. We "feel" that it is right to help others and not do anything to hurt them. Most of us even actively *want* to do everything in truth and love. Why aren't we *doing* it, though? For most of my life I know I couldn't. I'm certainly not doing it perfectly yet, but I'm way better than I used to be. Most days I feel like I'm living in love and joy and peace and truth. I want that for you, too. That's the only reason I'm writing this book. I can only see so many people personally.

I've been teaching the concepts explained here privately for twenty-five years—and I took it in the teeth many times for teaching them and using them with my clients before the scientific studies came out to prove them. Once considered fringe, these concepts are now cutting-edge science. For example, several mainstream doctors now agree with the idea that everything is energy, based on the growing body of scientific evidence. One is Dr. Mehmet Oz—"America's doctor"—who said on international TV back in 2007 that energy medicine is the next big frontier in medicine. I've come to call these concepts by the single name of Spiritual Physics, because they bring spirituality and science into a harmony and resonance that we can apply to any area of our lives in order to get real, lasting results. My hope is that this chapter will offer the understanding your belief needs to shift from placebo or nocebo to defacto—and get the same kind of results in your life that I have been consistently seeing for the last twenty-five years. And, of course, I am not suggesting you do this simply through willpower, at least not until you deprogram and reprogram what has been keeping you from doing that to this point in your life.

## THE PHYSICS OF SPIRITUAL PHYSICS

If Einstein's equation has proven that everything is energy, that means love is also energy—and operates on a frequency like any other kind of energy. In fact, love and light are the two sides of the same coin. Both have positive healing frequencies; light is the more physical manifestation of this energetic frequency, while love is the less physical manifestation. At a very different frequency, we have darkness and fear, which are also two sides of the same coin. Darkness is the more physical manifestation; fear is the less physical manifestation.

Did you know that an MRI machine doesn't take a photographic picture of your body? It creates a picture based on the energy frequencies it records. The "R" in MRI stands for "resonance," or frequency. MRI machines are programmed with hundreds of energy frequencies, such as the frequency of a healthy liver cell and the frequency of an unhealthy liver cell. When an MRI scans the body and picks up the frequency of an unhealthy liver cell, it makes a picture with a dark spot, because the MRI is picking up the frequency of darkness on your liver.

I've asked over two hundred doctors this question: "If your mind, body, and healing systems are in perfect working order, can you get sick in normal, day-to-day situations?" So far, the answer I've gotten every single time is "No." In normal, day-to-day situations (I'm not talking about visiting a foreign country and catching a nasty killer virus your body's never encountered before), if your physical immune system and your mental and spiritual healing systems are working perfectly, you really can't get sick.

Two things about our healing systems are important to note here. First, our healing systems govern not just our physical selves, but our whole selves—physical, mental, *and* spiritual. There are nonphysical aspects of your healing systems (in addition to your physical immune system) that help you feel love, joy, peace, and patience instead of anger, sadness, fear, anxiety, or worry. Second, we experience negative symptoms (pain, fear, disease, anger, etc.) not because there's a presence of the negative, but because there's a lack of the positive. According to the work of Dr. Caroline Leaf, we have no mechanisms—physical, emotional, or spiritual—that produce negative effects in our body. We only have mechanisms that produce the positive effects of health, vitality, and immunity.[8] Every single mechanism in our body operates to create health and happiness in its natural state. Believing disease is the natural state of our body is kind of like taking your broken down car to the dealer and asking, "Why did you build this car to make it do that?" Of course, the dealer will look puzzled and say, "We didn't! Something malfunctioned to make it break down. In fact, you haven't changed your oil for forty thousand miles!" Our bodies work the same way. When something negative happens in our life, it is always a malfunction of our positive systems.

So let me rephrase what I said before: as long as your mind and body are working the way they're supposed to, you can't get physically sick *and* you're going to feel good nonphysically—you literally cannot be lost in fear, anxiety, worry, sadness, anger, and other negative feelings.

Only one thing can cause your healing systems not to work correctly: fear. As we saw in the first chapter, when fear triggers your stress response, a fear frequency or a signal is sent from your memory banks to the hypothalamus in your brain, which turns the stress switch on. If your hypothalamus does not get that fear signal, it doesn't turn the stress switch on. (It's no coincidence that the other name for the stress response is "the fear response.") This reaction is part of your survival instinct, which helps keep you alive.

As we discussed in chapter 2, our stress response is only supposed to happen if our life is in imminent mortal danger at this moment. (When I say "stress," I'm not talking about healthy stress, or appropriately challenging our bodies, as we do in exercise. This kind of stress is often called "eustress," and we need it in our lives to stay healthy.) But that's not what's happening, is it? Many of us go into fight or flight ten, fifteen, or twenty times a day, to the point that stress is where we *live*.

When I did heart-rate variability testing for three years on the Healing Codes and other modalities, one of the questions I would ask subjects was "Do you feel stressed?" Over 90 percent of subjects who tested as being in significant clinical physiological stress at that moment answered that no, they did *not* feel stressed. Why? They were used to it. It had become the norm, when it should be the rare exception. We are living in stress, and we don't even know it.

Every destructive feeling we experience is based in fear. Wait a minute—surely there's one negative emotion that doesn't have anything to do with fear, right? Well, let's think about it: we feel anger when what we fear is happening right now. We feel anxiety and worry when we believe what we fear will happen in the future. We feel sadness and depression when what we fear has already happened, we believe we can't undo it, and our lives have changed forever—and that's where the hopelessness and helplessness come from. We feel unforgiving when we fear something is not right and fair and may never be right again. We feel rejection when we fear that someone isn't going to love or accept us, and there's nothing we can do about it (or they already have rejected us)—and we need to be accepted so desperately. I could go on and on. Truly every negative internal experience in your life comes, in some way, from fear and believing an untruth. All fear comes from an absence of love, just as darkness is always an absence of light.

A *fear-based* thought, emotion, or memory is one that increases stress (not including physical labor or exercise) when you are not in imminent mortal danger. Any time we are experiencing fear-based feelings (i.e., any negative emotion, belief, thought), we are turning our healing systems down or completely off. That means not only have we become susceptible to illness and disease, but if the situation continues long term, we are virtually guaranteed to become ill in the future. At the same time, we are turning our happiness down or off, our contentment down or off, our achievement and success down or off, and our satisfaction with life down or off.

Obviously, we don't want to live in fear and turn off our healing systems. So what is the antidote to our fear? *Love* is the antidote. Bernie Siegel, a world-renowned medical doctor, says in his book *Love, Medicine, and Miracles* that he has seen medical miracle after medical miracle from the power of love. And so have I. This is where the physics part comes in: the frequency of love directly counteracts the frequency of fear. Just to underscore the connection between love, light, and healing: the ancient Hebrew word for "healing" literally means "blinded by the light."

In 1952, a man named Lester Levenson was so unhealthy that after his second coronary episode, his doctors sent him home from the hospital to die. Taking just one step, they warned, could be enough to end his life on the spot. Needless to say, this dire prognosis thrust Levenson into a crisis, and he began to search for a solution beyond the realm of medical science, since it obviously couldn't help him anymore. He found it in love. He had a transformational *aha* experience about love much like I did, realizing that it was the solution to all his problems. It was just that simple and profound. He began to focus on loving everyone and everything, and letting go of all the thoughts and feelings that weren't based in love. As a result, his medical problem completely healed, and he spent the next forty years of his life teaching others to do what he had done through the Sedona Method and the Release Technique.[9] It all came down to the power of love to heal anything based in fear—including our physical symptoms. In contrast to fear-based, *love-based* thoughts, beliefs, and memories are those that decrease physical and nonphysical stress over the short term and long term.

The opposite of fear is love; in the presence of love, no fear can exist unless you're in a life-threatening situation this moment. The idea that love and fear are opposites may be new to you, as many think that the opposite of fear is peace. In one sense, this is true, because peace is a direct expression of love and derives from love. It is impossible to have true peace (not just situational peace) without having love. Similarly, if you have love, you *will* have peace, in spite of your circumstances. You may also be tempted to think that the opposite of love is not fear, but selfishness. Again, you would be right, on one level. But in the same way, selfishness is a direct expression of fear and derives from fear. If there is no fear, there is no selfishness (well, except for a five-year-old with an ice cream cone). As an adult, if you eliminate fear, you will naturally be kind and accepting and want to help others in need. It's like turning a light on in a dark room: the darkness disappears completely.

Love is the state from which all virtues flow: joy, peace, patience, acceptance, and belief. Fear is the state from which all physical and nonphysical malfunctions, blockage, failure, and harm flow. Fear cannot exist in a state of love, just as darkness cannot exist in an atmosphere filled with light. Love heals, fear kills. What we are talking about here is truly a matter of life or death—physically, emotionally, relationally, economically, and in every other conceivable way.

## THE SPIRITUALITY OF SPIRITUAL PHYSICS

To explain the spiritual side of Spiritual Physics, let's return to the concept of the spiritual heart, where the source of all our life issues resides. (As you'll remember from chapter 2, the spiritual heart is also what scientists call cellular memory, and others call the subconscious/unconscious mind.) The first time that the spiritual heart is mentioned in ancient Hebrew manuscripts makes it clear that the *imagination* is an integral part (or the language) of the spiritual heart—not words. Believe it or not, Einstein says that his greatest discovery wasn't the theory of relativity, or energy, or mathematics. It was that the imagination is more powerful than knowledge, because that was the source of all his discoveries.

However, instead of the word *imagination*, I use the word *image maker* to emphasize that we're talking about the creative force inside of us that generates images, and that we're not just talking about daydreaming. My spiritual mentor Larry Napier first taught me about the image maker—that it's how everything that exists came into being. Does an architect just go out and start building? Does a contractor just go out and start digging a hole? No. They see the final product as an image in their image maker first, then they put it on paper, and *then* they go out and create it. That was true for my Levi's, for a piece of chalk, for my camera, for Edison's lightbulb, and for Einstein's theory of relativity. Everything on planet Earth comes from the image maker, and every single human being has one. Learning to access it is the key to healing everything that ails us because it's the direct link to and language of the source, which is our spiritual heart.

The image maker is not a metaphor. It is real, just as real as this book in your hands (whether paper or electronic). So if it is real, is it standard medicine or alternative medicine? Neither. It is spiritual, which I know because science can't locate it. Science can find everything else in our bodies: we can locate our blood, our hormones, our organs, and the various systems of the body, and understand how they work. We can even see how we think by observing what parts of the brain light up when we are doing different things and thinking and dreaming different things. We have found and quantified the screen where we see actual physical things that exist in our environment through our physical optic systems. But we cannot find the screen that allows us to imagine and view images and pictures internally. I believe that we will never find it because it is in the spiritual realm. The spiritual heart is the container for the spirit, just as the body is the container for the soul.

Harvard neurosurgeon Eben Alexander, MD, had a life-altering vision on the edge of death, much like Einstein's vision of the theory of relativity and any other vision that ignites great discoveries and transformative insights. Yet this vision occurred when the physical mechanisms in his brain that might be responsible for such a vision were not functioning at all, and so it was clear to him, and to me, that his vision occurred in the spiritual realm. Before his near-death experience, Dr. Alexander did not believe in the existence of an afterlife or in the spiritual realm at all—primarily because science had never been able to locate any evidence of them. But after his experience, his beliefs about the existence of the spiritual realm and the afterlife changed so completely that he wrote the bestselling book *Proof of Heaven: A Neurosurgeon's Journey into the Afterlife* to explain why.[10] He related these experiences and the physical science behind them on national television.

According to Wikipedia, approximately 97 percent of people worldwide believe in the reality of a spiritual dimension, or in God. I think this percentage is so high because almost all of us experience the spiritual to some degree at certain times in our life. It's beyond words, and beyond the physical—just like our experience of love.

To me, this high percentage is one of the main indicators that this dimension does in reality actually exist. Why would I say that? Because historically, the predominant belief is the one with the most physical, measurable evidence. This is why Galileo was put in jail for saying what he observed about the earth, moon, and stars. If you just looked at the earth from our perspective, it appears flat and that everything revolves around us. In the 1800s, Dr. Ignaz Philipp Semmelweis was literally mocked and laughed out of medicine because he believed we have invisible things on our hands called germs that can cause infections. He advocated washing hands between delivering babies, and his survival rate was way higher than anyone else's because of that practice.

This is the norm throughout history, and the root of the age-old expression "I'll believe it when I see it." And yet, about this one issue of the existence of the spiritual, we see precisely the opposite: a 97 percent belief in something that is not measurable, that you can't see, and that has little to no empirical evidence that it exists. Wow! I don't know if you could find any other issue on the planet where there was 97 percent agreement, even about things that we can see and measure.

But even though science can't locate the spiritual, and even though 97 percent of us believe in a spiritual reality or in God despite a lack of physical evidence, we are entering an age where science is beginning to prove that the spiritual exists. In their book *How God Changes Your Brain*, neuroscientists Andrew Newberg and Mark Robert Waldman share extensive scientific evidence that the number one factor that improves brain function and health—even more than exercise—*is prayer and a corresponding belief in God or spiritual source.* They're not talking about going to church. They're neuroscientists following the science, reporting the evidence they've seen. Also, if prayer and believing in God/source/love has the biggest impact on brain function and health, it also means that it has the biggest impact on *everything* in your life, because your brain function affects everything—your cardiovascular system, your hormones, and perhaps most important, your control mechanism for stress.[11]

The language of our spiritual heart is pictures. Everything that has ever happened to us is recorded in our heart as images. Dr. Pierce Howard says in *The Owners' Manual for the Brain*, "All data is encoded and recalled in the form of pictures." Dr. Antonio Damasio, a neuroscientist who is head of the Brain and Creativity Institute at the University of Southern California—and is being mentioned in the same sentence with "Nobel Prize" a lot these days—says, "Imageless thought is impossible."

When we see our memories, it's as if they are on a screen in our mind, sometimes like we're watching a movie. I call this screen our *heart screen*: our view into our image maker. But just as science and medicine can't locate our image maker, they also cannot physically locate the screen to our imagination. Again, it's very real, but it's not in the physical realm—it's in the spiritual realm.

In our heart we have billions and billions and billions of pictures. You can think of your heart screen as a big, high-definition, holographic computer, smartphone, or tablet screen where the memories that are active right now are displayed, just like open files, icons, or pictures on your computer. Whatever is on the screen now determines your current experience. If you have fear on your screen, you are going to be experiencing stress in your physical body until the weak link breaks and you have some kind of specific negative symptom, which is often referred to as the weak-link theory. Every medical doctor I know on the planet subcribes to it because it is right.

Under continual stress, your body's and mind's weakest link will break first. With my wife, Hope, that meant depression. With me, it meant acid reflux. The weak link is different for every individual, based on all kinds of factors, including genetics. We've already said earlier that 95 percent of disease comes from stress. The 5 percent that is not from stress is genetic. This genetic tendency toward a specific disease *also came from stress*: it came from somewhere in your ancestry when a disease gene was unmasked because of stress. If the stress is removed from the person who currently has the disease gene—and the only way you can do that is by getting rid of the fear—the hypothalamus in the brain turns the stress switch off, and the stress leaves the body. The immune system can then heal the genetic tendency toward that particular disease.

Here's an example of how our heart screen determines our present experience. One day when I was at my house, we opened up a drawer and Hope about jumped through the ceiling, screaming bloody murder. I looked in the drawer and I didn't respond much at all, although I did chuckle just a little. Harry's rubber snake was in the drawer. That same day, a few minutes later, Hope saw something and said, "Oh, I just love that." I looked over and started to cry. She was looking at a rose. The last one I had seen was on my mother's casket. In both instances, Hope and I experienced the same physical circumstances at the same time but had 180-degree opposite reactions. Why? We had different pictures in our hearts for what we saw.

The problem is that about 99 percent of people don't have the first clue about 99 percent of what's on their heart screen. That's why people join program after program, take pill after pill, visit therapist after therapist, and they find themselves forty years later having spent tens of thousands of dollars and they still have their same problems, *or worse*. Usually they give up and die unchanged. But it doesn't have to be that way! They just weren't addressing the true source of their problem, which was the fear-based memories on their heart screen.

Based on the physics part of Spiritual Physics, we know that if there is fear on this screen, that means there is also darkness on the screen. Something happens: you're stuck in a traffic jam, you bite into a sandwich that is not as good as you hoped, somebody looks at you funny, the person next to you is wearing perfume you don't like—any one of a million things. This event comes in through the eyes and is transformed into an image, even if the data comes from another of the five senses. All data is encoded as images, remember. Even things we smell and hear and taste are encoded as images and recalled as images. Pictures are not just the language of the heart, they are the *universal* language, and they communicate at the speed of light—186,000 miles per second. Words take much longer, and you have to know that particular language.

Then, according to Dr. Lipton, this image goes down to the database of images accumulated from our personal and generational memories located in our spiritual heart, where it's compared to those millions of images to determine what our response will be. Hope and I both saw the rubber snake, but it brought up a negative image on her heart screen as soon as she looked at it. She had fear and darkness on her heart screen. I didn't. On my heart screen, when I looked at it, were love and light. What I saw in my imagination was Harry happily playing with the snake. I was fine.

Now, when I looked at the rose, I had a lot of images come up. I had some love remembering my mom, and I had some fear—some images with darkness, and some with light. I had a mixed response. What's on our heart screen immediately determines the physiology of our body. For example, when any amount of fear appears on your heart screen, you may feel sweaty, tension in your chest, or a headache. When this happens, don't focus on the physical symptoms. Yes, there's a physical component to your response, but it all comes from the heart screen, every bit of it. If you need to take the Tylenol, go ahead, but while you're taking it, start working on the source so that you don't have to take a Tylenol again tomorrow for the same thing.

Our programming is a big part of what determines what's on our heart screen. For Hope, her programming growing up said that she had to be "a good girl," or do everything that everyone wanted her to do. If she didn't do everything that everyone wanted her to do perfectly, she was a bad girl. The belief she has to be a good girl causes her to always try to be something that she's not necessarily feeling and comply with something that is not always her. For decades, that programming produced fear and darkness on Hope's heart screen, which continually spiked the stress on her body until the weak link broke and she became depressed. Why could she not get undepressed for twelve years, no matter what she did? Because she didn't know how to fix those underlying memories—she didn't even know what they were. Under the same circumstances, the same fear-based images showed up on her screen, and 99 percent of the time, they were fear and darkness. So she was depressed. She was anxious. She was fearful.

I've said this before, but it's worth repeating: everyone has some bad programming. No one is perfect. Humans have five possible brain states: alpha, beta, gamma, delta, and theta. During the first six years of life—and only during the first six years of our life—we are in a delta/theta brain state. In the delta/theta brain state, we don't have the ability to filter out information. For example, you may be five years old and in the backyard with your dad, playing Wiffle ball. You try to hit the Wiffle ball and miss, and your dad chuckles and says, "Well, you're never going to be a baseball player with a swing like that." You have no ability to filter that, and you just got brand-new hard-drive programming. No one *doesn't* have these kinds of memories! They're what I called "Popsicle memories." Plus, it's very difficult to deprogram something once it's programmed during this age. Research tells us that for children it takes a minimum of ten positive statements to neutralize one negative statement—yet most parents give ten negatives for one positive! Voilà— fear-based programming.

Even if by some miracle everyone does everything in love and truth 100 percent of the time, we can still inherit bad programming from past generations, or absorb it from others we are around. We all have some bad programming, and the heart screen is our direct link to heal it. Also, our heart screen is connected to the heart screens of everyone around us, particularly those closest to us, so that we are always broadcasting and receiving energy frequencies through a kind of "organic Wi-Fi" network. We will learn how to "tune in to" and "broadcast" love frequencies in chapter 8 when we talk about the Heart Screen tool.

Energy is never destroyed; it just changes forms. When you flip on the light switch in a completely dark room, it lights up every corner of the room. Where did the dark go? The correct answer is, it no longer exists. The definition of darkness is simply the absence of light. So when there's light, by definition there is no darkness. It works that way in the body, too, with fear and love. It's the same physics. When you pour love into fear, the fear doesn't exist anymore. It sounds strange to us because we haven't used this kind of language in this context. But let me remind you, this paradigm shift was predicted by Einstein back in 1905.

Whenever we shift paradigms in any significant way, those who have done well under the old paradigm often resist the new. For example, when the Wright Brothers first got started with their "flying machines," they went to the railroads. They said, "We are giving you the first shot at becoming the kings of the airways." The railroad people laughed in their faces and said nothing would ever replace the railroad. Today we could be going to the airport and getting on a plane from B&O Airlines—but nowadays you don't see "B&O" on anything, do you? They had an opportunity to shift to a new paradigm, but they were stuck in the old paradigm and have declined because of it.

A new paradigm for health, healing, and success, predicted for the last century, is happening right now. Are you going to be stuck in your old paradigm, or follow the new? It's not just coming—it's already here. In 2013, the American Psychological Association allowed the first energy medicine conference to offer continuing education credits[12] and is also on the verge of approving the first energy medicine modality for counseling and therapy—after twenty years of largely laughing at, mocking, and belittling the entire field. Why the reversal? Overwhelming practical evidence that the treatments are far faster and more effective and have no side effects.

These results are being noticed in the field of athletics as well. Just after college football coach James Franklin signed a $37 million contract with Penn State University in January 2014, after turning Vanderbilt University football into a winning program for the first time in one hundred years, he was interviewed by Dan Patrick on Patrick's syndicated television show about his success as a coach. Franklin's answers were, to say the least, unusual. When asked about goal setting (something almost all coaches do and greatly emphasize), Mr. Franklin said that he doesn't set external goals for his team. He said that if you set the wrong goal, that goal can end up being destructive. So the goals he sets for his players focus on the present moment and the present day: to be at their best spiritually, academically, physically, and socially. (We'll talk more about setting the right goals in the next chapter.) He said that with him, "It's all about relationships."[13]

That's right—one of the most successful coaches in the last one hundred years said on live national television that he prioritizes the spiritual in the present moment, and that he is all about relationships. By setting internal goals in the present moment, Franklin has succeeded where countless others have not, and he has done it with lesser players in terms of speed, strength, and ratings. Franklin is not the first coach to take this approach; over the years I've also heard Alabama head football coach Nick Saban (a four-time national champion) and New England Patriots head coach Bill Belichick (a three-time world champion) talk about teaching their players not to focus on the scoreboard or winning the game, but on doing their absolute best in the present moment. This is the essence of the Love Code, although I feel these coaches could have even better results with the tools in this book. Love in the present moment consistently produces superior peak performance. Fear, by nature, inhibits and constricts performance.

These reversals are the first of what will be an avalanche of change in the fields of psychology, self-help, medicine, athletics, peak performance, and success. In twenty years, I believe this approach will be the new norm, because it works. However, I don't want you to have to wait twenty years to be successful in your life. I want it for you in the next few months, and for the rest of your life.

We have known, or could have known, that the spiritual heart was the source of all the issues of our lives for thousands of years, but because we've had an old paradigm of separating the physical and the spiritual, we haven't been able to apply this spiritual knowledge to our physical body. You can't use a scalpel to cut out an issue of the heart. You can't take a pill to poison it out. The cut, burn, and poison method doesn't work on that. Neither do the alternative physical methods. So even if we've known how important the issues of the heart are, we haven't ever really applied this knowledge to health care, because health care as we know it had no methods or tools to truly heal these issues of the heart. And we certainly haven't applied it to our success issues.

Under the Spiritual Physics paradigm, the physical and the spiritual are in perfect, congruent harmony. In fact, real science is *always* in harmony with the spiritual. If the spiritual heart is the source of all our issues, then the only tool that can possibly heal the source is an energy tool—because the issues of the heart (i.e., our memories) are made of energy. We shouldn't be resisting this new paradigm; we should be celebrating! We're finally able to both identify and heal the real source of our problems.

Now, I've had a number of metaphorical rocks thrown at me. I've had a few so-called experts call me a huckster or a fraud because I teach these principles that unite the physical and the spiritual. But as I travel throughout the world, I see a very different picture. People are so excited to learn these principles and apply them, because they work in a way nothing else has ever worked. We've finally been able to get to and heal the source.

There may be a separation between church and state, but there is no separation between spirituality, success, and health. If you believe and act as if there is, the net result will be *your* separation from success and health.

The solution to our success issues is neither to focus on our problem, nor to continually ignore it. Both will cause your life experience to continue to deteriorate. The solution is to replace the darkness/fear/falsehood with light/love/truth—always! The source of light/love/truth is the source of the solution to any problem, while the source of darkness/fear/falsehood is the origin of every problem, whether it's terrorism, hunger, disease, poverty, or unhappiness. When the two meet, light/love/truth always win, for the same reason light fills a dark room, even if it may not be immediately apparent. Gandhi knew this to be true ("all through history the way of truth and love has always won"), as have all the great spiritual teachers.

In the long term:

*Love never fails!*
*Fear never succeeds!*

From now on, what is *your* choice?

Now that you understand the concepts of cellular memory and Spiritual Physics, we have just one more foundational principle to cover: how to set success goals rather than stress goals.

## chapter 4

# SET SUCCESS GOALS,
# NOT STRESS GOALS

The Love Code is to do everything you do in love, out of an inward state reprogrammed with love, joy, and peace, focusing on the present moment. As we said back in chapter 1, "everything you do" is determined by a goal—always. The problem is that most people are unaware of what their goals are, where they came from, whether they are right or wrong goals, where they're taking them, and, of course, how to change them. Ironically, many of us have very clear goals about the smaller things in life, such as personal hygiene, our clothing, and a clean house. I don't mean to minimize those things, but most of us would probably say those aren't the most important areas of our life.

I've worked with many people in the military (predominantly men, but some women) and a lot of women who tend to be perfectionists. They tend to be extremely disciplined about the external issues in their life: the house, the car, the laundry, the lawn, their children's outward behavior, and even high performance in their career. Yet many times they struggle with the internal issues that are not as concrete, such as their relationships and issues from their past.

When it comes to *those* areas, however, the things we want more than anything else, many of us tend to form and follow unconscious goals that lock us into vicious cycles of health problems, financial lack, mental poverty, and relational strife. These vicious cycles in turn lead us into the internal states of sadness, frustration, anxiety, despair, loneliness, and rejection—and, ultimately, failure in everything that matters.

At this point, I'd like to invite you to stop and pray or meditate for ten minutes and ask yourself: *Am I intentionally developing true, healthy, and right goals (in truth and love) for the things that are most important to me? The car may be immaculate, but how is my anger? I may have the laundry done—but how about my parenting?* Now that you know that our internal state drives our external circumstances, you understand how important it is to set goals for our internal state rather than run on unconscious, often unhelpful, programming. (Again, you'll learn how to diagnose and heal your own internal programming in Part II.)

Whether it's parenting or dealing with anger or any other area, if you realize that your goals haven't reflected what's truly most important to you, this chapter will help you set the goals that will lead to the success that's best for you, both internally and externally.

But even if you do have very clear and intentional goals for the most important areas in life, many people still tend to be focused on external circumstances achieved by willpower, which severely and inherently sabotages their chances of ever achieving that goal. Or they reach the goal and are still not happy and fulfilled long term. So here's the million-dollar question: How do we set the kinds of goals that lead us to success, rather than sabotage us?

For one of my clients, this was quite literally a million-dollar question. Several years ago, a gentleman came to me to heal some health issues in his life. After they were healed, he contacted me again to ask if I could help him with another problem. He said, "Hey, Doc. I've had a success goal for the last ten years that I've never been able to achieve.

I don't even know if you do things like that, but is there any chance you could help me with it?" I asked him to elaborate. He went on to tell me that he was one of the largest contractors in a rather small town. His goal for ten years had been to make a million dollars in one year. Not a million dollars gross for the company—a million dollars in his pocket. And in that ten years, the most he'd ever made was about half that. Still a great deal of money, but instead of being satisfied and enjoying it, he was constantly frustrated that he wasn't reaching his goal.

This gentleman had what you might call a type A, hard-driving personality. He pushed and pushed and pushed everybody and everything. He worked eighty hours a week and required his employees to work long hours as well, frequently not paying them for overtime. He was known to be sharp and caustic with his tongue, and he cut corners, so he did not have the best reputation in the contracting community. Every relationship he had was on edge, and his health had been getting worse for years, which was his original reason for coming to me.

So my next question for him was "Tell me about how you see your goal of making a million dollars in a year. Describe it for me. What do you do with the money? What does it change in your life?" He had no problem doing that. He had been looking at that "movie" on his heart screen every day for the last decade. He told me that he wanted to buy the mansion on the top of the hill that you could see from all over town. Yes, he wanted a new red sports car, too. Then there was the luxurious golfing vacation, and all the other usual toys.

When I asked him why he wanted the house on the hill and the red sports car, he told me it was so that everybody in town would see how successful he was and envy him. I knew that the problem wasn't the goal per se, but *why* he had set this goal. I told him I could help him, but in order for me to do so, we would have to do some surgery on his goals. He reluctantly agreed.

It was fine for him to want to make a million dollars in a year, but that part would change to a "desire," not his "goal." (We'll talk more about that difference later.) If he made the million dollars, he could buy a new house, but not the house on the top of the hill. He could get a new car, but not the red sports car. (Not that there's anything wrong with either of those per se—the problem was *why* he wanted them. For someone else, they may be totally appropriate.) We changed the golfing vacation to a family vacation. We eliminated some of the toys. We added giving some of the money to the less fortunate. We added spending some of his time and expertise personally working on a building service project, where he could give back to those less fortunate. We cut his hours to a maximum of fifty a week. We not only cut the hours of his employees, but we gave them all a raise and better benefits. We created time for exercise, meditation, long walks, a healthier lifestyle, and more family time than he thought he could stand . . . you get the idea.

His goal got a total overhaul. When it was all said and done, his *success desire* (not his success goal, as we'll define later) was to make a million dollars the next year, but to use the money for good, healthy, balanced things—in other words, "in love." His *success goal* was to focus on the present moment in love, doing what needed to be done to achieve his desire, but constantly giving up the million-dollar result to love/source/God. To do this he had to deprogram and reprogram his internal issues first. Then he would be capable of carrying out the goal, walking in the direction of his desire.

When I left him, he had just started deprogramming and reprogramming and was absolutely kicking and screaming. His exact words were "This is never going to work. If I hadn't just had my health issues healed, I would think that you were out of your mind."

I got a call from the contractor about a year and a half later. I literally didn't recognize his otherwise very distinct voice until he identified himself. His first words were "Hey, Doc, remember me?

The stressed-out contractor who thought you were crazy?" I'd often wondered what had happened with him and had prayed for him several times. He was certainly at high risk for trashing the whole program and going back to his previous lifestyle. Here's what he said: "Well, Doc—I did exactly what we agreed on, and I did not make a million dollars in that next year. *I made over a million and a half.* And I'm on track this year to make even more than that. To this day, I still don't have a clue how it happened—it was like magic. It was the easiest year of work I've ever had in my life."

He went on to tell me that virtually everything in his life had changed. He was healthy and happy, his relationships were wonderful, and his reputation around town had totally reversed. He now had a waiting list of people wanting him to do work for them because he did the best work in town, he had lowered his prices, and he no longer cut corners. His employees loved him and would never want to work anywhere else, and the whole office was full of joy, peace, and a camaraderie that no one had ever experienced before working there.

When the contractor deprogrammed, reprogrammed, and learned how to change his stress goals to success goals, his desired external circumstance came easily. I could fill several volumes with stories like these. The results are incredibly predictable. People who develop and actualize *success goals*, from the inspiration of the inward state they "really" want most, instead of the external circumstance they "think" they want most, always succeed. Always. People who don't, fail. Always.

## THE DIFFERENCE BETWEEN GOALS AND DESIRES

So let's get into some practical detail about how the contractor went from failure to success so quickly—and most important, how you can, too. As you've probably guessed, it has everything to do with the kind of goals you set. It's time to pull back the veil and explain exactly what determines whether you have a success goal or a stress goal.

## Defining Desire

First we'll start with defining a few terms. The first term is *desire* (or "hope"). A desire that results in success meets four criteria:

1. It has to be in truth.

2. It has to be in love.

3. It has to be in harmony with your ultimate success goal (from chapter 1).

4. It is typically in the future.

We've already mentioned the first two components, truth and love, in the context of belief: if something is to work in the long term, it must be done in truth and in love. But now it's time to get specific about what truth and love really mean.

1. The *truth* refers to the *objective* facts of the situation: required resources, needs, abilities, the marketplace, financial issues, time— essentially every objective fact relevant to achieving the desire, both circumstantially and externally. This is the "what" of the desire. For example, let's say a seventy-two-year-old gentleman told me he had a desire to be a starting quarterback in the NFL. I would have to ask him if this desire is in truth—in other words, is it in harmony with the objective facts of the situation?

2. Whether something is done in *love* refers to the *subjective* facts of the situation. It is the "why" of the desire. Why is this your desire in the first place? Who are you doing it for? What is the inspiration and motivation behind it? If it's predominantly selfish and someone is likely

to "lose" or to be harmed in some way, your desire doesn't meet the "love" criteria. The desire to be an NFL quarterback at age seventy-two could be based in love, just most likely not in truth. On the other hand, the contractor's original desire for a million dollars was based in truth (i.e., it was objectively achievable, given his current circumstances), but not in love, as we determined from discovering how he wanted to spend it. That means neither desire meets our definition of a success desire, and both would have to be revised in some way. The contractor, for instance, revised his desire by deciding to spend his time and money caring for others and giving to those less fortunate, and thus met the criteria of love.

One more thing about desires: they must be in harmony with your *ultimate success goal*. Take a moment to remind yourself of the internal state you answered for question 3 back in chapter 1 (if you received what you wanted most and the circumstances that would result, how would you feel?). That internal feeling or state is your ultimate success goal. It may have been peace, love, joy, safety, or any other positive internal state. It's why you do anything and everything that you do—so it's obviously counterproductive to have a desire that violates that ultimate internal success goal, feeling, and state.

I love going to the beach. It's a very spiritual, healing place for me. Let's think of going to the beach as my desire, and the peace I feel there as my ultimate success goal. Now, to actually get to the beach, I need to get specific: Which beach am I going to? How am I going to get there? What do I need to pack to enjoy it? At the same time, I need to be careful that the specifics of getting there don't violate what I've defined as my ultimate success goal: the peace that comes from love. If I don't leave myself enough time to pack for the trip and find I'm rushing around like a crazy person the morning I leave, then the way I'm going to the beach is, at least partially, negating the whole point of going to the beach in the first place. The same thing is true if I find out my niece is getting married at the same time I've planned my trip and my absence at the wedding would cause a great deal of personal and family stress. That's not to say I need to scrap the whole trip, but I do need to reevaluate and make some practical changes in my plan, so that the plan remains in peace and love, consistent with my ultimate success goal both now and in the future.

Here's a more practical example. Let's say a middle-aged father's ultimate success goal is peace as well, and his success desire is to go back to school and pursue an engineering degree. He has applied to a prestigious engineering program within commuting distance from his home, and he discovers he has been accepted. He's ecstatic! As he begins classes toward his degree, however, he realizes that pursuing this desire is fundamentally taking him away from his ultimate success goal of peace as it relates to his family: He's experiencing personal stress and pressure from his family at being overscheduled. This stress is a sign that he needs to reevaluate. Maybe he needs to do some internal work to deal with the source of the stress. Maybe he needs to consider a different degree program. Or maybe he does need to drop out of school entirely. The point is that we must never sacrifice our ultimate success goal (the internal state of love) for a success desire (the end-result external circumstance).

Finally, a desire is typically for something that hasn't happened yet. Another word for desire could be *hope*. It's something we desire internally, we believe in, we would like to have happen, we are working toward, but we don't know if it will happen for sure. A desire sets the direction that we walk in. Also, the critical thing about setting a desire is that we absolutely must give up all expectations of receiving it from the start, and every step along the way. You must surrender the end result to God/source/love, or to the goodness of other people—however you need to think about it to give it up completely.

## Defining Goal

Now let's define a *goal*. A goal, if it is to lead you to success, has to have all four of the following components:

1. It has to be in truth.

2. It has to be in love.

3. It has to be 100 percent under your control.

4. It is done in the present moment.

If it meets all four of these criteria, you have a *success goal*. That means it will work in the long term and lead you to success every time if you stay the course and have deprogrammed and reprogrammed first so that you can do it.

What primarily distinguishes a goal from a desire is number 3, that it must be 100 percent under your control—not 99 percent, not "most likely," but *totally* under your control. In other words, you can do it now, or at least for the next thirty minutes. If truth is the "what" and love is the "why," your control is the "how" of the goal. No exceptions. This component obviously limits what can be considered a success goal, but it makes all the difference.

This is also the part where most people have a problem. People are usually fine with truth and love, but when I tell them it needs to be 100 percent under their control, they typically get a funny expression on their face, akin to disappointment or frustration. For instance, the contractor's goal of making a million dollars personally from his business was not 100 percent under his control—so that could not be his goal. Same with the seventy-two-year-old's goal of becoming an NFL quarterback. Also, when we say "100 percent under your control," we're talking about healthy control, not unhealthy control. We talked about unhealthy control briefly in the last chapter: unhealthy control is seeking a result that's not 100 percent under your control, and that is not in truth and love.

Whenever I have someone question the notion that using willpower to pursue external expectations is counterproductive—usually because the opposite has been so popular for so long and seems natural—here is how I explain it. I tell them that another way to define pursuing external expectations (i.e., pursuing something as a goal that is not 100 percent under your control) solely with willpower is unhealthy control and worry. For example, over the years I have had clients say that their external expectations are totally, completely, 100 percent positive—without a trace of negative thoughts, feelings, or beliefs. I then ask them how they would feel, think, or believe if those expectations did not turn out the way they hoped they would. They tend to have a puzzled look on their face, and then they tell me that it would feel terrible. This reaction is likely because they have been counting on that end result and do not believe they will be okay with any other result, typically because they think if they completely believe, it *will* happen. So even if they were 100 percent positive in their conscious thinking, feeling, and believing, their unconscious and subconscious were not.

The number one job of the unconscious, remember, is to protect us from harm—not to produce the positive. So they were in internal conflict: they were positive consciously, but at least partially negative unconsciously. This internal disharmony creates stress, and remember, when the unconscious and conscious "disagree" over an issue, the unconscious always wins. The other factor is unhealthy control. Trying to force or manipulate an external circumstantial result that is *not* under your complete control is one of the most stressful things you can ever do, and most of us cannot keep it up to reach the desired result. Even if we do force the end result, we will typically *not* be happy, content, and fulfilled long term.

It's true that great results come from belief—but not from just any belief. All great results come from *believing the truth*. Healthy control is always based in love and truth. Healthy control is, quite simply, the right thing to do, the loving thing to do, and the best thing to do. Unhealthy control, on the other hand, will kill the result you're trying to achieve, as it is always fear based—and all fear comes from believing a lie. Worry (stress) and unhealthy control (the opposite of results-producing belief) are simply alternative ways of describing expectations and willpower. Worry equals expectations, and unhealthy control equals willpower alone. Expectations and willpower put us in disharmony with ourselves and in chronic stress—whether we are consciously aware of it or not.

So a goal needs to be 100 percent under your *healthy* control. If something is under your healthy control, you can do it in the present moment, right now. Also, you can easily tell the difference between healthy control and unhealthy control by their results. Healthy control usually produces peace and joy, while unhealthy control produces anxiety and stress. One of the wonderful side effects of this Success Blueprint is the elimination of anxiety from your life.

What if you've set a goal that doesn't meet one or more of the preceding criteria? Perhaps it's not in harmony with the truth. It may not be based in love. Or it may not be 100 percent under your control (like the majority of goals set by most people). Then you have what I call a *stress goal*, and put simply, you need to change your goal. Why? Having a stress goal is the fastest way I know to ensure failure. Even if it happens to be in truth and love (but not under your control), a stress goal will create expectations that in turn kill results and create unhappiness—the opposite of success.

Here's the easiest way to tell if you've set a stress goal or a success goal: if you are experiencing anxiety, anger, or any emotion in the anger family (irritation, frustration, etc.), you likely have set a stress goal and have some more work to do with deprogramming and reprogramming yourself to live in love. Stress is the direct physical symptom of fear, and anxiety is the direct nonphysical symptom of fear. Anxiety is the precursor of anger, or any emotion in the anger family. Some people are very aware of experiencing anger (and won't admit they are experiencing anxiety), while others are very aware of experiencing anxiety (and won't admit they are experiencing anger). The point is that if you experience either one, they are both signs of a stress goal.

Here's why. Whenever we experience pain (and lack of pleasure is also pain), we feel anger, anxiety, frustration, irritation, or any number of related emotions. That anger/anxiety causes us to focus on an end result: to fix the problem that caused the pain. If we were living in the present moment in love when the pain occurred, and if our goal becomes an end result, then we have also moved out of the present moment in love and into stress.

Comparison is often a part of this process. We might look around and ask, *How are other people doing? Are they in pain like me? If not, what are they doing that I can do that might get me out of pain?* Now, looking around at what other people are doing could be very healthy— for example, if you're having a problem and you remember hearing one of your friends talking about it, you may call them up and ask them how they solved it. What's unhealthy is looking around at others' external lives and assuming they don't have the problems you do, and getting angry.

That unhealthy comparison causes us to develop expectations. Based on what we see others doing, we think, *Maybe if I do what she's doing, it might get me out of pain.*

And that expectation causes us to create a stress goal. We focus on achieving an end result or external circumstance to avoid experiencing pain.

The problem is, it's not about the pain! That very first assumption that caused your anxiety—that you need to avoid pain at all costs—is what got you off the path of love and on the path of fear. The question isn't whether you're going to experience pain. You'll experience pain no matter what. The question is whether you're going to live in fear or love when you experience pain, and whether that pain will lead you toward success or failure.

So the pain is never the real problem; the pain is a test to see what your goal really is. If you see pain as the problem, you're going to be stressed all your life and just create more pain for yourself. Your goal should not be to fix the situation, but to respond to the situation in love.

On the other hand, if you are experiencing joy and peace regardless of your circumstances, you likely have set a success goal (consciously or unconsciously) and have been successfully deprogrammed and reprogrammed to live in love. Of course, even with success goals, you will experience disappointment when things don't always go the way you would prefer. The difference is that you bounce back from the disappointment quickly and do not ever fall into despair. Through it all, you experience a deep, abiding joy, peace, contentment, gratitude, and fulfillment, whatever circumstances or setbacks you face.

At this point you may still be thinking, *So what's the big deal about a little stress? Stress sharpens my mind, makes me pay attention, and gets me off my rear end to get things done.* If the evidence presented thus far about how stress leads to failure hasn't convinced you yet, consider this: Second only to the number of scientific studies done proving the negative effects of stress is the number done proving the negative effects of instant gratification. Predating Dr. Gilbert's and Dr. Lipton's studies by fifty years, multiple double-blind tests have shown that pursuing instant gratification (versus delayed gratification) consistently produces negative results in every area of life, including happiness, health, how much money you make—even your SAT scores. Instant gratification is itself based in our pain/pleasure response, which means when you are seeking instant gratification, you are choosing fear instead of love in response to pain.

Stress goals are *always* based on instant gratification, just as success goals always require us to delay gratification. In fact, delayed gratification is the essence of giving up the end result to God/source/love, and choosing love in the present—which is exactly what I've been saying is the key to success. Anything in opposition to this virtually ensures failure. The research on instant versus delayed gratification proves this exact thing. Everything in your life leads to success if you can appropriately delay gratification, and everything leads to failure if you choose instant gratification (unless it is the right and best thing for everyone in that instance). However, the delayed gratification needs to happen easily and naturally, not forced by willpower. When it's forced, it causes more stress. As you can probably guess, to ensure it will not be forced you need to deprogram and reprogram, which you will learn to do in Part II.

## TURNING YOUR STRESS GOALS INTO DESIRES

You can, however, take all the stress out of your stress goals by simply changing them to healthy *desires*. The difference between the two is the difference between long-term success and inevitable failure.

Let's say there's a big snowstorm and you need to walk to the grocery store, about a mile and a half away, to get some milk. The snow is already drifting, and between you and the store is a patch of woods riddled with tree roots and a lot of hidden hazards you probably won't see until you're right on top of them. But you know that the grocery store is right next to a tall radio antenna you can see above the trees, even from your house.

So here's the question: Do you walk toward the store looking up at the radio tower the whole way? No! You may look up at it occasionally, but if you want to actually get to the store, you're primarily focused on your next step—otherwise you'd twist your ankle or fall in a hole and never get to the store at all. If you look constantly at the end result, you'll never get there.

Believe me, when you're working toward your success goals, there are many potholes and tree roots along the way. For the most important things in life, the path is rarely straight and clear, and sometimes it's not even visible. Yet the experts are telling you to *focus on the radio tower*—visualize it, feel it, taste it, never take your eyes off the radio tower—or you may not get there. As a result of their advice, the landscape is littered with bodies of people who have tripped over tree roots and fallen down holes and never made it to where they were going, because they weren't paying attention to the next step.

The radio tower is your desire; it is not your goal. Your goal is to successfully take the next step, because you know that if you always successfully make the next step, one after the other, there's a really good chance you'll reach your desire. Now you do keep the radio tower in mind, and you glance at it from time to time—it sets your direction. But let's say you get halfway there and you're cold, you're tired, you're hungry, and you want to go home. About that time, you pass one of your neighbors. He asks where you're going, and you tell him you're going to the grocery store to get some milk. "Oh," he says. "You don't need to go all the way to the grocery store. There's a convenience store just a few yards from here that still has milk." You hadn't known about the convenience store. What would you do? You'd change your mind, say thank you very much, buy your milk at the convenience store, and get home in half the time! That's what it means to give up the end result: even as we focus on successfully taking the next step toward the desire we've set, we remain open to changing our desire if we determine another direction would be best for us. We just have to admit we don't know enough about the future to know if we'll continue to want that particular end result. Plus, an end result we might imagine as the worst thing that could ever happen to us may turn out to be the best thing for us in the long run.

I can't think of any better example than when Hope kicked me out of the house after three years of marriage. I thought it was the end of my life! But as you know, this incident turned out to be the single most positive turning point in my life. It led to a transformational *aha* that instantly reprogrammed me. It led to my discovering my life's work and is likely the linchpin for any success I experience today. In fact, the success I'm experiencing today is far beyond what I had ever imagined for my life twenty-five years ago. If I had focused on a specific end result for my career back then (which a lot of people were pressuring me to do), I would never have ended up where I am now, because what I do now didn't even exist back then!

I'm not the only one to have had an experience like this. When I speak to large groups, I often ask them, "How many of you have ever experienced something that seemed really bad in the moment, but months or years later, you realized it was really good, or even one of the best things that ever happened to you?" Invariably almost everyone raises their hand.

What I see most often are people shooting far too *low* for themselves in life. They are aiming for money (that million dollars), or a promotion, without the accompanying love, joy, peace, intimate, fulfilling relationships, and internal happiness. We talked about this back in chapter 1: when you set an end result as a goal, even if you achieve it, you often end up even more miserable than you were before, because you then realize it can't ever satisfy you internally.

The bottom line is that we can't always count on our rational, conscious thinking to determine the best end results for us—and our past experience proves it. The best thing we can do is to successfully live in the present moment in love and truth, in whatever we're doing.

If you ever get to the point where you can successfully live in the present moment in love and truth nearly all the time, I guarantee that you will feel and believe that you are outrageously successful, and most likely you will never want to trade places with anyone. As cliché as it sounds, this program is really about *having it all*. Internal love, joy, peace, and happiness *and* external success in health, finances, career, and relationships. Following this program is the only way I've found to do it, with the caveat of also being in right relationship with God/source/love, above all (for me).

We most naturally shift our stress goals into desires when we love someone. Let's say you and someone you truly love with all your heart both want to do something in particular today. When the other person tells you what he or she would like to do, and you see the sparkle in the other's eyes, you naturally sacrifice what you want in order to do what he or she wants want to do—even though you still want what you want. If you love this person with an agape love (not eros, as we explained in the introduction), you don't sacrifice what you want out of bitterness or duty. Love changes your have-to to a want-to. Love supersedes what you want. What you want is a desire—not a goal and not a need. In other words, if it doesn't happen, it doesn't affect your sense of identity, security, or significance.

This transition can be very difficult, because we are so used to the end result being everything. That's why you had it as a goal in the first place, right? It's all about results. As Vince Lombardi said, "Winning isn't the main thing, it's the only thing." For decades, I heard this quote just as it's written, as have you probably, in order to make the point that results are all that matter. I recently saw a documentary about Lombardi and absolutely jumped up and down and "woo-hooed" when I heard them mention that quote.[1] Apparently, Lombardi said that the quote and the way it had been interpreted had caused him great sadness, because he *never* intended it that way. His definition of winning—which is what he told his players all the time—was to leave the field having done their absolute best. It had nothing to do with the final score. So even Vince Lombardi defined winning based on the *process*, not the end result. In fact, the process *becomes* the end result.

## YOUR ULTIMATE SUCCESS GOAL *and* YOUR SPECIFIC SUCCESS GOALS

We have defined a success goal as follows: it must be based in truth and in love, and it must be 100 percent under your control, which therefore means it's almost always performed in the present moment. A success goal is the next step toward our desire; it determines the what, how, and why of what you do, while your desire is the radio tower—it determines the direction in which you walk. Back in chapter 1, we set our ultimate success goal, or the internal state we want most. But we need more than just our ultimate success goal to go through the daily tasks of life. We need *specific success goals* that tell us more precisely what we do, how we do it, and why we do it for each present moment, and that we are empowered to do without depending on willpower.

When it comes to setting specific success goals, the hardest part is finding something that's 100 percent under your healthy control. This component is where so many well-intentioned people get tripped up. How exactly do you exercise healthy control on a daily basis? The simplest way I have found is this: in any and every situation, your goal is to do everything you do in an inward state of truth and love for the next thirty minutes. That's right—it's the Love Code. It will result in healthy control every single time. And it even fits the requirement of being 100 percent under your control, once you use the deprogramming and reprogramming tools, because no one else can control your internal state except you.

Practically speaking, your desire will help you determine *what* you do for the next thirty minutes or so (your direction), but the Love Code will always tell you *how* and *why* to do it: in love, focusing on the present moment, and giving up the end result. In fact, the "what" is no longer your number one goal; it's the "how" and the "why." It's the *process*, not the end result—because your internal reality always determines your external results.

However, you may notice a slight difference in the wording of the Love Code here. First of all, we've now added "truth" in addition to love. Truth is very closely related to love, but now that we've explained the particular importance of living in accordance with the truth in chapter 3, hopefully the distinction will be all the more meaningful. Second, when I would simply advise people to "do whatever you do in truth and love, focusing on the present moment," I noticed many would struggle with putting this into practice. If you think about it, what I'm asking them to do is to live in love every moment for the rest of their life. Not surprisingly, that felt overwhelming to some people, particularly if they had already tried living in love unsuccessfully in the past, and it became another stressor in their life. But once I began suggesting they live in love for just the next thirty minutes, most people found that more doable. They may not be able to do "forever," but they could give it a try for the next thirty minutes. To be honest, if something is particularly pressuring me, sometimes I can't even do thirty minutes. I say to myself, *Forget thirty minutes. Can I do whatever I'm doing in love for the next five minutes?* I can usually do five minutes at a time, even under extreme pressure.

Now that we've explained the foundational principles behind how the Love Code works, we're ready to put the Love Code into practice, which we'll do in Part II.

# PUTTING THE LOVE CODE INTO ACTION

## chapter 5

# THREE TOOLS TO DEPROGRAM AND REPROGRAM YOUR HUMAN HARD DRIVE AND ITS SOFTWARE

Okay—we've finally reached the place where we can start putting it all together. As I begin this chapter, I have a drumroll going in my head and heart because I've been waiting for about twenty-five years to share this process with you—and only in the past couple years have I had all the pieces come together to make it complete, so that I could.

Decades ago I knew living in love in the present moment (out of an inward state that has been reprogrammed in love, joy, and peace) was the key to success. And long before I came around, many taught the same thing, including religious teachers, counselors, self-help gurus, and other motivational experts. I know I've said this before, but I need to say it again: the problem isn't that we don't know what to do. The problem is that over 99 percent of people cannot do it, based on the typical success blueprint we've all heard, namely (1) focus on the end result you want; (2) create a plan to get that end result; (3) use your willpower and personal effort to work that plan until you receive what you want.

Only relatively recently has science shown us why this blueprint leads us to failure rather than success through the research of Drs.

Lipton, Gilbert, Tiller, Weil, Sarno, and others. Unless your spiritual heart is *already* programmed for success, trying to go against your spiritual heart's programming with willpower alone is a million-to-one shot, because the spiritual heart (or what Dr. Lipton calls the subconscious mind) is a million times more powerful than the conscious mind. The problem is that most of us have human hard-drive viruses programming us for failure, based on internal fear memories. The unseen is always the parent of the seen. Expectations (a focus on end results) are a happiness killer. Our willpower alone will never get us the life we desire.

I know many of you have been trying to use your willpower to live in love in the present moment for a long time, and you've probably beaten yourself up because you haven't been able to do it. Some of you pretend to do it externally, but internally you are a mess. Perhaps you thought your problem was too big, or that you were doing something wrong. Perhaps you've wondered, as you compared yourself to other people's (apparent) success, whether something is wrong with you, since you haven't been able to do what you know you need to do. That's certainly how I felt before I experienced my transformational *aha* and I found the Three Tools. Based on the amazing success stories I read and the advice I heard, I just assumed there was something wrong with me if I couldn't do it, too. Let me say this clearly: IT IS NOT YOU! Please understand that. Remember the first principle in the list I gave you in chapter 1. Let the guilt and shame fall away. It was never you. You've just been trying to do something that has virtually been impossible for you with your current programming.

My sons are seven years apart. My oldest son, Harry, could always climb anything: he could climb trees, he could climb a pole, he could climb a hanging rope. When we'd visit buildings, he'd even shimmy up the big columns! We'd wonder where he went, and there he'd be, up in the air. Everyone around would be amazed, saying, "How did he do that?" Other kids his age couldn't do that. Now, of course, George, who was seven years younger, would watch his brother and think, *I can do that!*

In our backyard was a tall, straight sycamore tree that didn't have many low branches. Harry would jump up on that tree and squirm his way slowly up until he got to the first branch, and before you'd know it, he was at the top. One day, when Harry was twelve, he was sitting at the top of that sycamore tree and saw George at the bottom. He yelled, "George, come on up!"—knowing full well he couldn't come up. So five-year-old George said excitedly, "Dad, I'm going to climb the tree, okay?" I tried to reason with him. "George, you may not be able to climb that tree. Harry's bigger and stronger than you. There aren't any low branches. You're not going to be able to do it." He insisted he could. So finally I just took a step back and said, "Okay, go ahead, son." And inevitably, when he got stuck about seven feet up the trunk, still out of reach of the first branch, I had to help him come down.

We're like that a lot of times. We see other people at the top of the tree, so to speak—or at least, we think they are. So we say, "I'm going up there, too!" We run up and try to do the same thing with expectations and willpower. But what ends up happening is that they usually aren't really at the top of the tree like we thought they were; it just looked that way from our perspective on the ground. Or maybe they had a ladder, the right tool. Or maybe they want everyone to *think* they're at the top, when they really aren't. Or maybe they really are at the top but have completely different programming than you do. As for us, getting to the top of that tree without some additional help just isn't going to happen.

We may be acting like five-year-olds when we set these expectations and try to use willpower to achieve them. But just as a loving parent would have compassion and understanding for a child who acts in accordance with what the child thought was right at the time, we, too, should have compassion with ourselves. We just didn't know—we didn't have all the facts. It's just like when we all believed the earth was the center of the universe, or believed that the world was flat, or didn't know we had all these invisible organisms on our hands called germs. This book is offering you new technology to apply the knowledge that has always been true, for which we've only recently discovered scientific evidence.

The bottom line is that to have the success we desire, we either have to be that one in a million who can overcome subconscious programming with conscious willpower; or we need supernatural, miraculous help; or we need an entirely new blueprint and tools.

I've seen many, many miracles in my own life and in the lives of others, and I always advise prayer first, even to this day. But I also believe that we have some miraculous tools—a new technology—that can specifically program us for success without willpower. These tools load new software onto our human hard drive that automatically deprograms and reprograms us where it's needed. All we have to do is sit down at the computer, and use the keyboard, and we're able to do things we've never been able to do before.

## USING THE RIGHT TOOLS FOR THE JOB

We humans are multidimensional beings: physical, mental, and spiritual. If we want to become successful in life, we need to address all three of these levels, so that they are all healthy and working in harmony. In the next three chapters I'm going to introduce the Three Tools I've discovered and tested over the last twenty-five years that do just that: the Energy Medicine tool (for the physical), the Reprogramming Statements tool (for the mental), and the Heart Screen tool (for the spiritual). Again, understanding the *whole* truth results in belief that has real power. Now that you've learned more about the scientific and spiritual principles behind how these tools work, my hope is that the tools themselves will be easier to use and you will commit to using them over time.

I define the *physical* as everything in our physiology, down to the light or darkness frequencies, atoms, molecules, and cells. The *mental* includes the conscious mind, will, and emotions, or what I would generally refer to as our soul. The *spiritual* includes our unconscious mind, our subconscious mind, our conscience, and what I would generally refer to as our spirit. Now that we know everything is made of energy, based on the way energy works, when we address one of these aspects (such as the emotional), it will undoubtedly affect the other two. So when I say that each tool addresses a particular aspect of our being, I don't mean that the Energy Medicine tool will only address our physical symptoms; rather, I mean that this tool directly engages our physiology to produce healing in *all* the dimensions of our being: physical, mental, spiritual—and even circumstantial.

I realize I've made some pretty big claims about these Three Tools, and for good reason: I've never seen them fail to work to produce success in any of my clients that I have worked with personally (in their words, not mine), if they were used exactly the way I taught over an extended period of time.[1] I have seen these tools work for people with every worldview imaginable, both sexes, and all ages. I have found no difference in their effectiveness based on any of these factors. They seem to work in the same way that gravity works for everyone, whether you believe in gravity or not.

Note that the following instructions are suggestions, not rules. You are free to mix and match and practice these tools in the way that feels best to you. As I work with clients, I tend to "customize" the tool to fit the individual, the situation, and the particular set of issues. Obviously

I can't do that for each individual in a book. So I have developed a general process to follow for each tool that will work consistently and predictably for virtually any person and any circumstance, based on repeated testing and retesting. These instructions will work for you if you follow them, but if the instructions become burdensome, feel free to customize them for yourself. There really isn't a wrong way to use the tools.

One more thing. As you read on, you may discover that you've used or seen a technique similar to one of these tools before. Although I discovered each of these tools in the context of my own private practice, that's not to say someone else hasn't discovered them privately on their own as well. And certainly they're based on principles that have been widely taught for many years. For example, you may have already used a similar kind of Energy Medicine tool that has at least partially helped your symptoms in some measurable way. But if the results didn't last long term, it might be that you need to address the spiritual or the emotional as well. When used alone, these tools can work wonderfully, but because they each only address one aspect of what is typically a three-part problem, they may not always work alone long term, or completely. I believe that's why many techniques don't do the complete job consistently. One technique almost never addresses all three areas of our being, which all need to be healed and put into harmony to complete our success or healing.

To get full healing at the source of the success problems that plague you most, I'd suggest trying all three. One of the primary reasons I wrote this book was to give you *all* the tools you need to heal your source issues for good (no matter how your symptoms manifest themselves), to infuse new success programming into your human hard drive, and then to experience outrageous success for the rest of your life. But as you try these tools, you may find that one or two seem to produce better results than the others for you. That's fine—use the tool or combination of tools that provides the best results. But you can't know for sure which ones provide the best results for you until you try them all over a period of time.

After we discuss all three tools, you'll find instructions for using all three of the tools in one technique for maximum efficiency and results. You can use this "combination tool" for as little as five minutes, or for as long as you like. However, I recommend trying each tool separately first to become familiar with how it works for you.

*chapter 6*

# THE ENERGY MEDICINE TOOL: HEALING SOURCE ISSUES THROUGH THE BODY

In my experience, the Energy Medicine tool has the most powerful effect for most people, right off the bat. *Energy medicine* applies energy to specific points on our physical body to heal a symptom or a problem. Energy medicine has been a hot topic in health for at least the last fifteen years, and we're learning more every day about its applications. Several mainstream doctors, based on the growing body of scientific evidence I've detailed in the previous chapters, believe that applying our understanding of energy to our health practices may lead to breakthroughs we have never seen before. Donna Eden, author of the classic book *Energy Medicine*, has documented the resolution of thousands of stubborn problems that medical science simply couldn't fix. Based on her more than thirty years' experience healing and teaching around the world, Eden has seen energy medicine resolve terminal bronchitis, revive a flatlined heart attack victim, and reverse severe mental disability, along with witnessing thousands more equally dramatic results.[1]

Only in the last year did I discover that even Sigmund Freud used a technique similar to mine in his psychotherapy. Yes, *that* Freud—the famous Austrian neurologist and medical doctor who is considered to be the father of psychotherapy, psychiatry, counseling, and therapy. Believe it or not, energy medicine was his go-to intervention when all else would fail. In his own writings, he said, "I can safely say that it has scarcely ever left me in the lurch."[2] In a way, he was the first to show the world that the nonphysical changes the physical. Freud may not have known why it worked, but he knew that the moment he used this technique, his patients' deeper issues would come up. The Energy Medicine tool I'll show you includes the same position Freud used on his patients (hands over the forehead), although I've added two other positions, which I believe makes it significantly more powerful.

Energy medicine is nothing weird, mystical, or even spiritual. It is, in fact, physical (i.e., based in physics). In 1905, Einstein proved that everything boils down to energy ($E = mc^2$). In other words, every cell in your body runs on electrical energy, and every cell has its own energy power plant called the mitochondria. As long as the cell has plenty of positive energy, it's healthy. If it doesn't have enough energy, or it is infected with negative energy, it starts to become unhealthy. And we can diagnostically measure the energy level of our cells through CT scans, MRIs, and other similar tests.

Energy medicine is simply trying to infuse positive, healthy energy into cells that have a deficit of this energy. That's all it is. Energy medicine in its early forms actually predates Western medicine. Since Albert Einstein's discovery, Nobel Prize winners have predicted that someday we would figure out how to apply these principles to health effectively and that it would change the landscape of medicine and health, just as energy working through electronics, Wi-Fi, and computers has changed virtually every other technology field in the world since 1905. And as I said in chapter 3, it's happening right now.

The point is that energy medicine in general is not new; it's just that with an increased understanding of how energy is the source of every problem, only recently has medical science been able to document how powerful it really is, why it can be so effective, and how it now allows us to do things we have not been able to accomplish before.

## HOW THE ENERGY MEDICINE TOOL WORKS

The principle behind how the Energy Medicine tool works is quite simple. Everything in the body works on energy: every cell, thought, and feeling. Energy is also constantly pouring out of your body, most of it from your hands.[3] When you place your hands on specific points of your body, you're putting usable healing energy back into your body. When you put more usable energy into the body, it can do more work, and it can use the extra energy to fix problems. Remember that at their root, our issues exist only as internal energy patterns, not as bone, blood, or tissue. Physics 101 says that these energy patterns can be changed by another energy pattern. I believe that's exactly what Freud did for his patients, and what I have done for mine for the past twenty-five years.

The Energy Medicine tool uses three positions: the heart, the forehead, and the crown. These areas house the physical parts of our body that directly affect (or are affected by) the stress response, as well as the control mechanisms for every cell in the body. You can use the Energy Medicine tool on yourself, you can use it on someone else, or someone else can use it on you. I have found that results are more powerful if someone else can do it on you, which is what Freud did with his patients and what I have done with my clients.

### The Heart Position

In the heart position, you place one hand (either left or right), palm down, on your upper chest (over your heart), and place your other hand, also palm down, over the first.

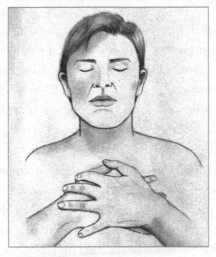

The Heart Position

For this position and for the others that follow, you have two options: you can either rest your hands in this position and hold for one to three minutes, which is how Freud used this tool, or you can move your hands gently in a circular motion (clockwise or counterclockwise, whatever is most natural), slowly moving the skin over the bone (not rubbing the skin), switching directions every fifteen seconds or so, for one to three minutes. This option is what I have used with most of my clients, and I've found it to be about twice as effective as just holding your hands still, in that it seems to generate results twice as fast. However, if for any reason you are not able to move your hands in a circular motion, the resting position will generate the same results, although it may take longer.

This position pours energy into your cardiovascular system and your thymus, as well as key energy medicine points for your immune system. The thymus is an integral part of our immune system: it governs the release of our hormones and chemicals throughout the glandular system. In fact, some doctors say that it *is* your immune system: as the thymus goes, so our immune system goes. Interestingly,

it functions at its peak when we're much younger—particularly at
birth and just before puberty. Research is being done right now to see
if activating the thymus to higher levels of functioning may heal cancer
and many other diseases.

Also housed in the chest is our cardiovascular system, which has
an electromagnetic field fifty to one hundred times stronger than the
brain's. I believe (as do other doctors) that if we think of the central
nervous system (which includes the brain) as the control mechanism
for our body, the cardiovascular system is the primary transmitter
and receiver: it resonates out the frequencies mandated by the central
nervous system. If that's true, then together the central nervous system,
brain, the glandular hormonal system, and the cardiovascular system
govern all the control mechanisms in our body, both physical and
nonphysical (including mind and spirit)—which are the same areas
we're pouring energy into with the Energy Medicine tool.

## The Forehead Position

In the forehead position, you place one hand (either left or right) over
your forehead, with your little finger just beneath your eyebrows (just
barely grazing the bridge of the nose), and your other hand on top
of that hand, both with palms down. Again, you can either rest your
hands in this position for one to three minutes or, for faster results,
move them in a circular motion, moving the skin over the bones,
switching directions every ten to fifteen seconds, for one to three
minutes. You don't even have to use a circular motion if back and forth
is more comfortable, but I have found the circular motion to have the
fastest results.

This position is what Freud would use with his patients: he would
put his hand on the patient's forehead. This technique works even better
when used in conjunction with the heart position and the crown
position (which Freud did not do). As a medical doctor Freud would

have known what *physical* mechanisms were located in this area, but he didn't know why it would so consistently bring up *psychological* issues when his other techniques did not. Now we do.

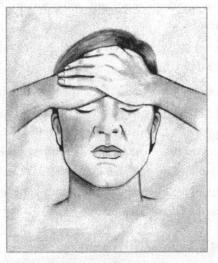

The Forehead Position

When you pour energy into the forehead, you're stimulating some of the most significant physiological mechanisms in your body. First of all, you're stimulating your entire brain: not only your higher and lower brain, but also your left and right brain. According to Roger Sperry's split-brain experiments in 1972 (for which he won the Nobel Prize), the right brain includes our limbic system and our reticular formation, which govern wisdom, meaning, feelings, beliefs, action, and images. Our left brain governs words, logic, and rational reasoning only (i.e., not action and not meaning). You're also pouring energy into the third eye chakra, one of the most powerful energy centers in the body.

Also, based on Sperry's original research, I personally believe the right brain may be one of the main control center locations of the spiritual heart, which is the "container" for our spirit: our unconscious, subconscious, conscience, and the so-called last frontier—everything else we don't even know about yet. In the same way, I also believe that the main control center for our soul, in addition to our body, may be the left brain—our conscious mind, will, and emotions. And all that is behind the forehead!

## The Crown Position

For the crown position, place one hand (either left or right) on the top of your head, or your crown, and your other hand on top of that hand, both with palms down. This position not only activates all the same physiological mechanisms of the forehead position (albeit from a different angle), but also the spinal column/vertebrae and the crown chakra, another powerful energy medicine point that many feel governs our connection to the spiritual realm.

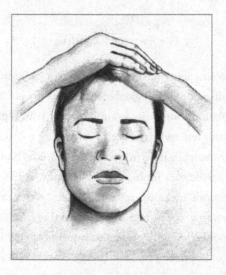

The Crown Position

Now you see how this physiological tool addresses all three aspects of our being: the physical, mental, and spiritual. When you apply energy to these three areas—the heart, the forehead, and the crown—you're physically increasing blood flow and functionality to the control centers for every cell, every thought, every emotion, and every belief, as well as to your heart, third eye, and crown chakras, the three most powerful energy centers in the body. In short, you're activating and providing more power to the control mechanisms for everything in your life: physical and nonphysical, conscious and unconscious, internal and external, your health, your relationships, your prosperity . . . *everything*.

Using the Energy Medicine tool is like putting gas in the lawn mower, hooking the propane tank to your grill, or giving food and water to a starving person. You're giving your body the power to do what it needs to do. In its current state, it might be able to function in ordinary ways. But with this tool, it can do the *extra*ordinary—it can heal our memories, thoughts, and feelings, which is what we want, and how our bodies were designed to function in the first place.

I agree with Freud. This tool, especially when using all three positions, has scarcely ever left me in a lurch. It's the one I've relied on most often, and for the longest period of time.

## USING THE ENERGY MEDICINE TOOL

You can use the Energy Medicine tool in two ways. The first is when anything's bothering you in the moment, such as anxiety, a headache, pain, or any negative emotion. Here's what to do:

1. First, think about one issue that's bothering you, and rate your problem at a level between 0 and 10. Even though you may

have a list of issues you'd like to address, just focus on one issue at a time, ideally the one that bothers you the most. Perhaps you'd rate this problem at a 7—not the worst you've ever had, but clearly significant. (If you have trouble rating things, don't worry about it. Just determine whether or not it's bothering you.)

2. **Close your eyes and relax. Say a short, simple, sincere prayer from your heart asking for whatever's causing your problem to be healed (i.e., the underlying spiritual issues).** As I explained when we were discussing affirmations, this prayer needs to be said in truth and love (as opposed to stating what is not currently true, or stating a desire for something that will hurt or disadvantage someone else). Express a true desire for your problem to be healed, rather than stating that it's already healed, and offer your prayer in love, expressing your desire for a result that helps everyone and has no losers. For example, if you were experiencing anxiety about something you had to do at work, you could say, "I ask for whatever's causing my anxiety to be completely healed at the source. I ask to be released from this anxiety so I can be freed to be a better worker (a better parent, a better spouse, etc.), and that it will be a win-win-win result for everyone involved." Instead of anxiety, you could substitute anger or a stomachache or anything else that's bothering you. Pray from the heart, giving up the end results and willpower, and allowing the process, light, and love to do their work in you.

3. **Begin with the heart position and place your hands on your heart.** Move your hands into the heart position as described on page 128. Now focus on your problem, but don't try to change it. Simply observe it. Alternatively, you can also relax and focus

on positive images that represent love and light to you. Focus on whatever feels best and right. Personally I like to focus on the problem itself and see it begin to melt away. For example, for anxiety, calmly observe the image of anxiety occasionally on your heart screen, and whether you notice any change.

4. **Keeping hands stacked, either hold the position or move your hands in a circular motion, lightly moving the skin over the bone clockwise or counterclockwise, switching directions every ten to fifteen seconds, as described on page 129.** Remember, adding the circular motion simply accelerates the tool's effectiveness; if you have a handicap such that you are unable to add the circular motion, or if you get tired, it's fine to just hold your hands in position. Omitting the circular motion won't compromise the overall effectiveness of the technique.

5. **Hold this position for one to three minutes.** You don't have to time it exactly, and the length of time you choose is mostly up to you. However, I recommend beginning with one minute, because longer periods can trigger a healing response for some. A healing response is a headache or other new, negative symptom experienced during a healing technique, and it's common for approximately 10 percent of individuals. It simply means you're trying to do too much at once. If you experience a healing response, simply switch to the next position. If that position also feels uncomfortable, simply stop and let your body catch up. Otherwise, continue relaxing and occasionally observe your symptom (to see if anything is changing) for the duration of this position.

6. **When the time is up, switch to the next position: your forehead.** Move your hands into the forehead position, as shown on pages 130–131. If you choose and are able, move your hands

in a circular motion, switching directions every ten to fifteen seconds for as long as it's comfortable. Just relax the entire time, occasionally observing the problem for change, but remember, just observe it—don't try to make anything happen. Hold this position for another one to three minutes. Note: You don't have to switch directions when moving your hands in a circular motion—let whatever feels best to you be the rule.

7. **When time is up, switch to the final position: the crown.** Move your hands into the crown position, as shown on page 132. Follow the same procedure as the previous two positions: move your hands in a circular motion, switching directions every ten to fifteen seconds for as long as it's comfortable; and observe your problem calmly for one to three minutes.

8. **Repeat the cycle of the three positions two to three times per day until you would rate your problem or negative feelings at below a 1 (i.e., it doesn't bother you anymore).** For a single session, you can repeat the three-position cycle as many times as you like as long as you are not having a healing response, but I would suggest repeating the three positions two to three times in one sitting, or for about ten minutes at a time once or twice a day. A single session may be enough to heal the source of many issues, but some issues can take days, weeks, or even months to fully resolve. If your issue still bothers you after one day, you can use this tool two or three times a day for as many days as it takes to get below a 1 (which means the original problem doesn't bother you anymore, even in stressful external circumstances).

9. **Please do not worry about the timing**—however long it takes for you to get below a 1 is the right amount of time for you. What's important is to do it correctly and consistently.

You can try the Energy Medicine tool right now on yourself with any physical or internal symptom that's currently bothering you. You can also use it on another person, or anyone who might not be able to do it for themselves, such as babies, pets, or an older person. As I said earlier, I have found results to be most powerful when someone is able to use the tool on another.

The results can be quite powerful and almost instantaneous, as they were with a medical doctor I met in Spain at one of my seminars in 2012. After the seminar ended, this doctor made a point to ask if she could talk with me. We found a private room for our conversation, and what soon emerged were her own unresolved issues—all based on external expectations and a life of constant willpower to the max. It came down to the fact that she had become a medical doctor to please her family, not because it was what she really wanted to do. I worked with her using only the Energy Medicine tool—and we resolved twenty issues in twenty minutes.

She told me the difference was immediate and unlike anything she had ever experienced. She felt love, joy, peace, freedom, and energy. More than that, she no longer wanted to practice medicine to please her parents, but to help people—in particular, she wanted to work with patients to heal the true source issues of their symptoms, in the same way this tool had helped her. When I heard from her six months later, she hadn't had a relapse on any of the twenty issues—they were all still completely resolved.

Now, these kinds of results don't usually happen in one day, as they did for her. More important, they happened without her trying to make them happen, or even expecting them to happen. When we healed those twenty issues with the Energy Medicine tool, her focus naturally shifted to love, joy, and peace in the present moment with no effort—yet *none* of her external circumstances had changed. Everything was based on an internal change.

That's one way you can use the Energy Medicine tool: on specific symptoms you're experiencing right now. A second way is to use it preventatively if you don't currently have issues or even after you heal. You can use this tool for five to ten minutes, two to three times per day, just to pull the plug on the day's stress. You can even use it while watching TV or doing something similar. I have had many clients who've done it this way with great results; however, it is still best to perform it in the meditative form detailed earlier—and this preventative approach should be used in addition to, not instead of, healing specific issues with the tool.

Finally, a third way is with the more formal forty-day deprogramming and reprogramming process: the Love Code 40-Day Success Blueprint. Rather than addressing a single symptom, the Success Blueprint is designed to help people who prefer a detailed, step-by-step process to help them achieve long-term success in a specific area in their life, such as starting a business, improving their parenting, achieving something in their career or sports, starting a nonprofit organization, moving to a new location, or anything that could be defined as a love-based calling or success. We'll cover this Success Blueprint in detail in chapter 11.

## chapter 7

# THE REPROGRAMMING STATEMENTS TOOL: HEALING SOURCE ISSUES THROUGH THE MIND

———

The Reprogramming Statements tool primarily heals the logical and analytical left brain, addressing both the mind (which includes the will and emotions) and the soul. But this tool also affects the subconscious heart and spirit, as well as the physiology. The language of the mind is words.

First, let's look at how the frequencies of love and fear play out in our lives (see chart on page 140).

The items on the left all generate and flow from love and light frequencies, while those on the right generate and flow from fear and dark frequencies. What determines whether you experience the left column or the right column is whether you believe the truth or a lie about that particular issue. The lie always takes you to fear, and from fear to the negative experiences listed above. The truth always takes you to love, which produces all virtues listed above. The Reprogramming Statements can replace and transform the frequency of fear and its negative chain reaction with the frequency of love and its positive chain reaction.

| LOVE | FEAR |
|---|---|
| Joy | Sadness, hopelessness, helplessness |
| Peace | Anxiety, worry |
| Patience, right goals | Anger, wrong goals |
| Kindness, acceptance | Rejection |
| Goodness, nonjudgment, forgiveness | Guilt, shame, judgment, or unforgiveness[1] |
| Trust, faith, hope, belief | Unhealthy control to manipulate circumstances for desired results |
| Humility, or believing the truth about self | Believing a lie about self (whether inferior or superior) |
| Self-control | Unhealthy control over thoughts, feelings, beliefs, and actions |

Because there are twelve categories of Reprogramming Statements, this chapter is longer and more complicated than probably any other. But don't let it overwhelm you. I have had a good number of clients who experienced reprogramming from one statement only, or one section that they really resonated with. They would pray, meditate, and repeat that statement for days or weeks until it was resolved, and that resolution would be their success turning point. So if you resonate with some statements more than others, feel free to focus on those. You can come back later and work through the other statements, until you have addressed all the issues you need to address. Feel free to use the statements however they work and feel best for you—there really isn't a wrong way to use them.

## HOW THE REPROGRAMMING STATEMENTS WORK

Psychologically and spiritually speaking, I believe that every issue you can ever have is rooted in the following list of actions and reactions (think of a long string of dominoes). They work like a flowchart or a chain reaction. (See chart on page 142.)

Any issue you can experience always involves all these actions, happening in this order (for the most part), to create either a positive or negative domino effect. You can be in one or more of these stages at any one time, but to make it to stage 12, you have to have been through stages 1 through 11. As we learned from Dr. Caroline Leaf, our bodies contain no mechanism, physical or nonphysical, for the negative—only for the positive. So experiencing the negative *always* indicates a malfunction of the positive, just like a computer virus. Get rid of the malfunction—the virus—and the positive starts to work again the way it was designed. The negative result always boils down to a memory with a lie in it, which is made of energy. Use the right energy tool to fix the memory—pull the lie out—and the symptoms will automatically start to go away, thus creating the positive version of the domino effect.

Note that it is possible to have the positive result in one area of your life, and the negative in another. You can experience happiness, health, and success in your marriage, but experience unhappiness, illness, and failure at work. If your programming contains both truth and lies, you can even have positive and negative results with the same issue. You may make millions of dollars but be filled with anxiety and unhappiness, or you may have few material goods but be completely happy and healthy.

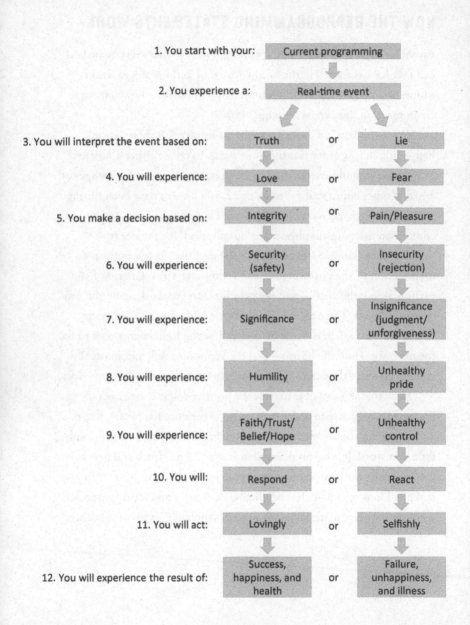

1. You start with your: **Current programming**

2. You experience a: **Real-time event**

3. You will interpret the event based on: **Truth** or **Lie**

4. You will experience: **Love** or **Fear**

5. You make a decision based on: **Integrity** or **Pain/Pleasure**

6. You will experience: **Security (safety)** or **Insecurity (rejection)**

7. You will experience: **Significance** or **Insignificance (judgment/unforgiveness)**

8. You will experience: **Humility** or **Unhealthy pride**

9. You will experience: **Faith/Trust/Belief/Hope** or **Unhealthy control**

10. You will: **Respond** or **React**

11. You will act: **Lovingly** or **Selfishly**

12. You will experience the result of: **Success, happiness, and health** or **Failure, unhappiness, and illness**

## THE CORE ISSUES OF SECURITY AND SIGNIFICANCE

The core issues at the center of this chain reaction are *security* and *significance*. All the events that precede these core issues determine whether you have problems with these issues, and all the events that follow security and significance flow directly from these issues. Security and significance are so important because they directly relate to issues of identity.

Security relates to our sense of acceptance or rejection of others, by others, and self. In my twenty-five years of working with clients around the world, I have never worked with anyone who had a serious health or psychological issue who did not also have a rejection issue. It may have been on the playground in kindergarten or from a well-meaning adult who said something relatively innocent, but as children in the delta/theta brain wave state, we didn't have the ability to filter (such as our "Popsicle memories"). Or we may have been truly abused or mistreated—physically or emotionally. The opposite of rejection is acceptance, or kindness, which is why one of the most powerful things we can ever do to help others is simply to be kind to them. Of course, this includes being kind to ourselves. But unlike significance, security is both internal and external. Security also involves our sense of safety, or whether basic needs are being met in our external circumstances, such as food, shelter, and protection.

Significance relates to our feeling of self-worth: what we believe we can and can't do, and our experience of guilt, shame, measuring up or not measuring up, forgiving or not forgiving, and judging ourselves and others. In other words, our significance represents who we are. Our experience of significance is almost exclusively internal and comes from our subconscious memory banks and beliefs.

Our sense of security and significance are created inside us through our ancestry *and* during our first few years of life, based on whether we experience fear or love in any and every given situation. If we experience love, as long as our basic needs are being met, we'll by and large experience security and significance in that situation. If we experience fear, then we'll feel insecure and insignificant—in other words, we'll feel guilt, shame, rejection, and the feeling that we don't measure up.

Based on whether we're feeling secure and significant (or not), we'll either experience the world through the lens of belief, faith, trust, and hope, or we'll have unhealthy control issues. The control issues mean we're trying to force a certain end result (expectation) by willpower that we believe we must have in order to be okay, which is in turn based on seeking pleasure and avoiding pain. Our programming tells us that we cannot trust and believe, because in the past we have received pain without love. Remember, if we're primarily seeking pleasure and avoiding pain, we're living as if we're still five years old. If we find ourselves living that way as an adult, that means we have a human hard-drive virus about that issue. We have something in our subconscious mind that's giving our brain the wrong instructions and keeping it in a dangerous and destructive loop. As we learned in chapter 2, we become "infected" with human hard-drive viruses when we form a wrong interpretation of an event. If you are experiencing both pain and a lack of pleasure in a particular situation, and our most basic programming says pain equals bad and pleasure equals good, you are extremely likely to believe a lie about your current circumstance. Believing a lie in turn creates a fear-based memory that governs our response in all other future similar situations and becomes part of our internal programming and beliefs, starting the vicious cycle of all the negative results listed on page 12.

On the other hand, if you have experienced love in a particular situation, then you don't live in fear of the end result when a similar situation occurs in the future. You're able to trust and believe from a place of peace, relaxation, and living in the present moment, setting into motion all the positive results on page 12–13.

Also, there's a very important implication here you may have already realized. In my opinion and experience, almost every issue is *a relationship issue!* Love does not exist outside the context of a relationship. So all fear has a relationship problem at its root, whether it's a relationship with yourself, God, others, animals, or nature. Just this year I have been reunited with my long-lost brother—we had not been in contact for forty years. I feel like a part of me that was dead has come back to life. It is an indescribable feeling that has healed me internally in a way that is way beyond words or measurement, and one that I didn't even realize needed healing. I had no idea how much the loss of my brother had affected my life and health negatively over all those years.

I believe this reality is common to everyone. Your security and significance are always formed in the context of relationships (except when you're in a life-threatening situation or experiencing a lack in your basic physical needs and safety). Even if you think your issue is solely financial, health related, or related to some other external condition, if fear/pain/pleasure are involved, it has to be rooted in a relationship issue. So, if you use the Success Blueprint in chapter 11, I highly advise using the forty-day process on *relationship* success goals. Heal your relationship issues, and you heal the great majority of your success issues—usually all of them.

That's exactly what the Reprogramming Statements help you do: they deprogram the negative for every key event, and reprogram us with the positive so we can be happy, healthy, and successful in any area—the way we are designed to be.

Note: These Reprogramming Statements, unlike many affirmations, are based in truth and love and help get our heart and mind back to the perfect state they were in when we were first born and our human hard drives were virus free. I've used these statements successfully for twenty-five years, with people all over the world.

## USING THE REPROGRAMMING STATEMENTS

Here is the full list of Reprogramming Statements:

1. I desire and pray/ask to believe the whole truth and only the truth about who and what I am, and who and what I'm not.

2. I desire and pray/ask to act on and believe the whole truth and only the truth about my current circumstances, not lies based on internal untruths in my programming.

3. I desire and pray/ask to believe the whole truth and only the truth in my heart, soul, spirit, and mind, and no longer believe anything that is untrue.

4. I desire and pray/ask to give up the pain/pleasure way of looking at my life in order to live in integrity and have the best life for me.

5. I desire and pray/ask to think, feel, believe, act, and do everything in love, not fear—in my heart, spirit, soul, mind, and body.

6. I desire and pray/ask to give up the fear, falsehood, and rejection regarding my security, acceptance, and safety, so that I can have security, acceptance, and safety.

7. I desire and pray/ask to give up insignificance, unforgiveness, judgment, false identity, and false self-worth so that I can have significance, forgiveness, nonjudgment, true identity, and true self-worth.

**8.** I desire and pray/ask to give up the wrong beliefs of superiority and inferiority about who and what I am, in order to experience the truth about who I really am, which is fantastic, but no better or worse than anyone else.

**9.** I desire and pray/ask to give up unhealthy control designed to ensure a certain end result so that I will have faith, trust, hope, and belief and therefore have the best results in my life.

**10.** I desire and pray/ask to give up reacting out of pain and pleasure and respond in truth and love.

**11.** I desire and pray/ask to live in the present moment in love regardless of the results.

**12.** I desire and pray/ask to give up achieving success, happiness, and health so that I can be successful, happy, and healthy.

To use these Reprogramming Statements as a tool to deprogram your human hard-drive viruses and reprogram yourself with the truth, simply bring to mind a particular issue or problem and begin with the first statement. Note that "I desire" is referring not to expectations, but to hope, which is love based rather than fear based.

Say the first statement and determine whether you believe it or not, based on your subjective feelings (which can be physical or nonphysical). For example, the first statement is "I desire and pray/ask to believe the whole truth and only the truth about who and what I am, and who and what I'm not." Say this statement for yourself, either out loud or silently. Try to discern whether you feel anything negative, or any resistance, and note exactly what you feel and where you feel it in your body. Most people experience the negativity in their body as a pressure or heaviness. (If you think about it long enough, you might even get a headache or stomachache, but I don't want you to think about it that long.) Keep repeating this statement until you truly believe it. You know you truly believe it when that negative emotion, tension, tightness, heaviness, or pain has gone away. If you don't feel it in your body, go by your thoughts and emotions.

Once you believe the first statement, move on to the second statement, following the same procedure: make the statement for yourself, determine whether you believe it (i.e., whether you have any negative feelings or sense of heaviness), and repeat it until you believe it and any heaviness, pressure, or pain has gone away. Then move on to the next statement, and then the next until you have gone through all twelve statements.

**1. Current programming.** We don't see things as they are; we see things as we are. And the way we see things has to do with our programming, just as with a computer. Our current programming comes from past generations and our own life experience, based on what we have inherited, learned, absorbed, observed, or done. We *all* end up with truth and lies in our programming, no matter how well intentioned our parents were or how perfectly we try to live. But if we want to live the life we want, we have to get rid of our fear-based, false programming.

Please understand: your programming is not *you*. If you have human hard-drive viruses, think of them as splinters inside your spiritual heart that are causing a negative chain reaction. Don't take ownership of any lies in your programming. We're going to use this tool to remove the splinters and allow you to work the way you were made to work: constantly producing happiness, health, and success. The first step is to reprogram you with the truth: the whole truth and only the truth.

> I desire and pray/ask to believe the whole truth and only the truth about who and what I am, and who and what I'm not.

Say this statement either aloud or to yourself. If this statement feels 100 percent true to you and you feel no resistance to it, move on to the next statement. If you feel any resistance to it, repeat it to yourself until the resistance is gone and you believe this statement is 100 percent true, and move on to the next statement.

**2. Current "real-time" circumstances occur, and our unconscious automatically compares our current external circumstances to our current internal programming.** I put scare quotes around "real-time" because in my experience, 99 percent of people do not see their circumstances as they really are and act on them in truth. They see them and act on them based on their programming—which, again, is typically fear based. Instantaneously, in the blink of an eye, our unconscious and subconscious mind determine the appropriate thoughts, feelings, and beliefs based on our current programming, *not* based on our current circumstances. Whenever you experience fear, anger, anxiety, sadness, or any other kind of negative feeling or emotion, and your life is not necessarily in danger, it just means your programming about that issue is fear based, and it will lead you straight to all the negative results you don't want! We want to be able to choose the right action to experience all the happiness, health, and success we *do* want. To choose the right action, we need the right programming.

> I desire and pray/ask to act on and believe the whole truth and
> only the truth about my current circumstances, not lies based on
> internal untruths in my programming.

Say this statement either aloud or to yourself. If this statement feels 100 percent true to you and you feel no resistance to it, move on to the next statement. If you feel any resistance to it, repeat it to yourself until the resistance is gone and you believe this statement is 100 percent true, and move on to the next statement.

**3. Falsehood or truth.** Every lie is a misinterpretation of the truth; that's why lies are so easy to rationalize. There *is* some truth in there. The problem is that it's not the whole truth, or only the truth. The whole truth always points the way to love, while falsehood always points the way to fear. In order to save time and pain, hit the issue at the truth/falsehood level. Train yourself to know when you're believing a lie, and don't act until you have the truth.

> I desire and pray/ask to believe the whole truth and only the truth in my heart, soul, spirit, and mind, and no longer believe anything that is untrue.

Say this statement either aloud or to yourself. If this statement feels 100 percent true to you and you feel no resistance to it, move on to the next statement. If you feel any resistance to it, repeat it to yourself until the resistance is gone and you believe this statement is 100 percent true, and move on to the next statement.

**4. Pain/pleasure or integrity.** We've already talked about our pain/pleasure programming: it's the simple equation of pleasure = good and pain = bad, no matter what. This programming is appropriate for the first six years of our life, while our survival instincts are naturally on high alert, but by about age six or eight, we're supposed to shift from this programming to making decisions based on *integrity*—what is true, loving, good, and helpful. In fact, living with integrity and living according to our pain/pleasure programming are mutually exclusive: you can't do both.

> I desire and pray/ask to give up the pain/pleasure way of looking at my life in order to live in integrity and have the best life for me.

Say this statement either aloud or to yourself. If this statement feels 100 percent true to you and you feel no resistance to it, move on to the next statement. If you feel any resistance to it, repeat it to yourself until the resistance is gone and you believe this statement is 100 percent true, and move on to the next statement.

**5. Fear or love.** When confronted with pain or lack of pleasure, which happens to all of us multiple times every day, we have a choice: Do we address the situation in love, or in fear? We may well experience pain and negative circumstances either way, but whether you respond in fear or love results in different ways of thinking, believing, feeling, and acting. Fear leads to everything you don't want in your life; love leads to everything you do want. The problem for most people is that even when they choose love, if the pain doesn't go away or pleasure doesn't come pretty quickly, they jump the track, return to fear, and try to force what they want. If they would have just stayed on the love track, they would have gotten everything they wanted and more.

> I desire and pray/ask to think, feel, believe, act, and do everything in love, not fear—in my heart, spirit, soul, mind, and body.

Say this statement either aloud or to yourself. If this statement feels 100 percent true to you and you feel no resistance to it, move on to the next statement. If you feel any resistance to it, repeat it to yourself until the resistance is gone and you believe this statement is 100 percent true, and move on to the next statement.

**6. Insecurity or security.** Security is one of the two core identity issues mentioned earlier. It (and significance) is a linchpin issue for everything in this entire list: all of the issues prior affect our sense of security and significance, and all the issues following flow from them. Our security and significance are inextricably linked. Sometimes our sense of security precedes our sense of significance and thus affects it; sometimes our significance precedes our security and thus affects it.

Our sense of security is both external (Am I physically safe and do I have my basic needs met in my surroundings?) and internal (Am I a person others would want to be in relationship with?). It has to do with whether we feel safe and accepted, or feel unsafe and rejected.

> I desire and pray/ask to give up the fear, falsehood, and rejection regarding my security, acceptance, and safety.

Say this statement either aloud or to yourself. If this statement feels 100 percent true to you and you feel no resistance to it, move on to the next statement. If you feel any resistance to it, repeat it to yourself until the resistance is gone and you believe this statement is 100 percent true, and move on to the next statement.

**7. Insignificance or significance.** The other of the two core identity issues, significance is almost exclusively an internal state. Our sense of significance answers the question Who am I? It specifically affects our ability to forgive (or not forgive) and to judge (or not judge). If we have a strong sense of significance, we are able to give everyone—including ourselves—the benefit of the doubt, knowing that our job is not to judge people but to love them.

> I desire and pray/ask to give up insignificance, unforgiveness, judgment, false identity, and false self-worth so that I can have significance, forgiveness, nonjudgment, true identity, and true self-worth.

Say this statement either aloud or to yourself. If this statement feels 100 percent true to you and you feel no resistance to it, move on to the next statement. If you feel any resistance to it, repeat it to yourself until the resistance is gone and you believe this statement is 100 percent true.

**8. Pride or humility.** Humility is the most misunderstood quality on the planet. Humility does not mean weak or spineless. Humility means believing the truth about ourselves. And the truth is that we're all equal at our core. We all have the same basic worth and value as human beings: no matter where we live, no matter what our skin color is, no matter what we have, no matter who we are. We all have unlimited potential and goodness. Superiority and inferiority are equally false and thus equally bad. Both come from insignificance and insecurity. Humility also means not being so caught up with ourselves—being humble means being capable of focusing on others and the work at hand. But most people don't live that way—they're constantly comparing themselves to others and creating expectations based on those comparisons: *How am I doing? What are they thinking? Will they notice?* True humility, rooted in security and significance, knows that deep down you're of great value and worth, and that you're no better or worse than anyone else, so you don't have to pretend or hide.

> I desire and pray/ask to give up the wrong beliefs of superiority
> and inferiority about who and what I am, in order to experience
> the truth about who I really am, which is fantastic, but no better
> or worse than anyone else.

Say this statement either aloud or to yourself. If this statement feels 100 percent true to you and you feel no resistance to it, move on to the next statement. If you feel any resistance to it, repeat it to yourself until the resistance is gone and you believe this statement is 100 percent true, and move on to the next statement.

**9. Unhealthy control or faith/trust/belief/hope.** This category goes back to what we believe: placebo, nocebo, or defacto. Unhealthy control is the opposite of true belief, faith, and trust. It says, "I have to manipulate or control the situation to ensure I receive the end result that I want, because if I don't get the results I want, I won't be okay." In fact, living your life based on willpower and expectations *is* unhealthy control. As we already know, it's one of the most stressful things you can do; it's why expectations are a happiness killer.[2]

Healthy control, on the other hand, is directly linked to faith, belief, hope, and trust. It means we can give up end results, believing that we are fundamentally okay no matter what our external circumstances may bring. Note: Many believe that if they live this way, they won't get anything done. They believe that their willpower aimed at external expectations is what gets results. It actually works in precisely the opposite way: if you give up expectations and relying on willpower, you will get more done in less time, and be happy to boot.

> I desire and pray/ask to give up unhealthy control designed to
> ensure a certain end result so that I will have faith, trust, hope,
> and belief and therefore have the best results in my life.

Say this statement either aloud or to yourself. If this statement feels 100 percent true to you and you feel no resistance to it, move on to the next statement. If you feel any resistance to it, repeat it to yourself until the resistance is gone and you believe this statement is 100 percent true, and move on to the next statement.

**10. React or respond.** Reactions happen automatically as a result of our survival instinct and our pain/pleasure programming. When our foot instantly slams on the brake if a brake light flashes in front of us, or when we see a long line at the grocery store and get angry, we are *reacting*—and this reaction is part of the chain reaction that goes all the way back to our current programming. Some of that reactive programming can be good, such as our reaction to the brake light, in truly life-threatening situations. But any negative reaction to a non-life-threatening situation is a surefire sign of fear-based programming. Once we have the right programming, we become capable of responding to a situation with love in the present moment, rather than reacting in fear. However, even when we become capable of responding, we still have to *choose* to respond in love. Our pain/pleasure programming may still rear its head every once in a while, but we can choose to respond out of love in the present moment, no matter what our pain/pleasure reaction wants us to do.

> I desire and pray/ask to give up reacting out of pain and pleasure and respond in truth and love.

Say this statement either aloud or to yourself. If this statement feels 100 percent true to you and you feel no resistance to it, move on to the next statement. If you feel any resistance to it, repeat it to yourself until the resistance is gone and you believe this statement is 100 percent true, and move on to the next statement.

**II. Selfish actions or loving actions.** Once it's determined whether you will react or respond, the next step is to act. Do you act selfishly, or lovingly? This step isn't about what you do, but why you do it. Are you acting out of self-centeredness or other-centeredness—or toward yourself in love, rather than selfishness? If you decide you want to make as much money as possible, you could be motivated by greed, hoping to accumulate as many toys as you want. Or you could want to help your family get out of poverty, build an orphanage, or give it all away. Only you know the true motivation behind your actions. No matter what your actions are, they should be love based, not fear based.

> I desire and pray/ask to live in the present moment in love regardless of the results.

Say this statement either aloud or to yourself. If this statement feels 100 percent true to you and you feel no resistance to it, move on to the next statement. If you feel any resistance to it, repeat it to yourself until the resistance is gone and you believe this statement is 100 percent true, and move on to the next statement.

**12. Failure/unhappiness/illness or success/happiness/health.** If we're unhappy and unhealthy, that usually means we're basing our happiness on external circumstances and the pain/pleasure instinct. It also means we're extremely likely to fail at whatever we attempt. My definition of success, happiness, and health is feeling joy and peace in the present moment, regardless of external circumstances. The content of your programming—whether it includes lies, or the whole truth and only the truth—determines which experience you have, every time.

> I desire and pray/ask to give up achieving success, happiness, and health so that I can be successful, happy, and healthy.

Say this statement either aloud or to yourself. If you feel any resistance to it, repeat it to yourself until the resistance is gone and you believe this statement is 100 percent true.

Bear in mind that you won't be done with the Reprogramming Statements until you truly believe all of them the way they are written. Keep working through the statements until you can. Until then, I would do the statements once or twice per day regarding whatever issue you are working on. If you get stuck, feel free to post your question to our online community on Facebook or visit www.thelovecodenow.com for additional resources.

Once you have fully deprogrammed any viruses and reprogrammed your mind and spiritual heart with the truth at every stage of the chain reaction, you'll know that your current programming will create positive results every time. And it can make such a profound difference that people may not even recognize you!

One of my clients, a middle-aged woman, had—in her words—
tried every self-help program on the planet. She had problems with her
marriage and she was overweight, unhealthy, and unhappy. In fact, she
was one of the most negative, bitter people I had ever met—every time she
came to see me, she had a long list of all the ways people had wronged her.
She was bringing even me down! "If it wasn't for this, I would be healthy.
If this hadn't happened, I would have made a lot of money. The world is
a terrible place to live: the government is out to get you, people only think
about themselves, my husband is a lazy bum and doesn't ever want to do
anything I want to do." (Of course, most of this was not true—she was
misinterpreting reality as a result of her programming.)

I believed these Reprogramming Statements were a tool that
could help her. You can probably guess what she thought: this was the
stupidest thing she had ever heard of! She said, "Well, I've already tried
affirmations." I explained that these aren't affirmations; you only say these
things if you believe them. Plus, you only work on these statements if you
truly desire them in the first place, which is why the first statement in every
set begins with "I desire." (To me, desire, in this context, means hope.)

So she did the Reprogramming Statements at home on her own—
all the while telling me over and over that they weren't doing a thing for
her. But soon I noticed she was sounding a little different—a little more
positive, a little less bitter. Over time this improvement continued until
it became quite comical to me: when she'd call, she'd sound so positive
and so happy, but then would say, "But I don't think saying these
statements is doing anything."

She told me that one day, her best friend was having lunch with her
and said, "Okay, I've got to ask—what has been going on with you?
Have you been to a faith healer or something? Have you had some kind
of mystical experience? What has happened to you?" And my client
said, "What in the world are you talking about?" She didn't understand.

It was like the frog in the kettle: the change happened so slowly she couldn't tell what was happening. Eventually she confirmed it by asking other people who were close to her if they had noticed what her friend had. They said the same thing: "I've never seen anything like it." Even her husband admitted that he had been amazed at the change—but he didn't want to say anything because he was afraid it might disappear!

She had lost a significant amount of weight without trying, and she and her husband were having a lot more intimate time. And all we did were these Reprogramming Statements. After deprogramming and reprogramming herself, everything was different. Remove the viruses, and your brain is freed up to work properly.

## chapter 8

# THE HEART SCREEN TOOL: HEALING THE SOURCE ISSUES THROUGH SPIRITUALITY

————

The Heart Screen tool addresses the spiritual part of us—that is, our spiritual heart, cellular memories, unconscious, subconscious, conscience, and beyond. Specifically, this tool consciously and intentionally activates and uses our heart screen, a mechanism inside our being that is capable of deprogramming and reprogramming us at a spiritual level. As we learned in chapter 3, our heart screen is the real, internal screen on which we can see the pictures of the memories in our mind, much like we can see pictures on a computer, tablet, or smartphone screen. We use it every time we imagine something, whether real or made up.

To see your heart screen, just close your eyes. Now think about what you had for your last meal. Can you see it? Taste it? Smell it? Do you remember what was around you, or any conversation you were having? If you can, you just saw your heart screen. If you have trouble visualizing in general, try this: eat a piece of candy, noticing everything about the experience as you do—the taste, the texture, the smell, the feelings, and the physical sensations you have while eating it. Shortly afterward, close your eyes and recall eating the piece of candy. (If you'd rather not eat a piece of candy, you can do the same thing by going out in nature and staring at a flower. Then close your eyes and see the flower on your heart screen.) If you cannot visualize at all, it could be a result of brain damage (primarily from severe head trauma, and you would know if you had experienced this), or you have experienced so much pain in your life that your unconscious has disconnected access to your image maker out of your survival instinct because the images there are always so painful. Even these issues will many times improve or heal altogether when using this tool, so I encourage you to try using it no matter what.

The Heart Screen tool has the potential to dwarf the Energy Medicine tool and the Reprogramming Statements in terms of power and effectiveness. Why? This tool taps into our image maker, the source of the most powerful creative and destructive force on the planet since the dawn of time (see chapter 3). In fact, everything that has ever been created or destroyed by humanity was done through our image maker first and could not have occurred without it.

## HOW THE HEART SCREEN TOOL WORKS

As I explained in chapter 3, your heart screen is the screen for your imagination. It is your view into your spiritual heart, or your human hard drive, which includes your unconscious, subconscious, and conscious mind. However, I prefer the term *image maker* because *imagination* tends to convey daydreaming or fantasy, which is not at all what we are talking about here. We are talking about creating the perfect success for you by using the most powerful tool available.

Whatever appears on your heart screen determines what you experience, and there may be several or even many things on your heart screen at the same time—some you can see, and some you cannot. You can see what is in your conscious mind much as you can see what's on your smartphone screen, where you can delete and change what you see on the screen by pushing certain icons or changing settings. Your subconscious and unconscious mind are like the unseen deeper programming or hardware of your phone: you can only change these to a certain extent, because you never know exactly what's going on under there. Your phone's unseen programming or hardware may not respond to your changes, or it might even override them if the programming or hardware is strong enough and in disharmony with the changes you are trying to make. You can't do anything that the phone is not programmed to do.

So let's assume that your heart screen is split right across the middle into two parts: a top part and a bottom part. For the bottom part, or the unconscious side of your heart screen, you do not have any direct controls on the device to see or change what is on. You have to affect it through the part that you can see (the top, or conscious part), and by deprogramming and reprogramming—much like opening up the back of the device, where you need to have the right tools and know how to use them. Nevertheless, what is on the part you can't see (the unconscious) affects everything on the part you can see (conscious) and everything in your life, including your external circumstances.

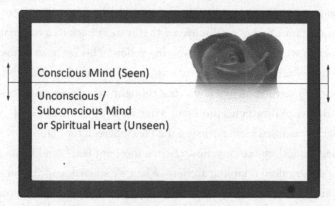

Conscious Mind (Seen)

Unconscious /
Subconscious Mind
or Spiritual Heart (Unseen)

The Two Parts of the Heart Screen

So if you're experiencing anger, you have a memory on your heart screen, conscious or not, that has anger in it. You have to. There is no other way you could be experiencing anger. If the anger memory is only on the unconscious part of your heart screen, you will not be able to remember it and see it. If it is on the conscious part as well as the unconscious, you will be able to remember it and see it on your heart screen. The same is true for any issue: low self-worth, sadness, or any other internal experience.

The more in disharmony the two parts of the screen are in terms of whether the images are fear based or love based, the more the unseen part will take over, mandate what is on the seen part, or even bypass it to mandate feelings, thought, and actions, if the unseen part deems it an emergency (whether real, imagined, or inherited).

One of the most dramatic examples I can remember is from one of my clients. He could not get through a single day without becoming so anxiety-ridden that he was virtually incapacitated. He began each day feeling fine, but somehow he would get triggered and didn't understand why. To be honest, I was stumped for a long time. But one day, as I was talking to him and doing some testing, we finally figured it out—his trigger was the color yellow. Whenever the color yellow was prominent in a current situation, he instantly went into extreme fight or flight. We discovered that it went back to a traumatic memory in which someone was wearing yellow. This reaction to the color yellow certainly wasn't conscious, but it was there—and it was far more powerful than any conscious thought, reasoning, or defense he could use to disarm his problem. After we deprogrammed and reprogrammed that memory using the Heart Screen tool (and the Healing Codes), the color yellow elicited love, not fear—and he no longer experienced crippling anxiety. When we started working on the issue, he was not conscious of the memory, so he could not see it on his heart screen (i.e., in his imagination). Once we found it, he could remember and see it.

The Heart Screen tool is a very powerful way to tap into the power of our subconscious and unconscious mind, which not only is exponentially more powerful than our conscious mind, but controls our conscious mind and body. But the great thing about the heart screen is that we can access it from the conscious mind, not just our subconscious or unconscious mind. Remember, the top part of your heart screen is conscious; you can see it. And what happens on the conscious part of the screen affects what's on the part you can't see (the unconscious part)—it can have a healing effect on the unconscious part of the screen. As you reprogram and deprogram your heart screen over time, you will be able to choose what you want to see and what you don't want to see on your heart screen. In other words, you will be able to choose what you experience and what you don't, which can determine your health, wealth, relationships, happiness, and success in any area.

## USING THE HEART SCREEN TOOL

Now let's talk about the actual screen and how to use it for yourself. You can follow the steps below, or visit www.thelovecodenow .com, where you can listen to my hour-long audio description and demonstration of the Heart Screen tool.

1. Picture a blank screen in your mind, such as a smartphone screen, tablet screen, computer screen, or TV screen— whatever is vivid and meaningful for you. In my experience, the bigger the better. Imagine a horizontal line through

the middle of the screen, denoting the conscious part and unconscious part of your heart screen. You can see what's on the upper part of the screen (the conscious part), but not what's on the bottom part (the unconscious part). By the way, if imagining your heart screen as a literal screen trips you up, just skip this step. You have been using this screen all your life without thinking about it. The Heart Screen tool is about taking control of the steering wheel, so to speak—not just in your imagination, but to create a new reality in mind, spirit, and body.

2. Now take your own spiritual temperature: What are you experiencing right now that is different from what you want to be experiencing? As an example, let's say you're experiencing anger and don't want to be.

3. Say a simple, sincere prayer from your heart, asking to see the anger that is on your heart screen. Don't make it happen; let it happen. Allow the anger pictures on your heart screen to materialize, in words, pictures, memories of past experiences, or however it happens. If nothing happens, try placing the word *anger* on the screen, and then just relax and let it sit there and see what happens. Perhaps you most vividly experience the anger as a feeling of exploding, or a screaming, red face, or your father yelling at you when you were young. Since your anger is conscious, because you are aware that you're experiencing it, picture this anger image on the conscious part. Note that even though the experience is conscious, it is also on the unconscious part (although you don't know what memory is being shown there); otherwise, it would not be a conscious problem for long. The unconscious

is so much more powerful than the conscious that if the two "disagreed," the unconscious would pretty quickly change the conscious picture and your subsequent experience (your feelings, actions, and physiology).

4. Once you experience seeing your anger or other negative emotion, memory, belief, person, place, or thing on your heart screen, ask and pray that this anger will no longer be on your heart screen and that it will be healed to the point that it does not exist anywhere in you anymore—not on the screen, and not in your memories. For instance, you might say, "Let the light and love of God be on my heart screen, and nothing else." Or, if you don't believe in God, simply say, "Let light and love be on my heart screen, and nothing else."

5. Then picture this light and love on your heart screen in images, whether as a blue sky, children, a sunset, true love, flowers, the divine light of God/source/love, or a beautiful view of the beach or the mountains. As with the Energy Medicine tool, just observe the images of light and love on your heart screen, rather than trying to force them to appear. You will eventually see the light and love spread to the unconscious part and heal whatever memories are there, removing the lie, fear, and darkness and changing them to truth, love, and light. You may see the word *anger*, then the light and love dissolving it, and then the light and love spreading to the part of the screen you can't see, and from there to all the related memories (conscious and unconscious). This change frequently happens in a matter of minutes, but it could take days, weeks, or even months in extreme cases,

such as when long-term fear programming has resulted in deep, recurrent negative cycles (and depending on how skilled you are at the process). You will know that the memory has been deprogrammed and reprogrammed when you no longer experience any negative feeling or emotion when you think about or visualize that image of anger, or when the circumstances that typically trigger anger happen again in your life.

6. Until you have been fully deprogrammed and reprogrammed about your issue as described, use this tool as a prayer/meditation once or twice a day. How long you use the tool in one sitting completely depends on you. Allow yourself to really be transported into the inner world, like you are in your own gigantic internal movie theater. If what is happening on the screen is scary to you, feel free to mentally take someone you love and who loves you into the theater with you. If you can't think of anyone, I would be honored to go there with you. (I assure you that I do love you. Maybe someday we will meet and I can prove that to you.)

One of my clients was the kind of a guy you'd call a "man's man," with a gruff demeanor. When I first met him, he just wanted to "fix this." For him, "this" was his arthritis: it was limiting his ability to work, which was causing him stress, which in turn was causing him to distance himself from his family, which was causing family relationship problems, and so on. Interestingly, he was into meditation, particularly the ancient Eastern type of meditation that focuses on emptying your mind. There's an obvious benefit to emptying your mind: it takes the focus away from your problems and your stress, kind of like changing the channel. It may provide relief in and of itself, but it doesn't heal the source issues, in my experience. You would need to do it for hours a day every day if you wanted to sustain the relief. In fact, many people I've counseled have tried meditation and finally decided to quit because even though it helped for a short time, they didn't feel it actually healed anything long term, and they didn't have hours a day to do it.

Now, for the record, I believe traditional meditation is terrific! It's an awesome discovery that has benefited millions. To the body's physiology, one to three hours of daily meditation is similar to taking a nap, and every study I have ever seen on taking a short nap every day is very positive. Also, it is of great benefit to quiet or empty your mind if your mind is filled with fear, falsehood, and darkness (i.e., stress).

However, here's the point: if your mind is filled with light, love, and truth, and therefore absent of fear, falsehood, and darkness, your mind does not need to be quieted! It is designed to work twenty-four hours a day, and it will do that no matter what—you couldn't stop it if you tried. Simply quieting your mind if it is in stress is a coping mechanism, not a healing one. Yes, you will feel more relaxed. Yes, your blood pressure will get better. Yes, your emotions will improve. You'll likely experience many other positive symptoms as well. But the moment you stop meditating for hours a day, all your negative symptoms will return, because you never healed them; you were just coping.

The Heart Screen meditation is the opposite. It's not about emptying your mind; it's about hyperfocusing (in relaxed peace) on the mechanism that controls the problem—and that mechanism is activated by the mind. The heart screen and image maker together form the mind and body's self-healing program and mechanism. The solution is not to disengage it (i.e., focus on nothing, or shut it down), but to engage it to heal the source of the internal stress and fear in our mind, heart, and body. The Heart Screen tool will do everything that meditation does, usually in a fraction of the time. But it will also heal the source, rather than just allowing you to cope with it.

I explained this concept to my client, and he was really intrigued— but skeptical. His tone was never warm, but rather information-gathering. He said, "So if I do the Heart Screen meditation, I won't have to keep doing it over and over?" That was the clincher. If he could find a solution that didn't involve talking all the time (or paying a lot of money), but was something he could do at home on his own, he would try it.

He called me back about a month later. I hardly recognized his voice. He talked to me as if I was his best friend in the world; he just raved and raved. He said, "This is what I've been looking for all my life." He no longer had arthritis pain, he was back to working at full force, and he could spend time with his family. The Heart Screen tool had reversed his vicious cycle into a virtuous one. He had achieved true success for him.

Back when I was doing my doctoral program, I remember a meditation technique one of our professors taught us to address test anxiety. He invited us to visualize ourselves at our favorite place, under the perfect circumstances, and as if it were happening in that moment. We might be on the beach at a tropical island, reclined on a lounge chair on the white sand, sipping a drink, soaking in the sun, and watching the blue-green waves rolling in rhythmically. We might be alone, or we might be with the person we love most. We picture ourselves in that place, under the perfect circumstances, in the moment, as vividly as we can. This technique helps lower anxiety whenever you're experiencing external circumstances that are stressful to you, such as taking a test.

Like anything else, it typically takes practice for maximum effectiveness. The more we practice this technique, the more quickly we'll be able to visualize ourselves in that perfect place, and the more quickly we can neutralize the stress we're feeling in any situation that triggers the stress response. Eventually, with practice, I could get to "that place" and de-stress for a test in about ten seconds, even if people were all around me. But, of course, this visualization wasn't real. The current circumstances still triggered the stress response every time, proving the technique to be simply another coping mechanism—albeit an effective one.

The Heart Screen tool multiplies the power of that visualization a hundredfold. It places that love-based, perfect picture in your spiritual heart so those external circumstances never trigger your stress response in the first place. It is not a normal meditation or coping mechanism. It is real. What you see on your heart screen determines what happens in your heart—which in turn determines what happens in your external life. This has been happening in you your whole life; you just didn't know it, or how to use it to heal yourself.

The Heart Screen tool is the key to experiencing truly miraculous results; spending whatever time it takes to master it is well worth the effort. I've found that the Three Tools discussed here correspond loosely with natural differences in our learning styles. If we tend to be a touchy/feely, experiential type of learner, we'll have an easier time using the Energy Medicine tool. If we tend to be an analytical/verbal learner, we'll have an easier time using the Reprogramming Statements. And if we're visual learners, we'll have an easier time using the Heart Screen tool. But I've also found that, generally speaking, even though the Heart Screen tool may not produce results as immediately dramatic as the Energy Medicine tool, its results can be even more profound over time. It may take a week for the visual learners, and four months for a nonvisual learner—but I would advise one hundred people out of one hundred to practice using the Heart Screen tool until they get results. It may be more of a struggle for certain personalities, but you really can *consciously* change what's on your heart screen with the flip of this switch.

## YOUR SPIRITUAL HEART TECHNOLOGY

Not only do we have access to our own internal heart screen, our heart screen communicates with others' heart screens as well, continuously. We function much like a smartphone or a computer—or, more accurately, as I have said previously, they were designed to function like us. We also now know that the Internet, or what we aptly call the World Wide Web, also was designed to function the way humans do (whether intentionally or not). I call the real-life equivalent to the Internet connection between computers for human heart screens our *spiritual heart technology.*

Just as our computers constantly send and receive data wirelessly, invisibly, and constantly with every computer connected to the web, our individual heart screens also constantly send and receive energy data from every heart screen on the planet, and this data thus constantly affects our current experience and health, as well as that of others we are connected to.

It's as if our heart screens are connected to one another via an "organic Wi-Fi," affecting our thoughts, feelings, behavior, and physiology instantly and constantly. So our spiritual heart technology is connected internally to our generational and personal memories on our own heart screen, and externally to the heart screens of everyone we're related to and close to, our recent contacts, and the people right around us. All the data we receive from other heart screens is being run through our programming, constantly rewriting and tweaking it, and whether we realize it or not, this data from other heart screens played a big role in the original formation of our programming.

Physicists have been able to verify the existence of the heart screen and our spiritual heart technology with experiments dating back seven decades, beginning with Albert Einstein. The Einstein, Podasky, and Rosen experiment in 1935, which identified the effect called "action at a distance," is one of the most famous experiments ever done in science. The results of the experiment corroborated what Einstein believed to be true and expected to happen. Yet for years, it has been commonly known as "spooky" action at a distance, because even though physicists know it happens, they still can't explain how it happens.

This experiment has been replicated many times since 1935 with the same results. If you mention this experiment to physicists today (and I highly recommend you do), they'll likely put their hands over their faces and say, "Oh no, not the spooky action-at-a-distance experiments!" Even though it is a known and proven phenomenon, they can't explain it.

Here's how a world-class physicist explained one of the "spooky action-at-a-distance" experiments to me. The experiment began when two people who had never met before introduced themselves and shared cursory personal information, such as their names, their hometowns, how many children they had, and so on—just enough to make each other's acquaintance. Then they were separated and put in Faraday cages, situated so each participant could not see what was happening with the other person. A Faraday cage is constructed so that normal electricity and energy cannot penetrate it. If you had five bars on your phone and stepped into a Faraday cage, it would instantly go to zero and say "no service." But quantum energy *can* get through. Inside their separate Faraday cages, the scientists hooked the two people up to diagnostic equipment that measures physiological responses and neurological responses. One scientist shone a penlight into one person's eyes in the individual's Faraday cage, while the other, out of sight, rested comfortably. When the penlight was shone into the person's eyes, the needles on all the diagnostic equipment went crazy. Here's the spooky part: the needles also went crazy on the *other* person's machines, registering exactly the same physiological response, even though the other person not only did not experience it, but also had no knowledge of the companion's experience.

The action-at-a-distance experiments show us that we are constantly connected to others around us through quantum energy, especially those whom we are closest to or have had the most recent contact with, just like being connected wirelessly to the Web. We may even be connected to everyone on the planet to some degree. We are, in fact, constantly transferring data, both consciously and unconsciously, to those we are connected to, and that data can instantly affect the physiology of everyone involved.

One Department of Defense study[1] shows even more clearly how the energy we broadcast immediately affects individual cells, either stressing them (if we broadcast fear) or eliminating their stress (if we broadcast love). In this 1998 experiment, cells were scraped from the roof of the participant's mouth and taken to another location fifty miles away. The participant was then shown violent images on TV and registered the expected cluster of stress-response physiological changes: galvanic skin response, increased heart rate, changes in neurological activity, and the like. Fifty miles away, at the same moment the participant was registering symptoms of the physiological stress response, the *scraped cells* also registered the same physiological stress response.

Next, the participant was shown a calming show on television, and his physiological responses registered this calming effect. Fifty miles away, again at the same time, the scraped cells also showed this calmed physiological response. In fact, the participant's cells continued to show exactly the same physiological response as the participant himself even when the experiments continued *five days* after being detached from the person, still fifty miles away.

Dr. Masaru Emoto's bestselling book, *The Hidden Message of Water* (Atria, 2005), and landmark research show us that even words, thought or spoken, can change the molecular structure of frozen water crystals. Fear-based words change the molecular structure to a grotesque, dark, distorted shape and color, while love-based words change the molecule to a breathtakingly beautiful kaleidoscopic snowflake of light when viewed through a microscope.

An Institute of HeartMath study shows that love-based thoughts or spoken words have a healing effect on DNA, while fear-based thoughts and words have a stressful, damaging effect. In one study, when individuals held a test tube with human DNA and thought positive, healing thoughts, the DNA showed the same kind of harmonious patterns Dr. Emoto's love-based words produced in molecules. Similarly, when these individuals thought negative, destructive thoughts, the DNA became chaotic.[2]

Again, our heart screen and our spiritual heart technology are not metaphors. They are real. Fear and love data are constantly affecting your own cells this way right now (and thus your physiology,

thoughts, feelings, beliefs, and external circumstances). This fear
and love data could be from your programming, your generational
memories, your own choices, and *from other people you're connected
to and don't even know it.* Of course, whenever we start to feel low,
we don't automatically think, *Oh, right. Three days ago, I talked to
my friend, and she was really low. That's probably why I'm feeling
low.* No! Our mind tries to come up with a reason why we're feeling
low, so we can use our willpower to avoid pain and seek pleasure, and
we look around and blame our spouse, kick the dog, or honk the horn
at the car in front of us.

Understanding the scientific basis behind our spiritual heart
technology takes the adage "Be careful who your friends are" to a
whole new level! At the same time, if you deprogram and reprogram
in love and light, and choose to live in the present moment, you
can be a powerful healing presence to everyone you meet. Love and
light always overcome fear and darkness. So if you consciously
only transmit and receive love, your energetic field will be like a bug
zapper against any fear or stress frequencies coming your way. And
that can have profoundly positive effects on others' lives, including
your own.

One of my clients had not spoken to her daughter in ten years.
When she first called me, she said, "I've got a problem, and it's my
daughter." I finally convinced her not to worry about her daughter
and to just focus on healing the issue in herself. Several months later,
as she worked on deprogramming and reprogramming, she felt herself
getting better and better. One day she called me and was weeping.
She said, "I was doing the deprogramming and reprogramming work
this morning and I felt the last little bit of unforgiveness and anger
go away. I knew it was finally, completely healed. At that moment
the doorbell rang, and it was my daughter, weeping, standing at my

door with her arms open, saying, 'Mom, I'm so sorry. Will you please forgive me?'"

Our coaches, who have worked with me for twelve years, also have many stories like these. You can become a healing influence on everyone you meet simply by deprogramming and reprogramming yourself to constantly transmit love.

Here's my question: Would you like to take charge of your spiritual heart technology and control whether you receive love or fear from others' heart screens, or would you rather be at the mercy of all the anger, fear, and stress being transmitted to you every moment from people all around you? Just as you can sit at the keyboard and set your Internet settings so that you can choose what kind of data your computer receives and transmits, you can choose to receive and send only love frequencies.

These pathways and connections do not have to be created; they have existed since we were in utero. The Heart Screen technique allows us to consciously use these existing pathways to "tune into love"—love in you, around you, in your cells and memories, and in everyone else's cells and memories to whom you are connected. You can control where you "tune" your station.

Personally, I like listening to Pandora. I pick my music group, and it finds all the music that is like that group without my having to manually search and create a playlist, or keep changing the radio station. In a similar way, you can consciously and constantly tune in to your love station using pathways that are already there. Until you are deprogrammed and reprogrammed, you may not be able to do this to the extent you would like. But consciously tuning in to love will help you change that programming, and it will be surprisingly easy and effective after you have reprogrammed using the principles and tools in this book.

Let's take a moment to look at how "tuning into love" chemically works in us. Oxytocin is often called the "love hormone." In addition to being released in our brain when we feel "in love," it is also released by sex, eating ice cream, or any enjoyable activity. It is quite literally, both physically and nonphysically, the diametrical opposite of the fear/stress response. Remember, we are built and designed to live in love, not fear—living in fear is a malfunction. Nevertheless, you're not going to engage in these enjoyable activities constantly, and it wouldn't be good for you if you did.

However, Dr. Margaret Altemus and Dr. Rebecca Turner, in a study on oxytocin, found that recalling a love relationship memory can cause oxytocin to be released in the brain.[3] Similarly, Dr. Daniel Amen found that recalling fear-based memories can cause the same negative, fear-based hormones and chemicals to be released in the brain as when the event originally happened. As we mentioned in the introduction, the clinical effects of the stress/fear response and those of oxytocin when released in the brain include the following:[4]

These two lists are the very definition of failure and success, and the ultimate source of both are our fear-based and love-based memories. A fear-based memory turns on the stress response, which releases cortisol in the brain, which results in all the symptoms on the left. A love-based memory that has been activated on the heart screen can release oxytocin in the brain, which results in all the symptoms on the right. Here's the great news: you get to choose which experience you have! You can decide to keep your fear-based programming and constantly turn on the stress, cortisol, and failure switch, or you can deprogram the fear, reprogram with love, focus on living in love in the present moment, and turn on the love, oxytocin, and success switch!

| CLINICAL EFFECTS OF CORTISOL (Released by Fear/Stress) | CLINICAL EFFECTS OF OXYTOCIN (Released by Love) |
| --- | --- |
| Dumbs us down | Enhances relationships |
| Makes us sick | Increases parental bonding |
| Drains energy | Results in love, joy, and peace |
| Suppresses the immune system | Increases immune function |
| Increases pain | Reduces stress |
| Raises blood pressure | Lowers blood pressure |
| Closes cells | Opens cells |
| Destroys relationships | Counteracts addiction and withdrawal |
| Causes fear, anger, depression, confusion, shame, and worth and identity issues | Stimulates human growth hormone |
| Causes us to approach everything from a negative perspective (even if we put on a happy face) | Increases trust and wise judgment |
| | Modulates appetite, healthy digestion, and metabolism |
| | Promotes healing |
| | Stimulates relaxation |
| | Stimulates non-stress energy |
| | Stimulates higher neurological activity |

Based on my own experience and what my clients have told me over the past twenty-five years, I believe that when we are deprogrammed of fear and reprogrammed with love, and then choose to live in love, focusing on the present moment, we also create a steady release of oxytocin in the brain. After all, my clients report exactly the same kind of experience after they are deprogrammed and reprogrammed and put the Love Code into practice: they feel as if they're twenty years old again, full of energy, thinking more clearly, healthier, and more positive.

Do you remember how you felt when you fell head over heels in love? Didn't you feel the same way: more energetic, less stressed, more vibrant, and healthier than ever? That's what happens when oxytocin is released in your brain. The problem, of course, is that you fall out of love. If you are able to deprogram and reprogram your spiritual heart, mind, and body and then focus on love in the present moment, it would be like falling in love and never falling out of love again. There may be nothing else on the planet that can make us feel this way!

After you deprogram and reprogram, you can take control of your spiritual heart technology in at least two ways. First you can make a conscious effort to tune into love, choosing to only experience, receive, and send light and love. Visualize nothing but light and love on your heart screen and visualize receiving and sending only light and love, every hour of every day, just as you learned to do with the Heart Screen tool. Light/love and fear/falsehood is in you, around you, and in those energy pathways—just like wireless data streams to and from your computer, tablet, or smartphone. Make this spiritual healing, cleanliness, and maintenance part of your daily practice, like brushing your teeth. After all, if you just go on the way you have been, you will continue to get and send and experience what you have been—which is usually stress, anxiety, anger, and sadness.

If you're not sure how to begin "tuning in to love," the good news is that in your heart you have a conscience, or what I call the "love compass"—ancient spiritual texts have referred to it as the law that is written on your heart.

Close your eyes and visualize being connected to every love-based memory inside you, including generational ones. Picture being connected to all your loved ones, friends, even people you don't know, and constantly sending and receiving love from all of them, 24/7. You don't have to worry about fear memories either internally or externally from others; the light always eliminates and overcomes the darkness, as does love with fear. You can overlay this practice onto every hour of your day: become "tuned in" to sending and receiving love energy, internally and externally—have it always running in the background, like background music while you work.

If this seems "out there" to you because you can't see it with your physical eyes, consider that you would probably never attempt to defy gravity, even though you have never seen it. Similarly, I imagine you believe in "sound," even though you have never seen a sound wave. You probably own a cell phone or smartphone, even though you can't see the incoming and outgoing energy signals that make it work. All these things mimic how we as living beings work—constantly sending and receiving energy. Only recently have we been able to prove many of the things that make your "love station" work.

The difference between this and a lot of other meditations and visualizations is that you are visualizing something that is absolutely real and happening right now, has been happening all your life, and will be happening for the rest of your life. It's not made up. You might think of this as "defacto" meditation, as opposed to "placebo" or "nocebo" meditation. We have just recently been able to prove and quantify many of these things. Your visualizing (imagining) it with my instructions is the only truly creative force on the planet. Everything is imaged before it happens. You are just, for the first time, using your image maker to create something internal with your spiritual heart technology.

In addition to consciously tuning in to love, a second helpful technique you can use with your spiritual heart technology is to focus on what I call a "love picture," or love memory, which is what Drs. Altemus and Turner found can cause a release of oxytocin in the brain. Imagine a memory where you felt completely and utterly loved, and visualize that love picture on your heart screen. If you don't have any love memories, you can create one using your image maker. As long as it is in truth and love, it will typically work great. We are creating and editing memories constantly anyway; plus, your memory of what happened and what *really* happened may be two very different things.

In one sense, whether a memory is real according to external circumstances or not is immaterial. It is always real (and is happening right now) to the spiritual heart and unconscious mind. You don't necessarily have to figure out if it is a real or false memory—just heal it, regardless. It can do similar damage to your cells and programming either way.

However, many have trouble using the two spiritual heart technology techniques because although they try to focus on a loving relationship memory, they are stressed and in fear of everything else. They want the benefits of the release of oxytocin in the brain, but become overwhelmed as they are flooded by the effects of cortisol and stress, physically and nonphysically—which is why you have to deprogram and reprogram for it to have maximum effect.

## chapter 9

# THE COMBINATION TECHNIQUE USING ALL THREE TOOLS

Although I recommend trying each tool separately to become familiar with how they work for you, I believe they work most effectively together.

Even though we've taken many pages to describe the Three Tools, the process itself is very brief and simple. You can use all three of these tools together in five minutes. In fact, after years of practice, I use them all the time in one minute.

You can use this combination tool in two ways. First, you can combine the Reprogramming Statements with the Energy Medicine tool and the Heart Screen tool, which is the way I'd recommend to start. Or, if you have an issue that's bothering you right now, you can substitute that particular issue for the Reprogramming Statements, whether it's your gallbladder, anxiety, or a particular relationship. Just follow the steps below, or visit www.thelovecodenow.com for a ten-minute audio that guides you through the process.

1. Begin by stating the first Reprogramming Statement to yourself: "I desire and pray/ask to believe the whole truth and only the truth about who and what I am, and who and what I'm not."

Or, if you'd like to work on a particular issue, identify that issue clearly in your mind.

2. Consider how you feel about that statement, or about having your particular issue heal or improve. Do you feel any fear, stress, or resistance, whether in your thoughts, your emotions, or your body? If you do, that's a sign that you have a source memory with fear in it regarding the statement or issue, and this combination tool will help heal the source of that fear. If you don't, and you're working with the Reprogramming Statements, you can move on to the next Reprogramming Statement until you do feel some resistance to the statement.

3. Once you have noticed some specific resistance to a Reprogramming Statement or to the healing of the issue, ask yourself, *When have I felt this way before?* To get as close as you can to the source, try to think of the earliest memory you have of feeling this way.

4. Say a prayer from your heart that you will be able to see the images on your heart screen that will heal the issue you're experiencing. Note: As you go through the process below, remain open to whatever appears on your heart screen. Many people have experienced amazing images on their heart screen that have resulted in far deeper healing than they had thought possible. So don't try to control the images that appear on your heart screen too much; simply allow the images to arise.

5. Now imagine on your heart screen the resistance or problem you're experiencing regarding the Reprogramming Statement or issue. If it's difficult to imagine that resistance on your heart screen, you may want to create a metaphorical image, such as an animal or a plant that needs nourishment or care. Or you

can just imagine the feeling you're experiencing. For example, if it's fear or anxiety, imagine the word *fear* or *anxiety* on your heart screen. Again, don't work too hard at the imaging; just relax and let it happen. If you just have a feeling right now and can't visualize anything, that's fine, too.

6. Place both hands over your heart (the first position of the Energy Medicine tool).

7. Imagine the light and love (of God), the source of your life, filling your heart screen. You might see a gentle and powerful light flowing in, bringing warmth and comfort into your heart screen. Let that light and love saturate your entire heart screen, including any resistance. You may see the resistance image change as a result, but don't try to make it change. You might want to take a few deep breaths into your belly; continue to relax into the experience.

8. Now shift both hands to your forehead (the second position of the Energy Medicine tool).

9. Imagine someone who knows you and loves you unconditionally, such as God, Jesus, a family member, or anyone else you admire and feel 100 percent safe with. With their presence, they are bringing even more of this light and love, so that the entire atmosphere seems to be in perfect harmony. Your problem or your feelings about the problem may be shifting as well, but let those images shift and change on their own. Whatever shows up on the heart screen is fine. Just let it happen.

10. Finally, shift both hands to your crown (the third position of the Energy Medicine tool).

11. Imagine the opposite feelings of what you were feeling before start to fill the heart screen. If you were feeling grief and

hopelessness before, imagine feelings of joy and hope filling your heart screen. Perhaps you see positive images, or you just feel positive feelings of love, joy, and peace, so that there is no more fear or impatience or frustration or anger. Allow that positive feeling or image to fill your heart screen, blending perfectly with the light and love surrounding you, and with the presence of your loved one, and your feeling of resistance.

**12.** Finally, place both hands back over your heart.

**13.** Imagine, amidst this light and love, a small child, perhaps six or nine years old. When you walk over to the child, you notice that the small child is you. You, as a child, are becoming aware of all this love and light surrounding you, and of God or your loved one right there. Perhaps before you were feeling alone, but you now see that there is love all around you. Now you notice another person coming onto the scene approaching the young child—and it's also you, now as an adult. The grown-up you kneels down before you as a child, embraces the child, and says, "I love you. It's all right now, I'm with you. You are not alone. It is not your fault. It's never been your fault." At that moment, you as a child realize you are loved deeply.

**14.** Continue to take everything in: the love and light (of God), the presence of God or your loved one, and you as an adult embracing and loving you as a child unconditionally are all blending together around you in perfect harmony. You know you are loved, and you know you are safe: you feel it in you and through you, deep in the core of your being. As you feel this love and embrace it, allow whatever images arise on your heart screen to simply be there.

**15.** To conclude, take a deep breath from your belly, nice and slow. Smile. Gently open your eyes, and know that you are loved.

## OUR PHYSICAL, EMOTIONAL, AND SPIRITUAL DIMENSIONS ARE ALL CONNECTED

Even though the Energy Medicine tool most powerfully affects your physiology, the Reprogramming Statements tool most powerfully affects your conscious mind (which in turn affects the unconscious mind), and the heart screen most powerfully affects your spiritual heart (which includes your unconscious and subconscious mind), all Three Tools overlap and affect one another. Also, resetting your experience with these tools is a skill you learn over time, like shooting a bow and arrow. I can now reset my experience in sixty seconds, though I certainly couldn't do that at first. The more you practice, the better you'll get. And as I said before, people with certain learning styles may have an easier time with one tool rather than another. Don't let that discourage you, and don't worry about how long it takes. The results will be worth it.

Now that we've made it to the end of this chapter, let me make one thing perfectly clear. I believe that the most important thing is to plug into God/source/love, every hour of every day, as I mentioned in chapter 3. I do this primarily through prayer. If you can do that, everything else *will* be okay. The second-most-important thing is living the Love Code theory, principles, and process. It is the path to success, and 99 percent of all people, in my experience, are on another path. Sometimes you just need the map to show you how to get on the right road. The least important things in this book are the Three Tools. Remember, you can accomplish the internal deprogramming and reprogramming that leads to transformation in any one of several ways: a transformational *aha* from meditation and prayer on principles of love and truth, a transformational *aha* from a near-death experience (whether physical or nonphysical), plugging into God/source/love (which may happen through prayer), or using tools specific to these issues, such as the Three Tools.

Having said this, if you can't get your unconscious and subconscious deprogrammed and reprogrammed any other way, they are still indispensable. However, I do know of several other energy medicine techniques that can produce similar results to the Energy Medicine tool I describe here, so feel free to use one of those if you are more comfortable with it.

Now that you understand how to use these Three Tools, I'm going to walk you through some basic diagnostics and a forty-day process to help you more easily diagnose the source behind your success issues, use these tools to deprogram and reprogram your spiritual heart, and achieve the success you want.

*chapter 10*

# BASIC DIAGNOSTICS: IDENTIFY AND HEAL THE SOURCE OF YOUR SUCCESS ISSUES

When I work with clients, almost everyone comes in needing some "basic deprogramming and reprogramming" before they can begin to work on their success goals and really start putting the Love Code into practice. In this chapter I've included three diagnostics for the deprogramming and reprogramming work: the Success Issues Finder test, which I advise everyone to start with, and two other diagnostic tools that are included as a bonus. For perhaps one client in ten, these last diagnostic tools have been extremely beneficial.

Be aware, though, that this kind of basic reprogramming can unearth your biggest, most intractable issues. Some of these issues may have lain dormant for years, decades, or even generations. If you begin to go through these diagnostics and feel like you're getting bogged down, or you just don't feel like tackling the underground issues before you start working on the one or two success issues you know you need help with, go ahead and start using the Three Tools on those issues or turn to the next chapter for the more detailed, step-by-step Success Blueprint. The Three Tools and/or the Success Blueprint will allow you to work on the same issues the diagnostics reveal in a more specific context—namely, how these issues are blocking you from the success you want right now. You can always return to this chapter to do the full deprogramming and reprogramming when you're ready.

But if you do have the interest and desire to work through these Basic Diagnostics, you'll find that working through your success issues will be quicker and easier. You will almost certainly be "surprised" by something you find through the Basic Diagnostics—it happens almost every time. That surprise may end up being a very important key to your success.

## DIAGNOSTIC 1: THE SUCCESS ISSUES FINDER

The first thing I'd highly advise you to do is go to www.thelovecodenow .com and take our Success Issues Finder test. It is the only test of its kind in the world (that we're aware of), and it's absolutely free to you because you bought this book. All over the world, doctors, CEOs, ministers, social workers, and teachers use it as their primary means for discovering the underlying source of problems for their clients and students—in other words, their human hard-drive viruses. This test diagnoses the root causes of all your problems and blocks to success, whether they're physical, emotional, spiritual, or even circumstantial.

The Success Issues Finder is a ten-minute spiritual diagnosis, though it's not at all religious. But it is called a spiritual diagnosis because it diagnoses the issues of the spiritual heart.

About twenty years ago, back when I discovered the ancient manuscripts about the issues of the heart, our unconscious and subconscious beliefs, and their effect on our health and everything else, I searched all over the world to find a test that could accurately diagnose these underlying source issues. I could not find one. I then desperately tried to create a test that could diagnose these issues. That attempt was unsuccessful. Fortunately one focus of my doctoral work in psychology was psychometrics, or the construction and administration of tests, and that's where I discovered several missing pieces. I went back to work on the test with a team of computer programmers, a clinical psychologist named Lorna Meinweiser, and Tom Costello, one of the most brilliant people I know—and voilà!—a few years later, the Heart Issues Finder was born, and after that, the Success Issues Finder.

Since then many people have shared with us that after decades of counseling and therapy, countless tests, libraries of self-help books, and unlimited prodding and poking (both physically and into their psyche), the Issues Finder tests uncovered the true source of their difficulties in ten minutes. How did they know? First, many of them just knew intuitively, like how you know when you're in love. But second, they also knew because when they started to focus for the first time on healing the true source as revealed in this assessment, their long-term symptoms magically melted away.

One note: After publishing *The Healing Code*, which gave people online access to the Heart Issues Finder (primarily for health issues), I was asked why I did not include a hard copy of the test in the book. The reason is simple: the test exists only online because it has a very complicated mathematical algorithm and is only practical as a computerized test. The same is true for the Success Issues Finder test. If offering you this wonderful tool was contingent upon it being replicated fully in the book (questions, scoring, and interpretation), then I would not be able to make it available to you. Immediately after you complete the test, it will produce an eight- to fifteen-page individualized interpretation of your underlying spiritual issues related to success in your life—in other words, all the details about the real sources of your success problems *and* their solutions, customized specifically for you. And you will be glad to know that one of the things I like best about the test is that it's free to you for buying this book. In fact, it's free to you and your family from now on. Take it once a month and, as you deprogram and reprogram, watch your underlying scores change.

## USING THE SUCCESS ISSUES FINDER TEST

Based on your answers to the questions, the Success Issues Finder test produces a scaled score (between −10 and +10) for sixteen different source issues that may lie behind the visible problems in your life and keep you from being successful. Your individualized interpretation will include a robust description of each of these potential issues:

- unforgiveness versus forgiveness

- harmful actions versus helpful actions

- wrong beliefs versus transforming beliefs

- selfishness versus love

- sadness/depression versus joy

- anxiety/fear versus peace

- impatience versus patience

- rejection/harshness versus kindness

- not being good enough versus goodness

- control versus trust

- unhealthy pride/ arrogance/image control versus humility

- unhealthy control versus healthy self-control

- internal states

- external focus

- goal setting

- success orientation

I invite you right now to go online to www.thelovecodenow.com and take the test for yourself. Be sure to answer the questions in light of how you feel most of the time—in other words, on an average day. If you're feeling bad, you may tend to answer the questions based on your bad feelings in the moment. Or perhaps you feel exceptionally good, and you answer the questions based on your exceptionally good feelings in the moment. This can skew the test, so for the most accurate reading, answer based on the way you usually feel. You can also take the test to identify the underlying causes related to one specific issue in your life, such as your job or a particular relationship. Simply answer every question (as much as possible) in light of that one issue. You can take the test multiple times to address as many specific issues as you want.

Once you receive the results of the assessment, first look at your lowest scores. Let's say your three lowest scores were Patience (−5), Peace (−3), and Love (−3). Those lowest scores likely identify the strongest source of the things bothering you most in your life—where you need success and healing the most. They also tend to be the source of whatever end-result goals you're setting and why you don't know what you truly want. The pain from these lowest-score issues causes you to focus on your external circumstances for relief. As we learned in chapter 2, we tend to misinterpret the source of our pain as arising from our external circumstances, rather than these underlying spiritual issues in our memories that are often generations old. As you look at your results, you'll see an interpretation of what your score in each of these areas practically means. For example, here's what the test says for a score of −5 for Patience:

> In the area of Patience, your scaled score is −5 on a scale of −10 to +10.
> *You may often feel impatient or angry when things don't happen as quickly as you want them to. When you want*

*something, you have trouble waiting for it. Your goals may often*
*be rooted in selfishness rather than in truth and love. You can*
*learn to set true love goals and find peace and joy in your life.*

Next, look at your highest scores. These are your strengths and
gifts—what you're best at. Use this knowledge in your relationships,
your career, and everything that you do, to enhance your results—the
way a sports team would play to its strengths. For example, I went to
college on a tennis scholarship. I really wasn't very good, but I was a
bulldog and hated to lose. So I would dive all over the court to get every
ball back, which would usually become frustrating to my opponent.
My weakest shot was my backhand, so I would compensate: I would
run around my backhand to hit a forehand. I would stand on the court
in a position that made it difficult for my opponent to hit it to my
backhand. All this compensation and protection took a lot of energy
and work, but it pretty effectively nullified a weakness. So I believe
in both approaches: eliminate your weaknesses and emphasize your
strengths. Do both! The Success Issues Finder will help you with that.

Don't be discouraged if your highest score doesn't seem very high.
Let's say your highest score was +2 for Self-Control. Here's what the
test would say:

In the area of Self-Control, your scaled score is +2 on a scale of
−10 to +10.

*You may have a sense of entitlement, that others should do*
*things for you, or that the world owes you success. Or you might*
*feel as though you are not capable of success and sometimes feel*
*like giving up. As you let go of old, harmful beliefs and toxic*
*cellular memories, you can live your life empowered by truth and*
*love.*

That may not sound much like a strength to you. But when you have strong, fear-based programming, that negative programming functions like a dam against your strengths, holding them back against their will. You may only have the tool of willpower at your disposal, trying to fight against a power exponentially stronger (i.e., the programming in your spiritual heart). But once you deprogram the fear from your spiritual heart and reprogram it with love using the Three Tools you learned in chapters 5 to 9, these strengths can be released like a flood. For now, use your conscious mind to apply love to your situation: believe that you are doing the best you can in every area— even where you show the lowest scores. Whatever your scores show, be kind to yourself, not condemning. We are going to change them.

## USING THE THREE TOOLS WITH THE SUCCESS ISSUES FINDER DIAGNOSTIC

Identifying exactly where the source of your success problems lies may be the missing key that unlocks everything for you. I had a client who was living in Los Angeles and working three jobs. She had tried every success program under the sun, yet still felt like she didn't know what the problem was. Everyone had told her something different, and she was running out of money. She took the Success Issues Finder test and discovered that External Focus was her lowest score. In an instant she knew that this issue was what was blocking her: she had already learned how an external focus inherently triggers our stress response and directly works against our success, and she was beginning to see how an external focus characterized the way she lived her life on a daily basis. Once she saw the connection, she prayed, meditated, and used the Three Tools to heal her underlying programming about this tendency. One year later she called me to tell me her income had increased 16 *times*. Not 16 percent, not $16,000 more, but 16 times. She said it all came down to the Success Issues Finder and being able to work directly on the true source of her success problems. I have even seen a number of instances when individuals identified the true source of their problem for the first time and the problem immediately healed, without doing anything else.

But as you know by now, identifying your source issues isn't usually enough to heal them. Fortunately, you now have the right tools to do just that. To heal the source issues identified by the Success Issues Finder, begin with your lowest score and use the Three Tools: the Energy Medicine and Heart Screen tools, and the Reprogramming Statements. To return to our earlier example, if Patience was your lowest score, think of a time when you felt particularly impatient. The earlier the memory, the better, as it gets closer to the original source memory. But if you can only remember how impatient you felt this morning, that's fine, too. You can use the Three Tools with this test in two ways: you can apply the Energy Medicine tool, the Heart Screen tool, or both to the specific issue with the lowest score, following the step-by-step instructions in chapters 6 to 8. Or you can use the combination technique in chapter 9, as the Reprogramming Statements will also ensure you go through every one of the source issues that could be the cause of your lowest score. You can use whatever approach appeals most to you; they produce the same results in different ways.

Continue applying these tools to your lowest score over the course of a month if needed, and retake the Success Issues Finder test at the end of the month to gauge your progress. Note: If you feel the issue is healed in one day, that's great; just take the test again the next day. You'll find that as the tools begin to heal the issue you're working on, your lowest score will rise and eventually won't be your lowest score anymore. When that happens, take your new lowest score and begin applying the Three Tools to that one, following the procedure.

The obvious goal is to have high, positive scores for every area. But I've found that as people apply these tools to their lowest test scores, they move through several natural benchmarks over time that are typically accompanied by a breakthrough that enables them to get to the next level of success. The first benchmark is when you have no negative scores; all your individual scores (measured from −10 to +10) are positive. The second benchmark is when every score is +3 and above. The third benchmark is when every score is +5. And the fourth benchmark is when every score is +7. To pace and manage your improvement, I encourage you to aim for the next benchmark rather than aiming for all +7s from the beginning. In addition to the fact that a breakthrough tends to accompany each benchmark, breaking the larger goal down into steps is far less daunting than trying to get from, say, −3s in most areas to +7s in every area. Most people find this approach feels much more doable.

When you reach the fourth benchmark of +7s in every category (and you will, if you follow the process in this book), you will be living in love, joy, peace, and truth, moment by moment, day in and day out, regardless of your external circumstances. You will be living in the high country, breathing the rare air few people ever breathe. You will feel as if you've achieved the greatest success you could ever achieve. But there's more: your new internal state will, over time, miraculously transform your externals. Of course, it's not really a miracle at all; you are simply living in harmony with the spiritual and physical laws of nature, the way you were designed to live.

In addition to the Success Issues Finder, the next two "bonus" diagnostics are additional, complementary ways to heal your subconscious issues with the Three Tools.

## DIAGNOSTIC 2: REVERSE GENIE QUESTIONS

Anxiety is an epidemic in our society today. Forty million adults
in the United States have been clinically diagnosed with an anxiety
disorder (18 percent of American adults), and this doesn't include the
far greater number who experience undiagnosed day-to-day anxiety
on a chronic and daily basis.[1] So many of us have become addicted to
fear, constantly living in stress, when fear should never be the primary
experience of our lives. As you know, the cause of our constant fear is
focusing on external circumstances and end results. Focus on internal
issues (love, joy, and peace), give up the end results, and the fear and
stress vanish.

Dr. Thomas Peris of Boston University did one of the largest
studies in history on people who live to be over a hundred years old.
He found that these people had a common tendency *not to worry*.[2]
Logically, this observation is consistent with the statement we've
made all along that stress is the cause of 95 percent of all disease and
illness. Since fear is the cause of stress, it makes sense that those who
do not worry (have no fear) would be vastly less likely to develop life-
shortening disease or illness. Biblical scholars have told me that the
Bible says "fear not" *365 times*. It would make perfect sense for the
creator/source of our body and mind to repeat this phrase so often,
knowing what fear, worry, and stress would do to us.

The Reverse Genie diagnostic identifies the fear at work in your
life right now. Remember the three ultimate success goal questions you
answered in chapter 1 that identified what you really wanted most? Just
in case you don't, here they are again:

   1. What do you want right now more than anything else (i.e.,
      your wish for the genie)?

2. If you got what you wanted most in question number 1, what would that do for you and what would it change in your life?

3. If you got the answers to both questions number 1 and number 2, how would you feel?

This second diagnostic also includes three questions, but in reverse. These questions will reveal what you're most afraid of—and thus what you need to deprogram and reprogram to get rid of your internal virus. You can answer each question now as we move through the explanation.

1. What are you more afraid of than anything else right now? Take the time you need to give this question some serious thought. When you have your answer, describe it in detail.

Your answer to question 1 reveals the negative circumstance you are currently most focused on with willpower, negative expectation, and stress. You believe that if it happens, you will not be okay. This circumstance is also what you are in the process of creating in your life right now. Why? First, it would not be possible for you to give that answer if that image was not already in your spiritual heart. You have to be able to see it in your spiritual heart, otherwise you wouldn't be able to form the words to describe it. Second, our heart does not differentiate what is real and what is imagined. What is imagined *is* real to the heart, so anything in our spiritual heart is actually happening right now to our heart, and thus to our body. Remember, the spiritual heart's experience is 100 percent surround-sound present tense. So whenever you see the picture of what you fear most, your heart changes the physiology of your body to respond to the emergency that is going on at that very moment in your heart in order to save your life. Every single time you think of what you fear most, you are putting yourself into fight or flight—and nothing has even happened externally.

**2.** If what you are most afraid of actually happened (your answer to question 1), how would that change your life and what would that do to you?

Your answer to question 2 goes a bit deeper: it reveals the underlying external circumstances in your life that you have and are afraid of losing, or that you don't have and are afraid of having imposed on you. As in question 1, your answer here also names the specific circumstances you are creating in your life this moment— possibly only because you fear them, not because they're likely to happen on their own. In other words, our fear makes the answer to number 2 (and number 1, for that matter) all the more likely to actually happen in the future, completely independent of its objective likelihood of happening on its own.

Frequently, all the imagined answers to question 2 would never occur under any circumstances. Statistics tell us that over 90 percent of the things we worry about never happen—and even if they do, they're almost never as difficult or terrible as we imagine. In his TED talk "The Surprising Science of Happiness," Dr. Dan Gilbert shares data from a research study with new lottery winners and new paraplegics.[3] At the beginning of the study, the new lottery winners' subjective state of happiness was dramatically higher than the new paraplegics'. Six months later, there was no difference. This is called psychological adaptation. (One note: Psychological adaptation is a coping mechanism, not a sign of healing. In fact, psychological adaptation typically means healing has *not* happened.)

The point of this example is that the things we believe would devastate our lives almost never do. However, many things we think are no big deal *will* in fact destroy our lives over time. The reason most people think their answer to number 2 would be so catastrophic is that they believe the circumstances resulting from question 1 would be the biggest problem of their life. But this is not true—in fact, this lie/ misinterpretation is the source of the fear. The truth is that the biggest problem of our life would be to answer question 1 from chapter 1 (what do you want right now more than anything else?) *with an external circumstance*—because pursuing an external circumstance above all else is what sets off our stress response and causes all our problems, as we've spent most of the book explaining.

Now, if our biggest problem would be answering question 1 from chapter 1 with an external circumstance, our *second* biggest problem would be our answer to question 3 of the Reverse Genie Diagnostic, and identifying this problem is the goal of this diagnostic.

> **3.** If your answers to questions 1 and 2 actually happened in your life, how would you feel?

Just as in chapter 1, where your answer to question 3 revealed what you really wanted, your answer to question 3 here reveals your real problem—very possibly, the biggest (or second biggest) problem of your life. It is the inward state that exists inside you right now that is probably causing more stress than any other. It comes from your memory banks, your pain/pleasure/fear programming, and your primary beliefs, thoughts, and feelings. This question can be very difficult to answer for many people. In my experience, people get to question 3 and completely break down, because their answer is truly the worst experience they can imagine. But the truth is that they are experiencing it *right now*. If it's in their spiritual heart and they're envisioning it on their heart screen, the spiritual heart is always living in the present tense, and according to your heart, it is not a matter of "if" it happens; it is happening in real life, this moment.

Fortunately, if you heal the source memories of your answer to question 3, you will likewise see a monumental difference in virtually every area of your life. Somewhere, in whatever area question 3 relates to, you are believing a lie—about yourself, others, God, your circumstances, or all of the above. Heal the lie, and your internal feeling *and* external circumstances will instantly begin to transform.

## THE REVERSE GENIE QUESTIONS IN ACTION: NEIL

When I work through these questions with clients, the top category of what people fear most these days has to do with finances. This was true for Neil, who had been laid off three months prior and had only been able to find odd jobs here and there since then. The stress was beginning to paralyze him, which caused him not to perform well during his job interviews, and that was sending him into a vicious negative cycle. His wife was at home with a toddler and an infant, and the amount in their savings account was starting to free-fall. When we began with question 1—What do you fear more than anything else right now?—Neil's answer was very specific: "I'm not going to have enough money at the end of the month to pay for groceries and food." Then I asked Neil question 2: "If at the end of the month you actually didn't have enough money to pay your mortgage and buy enough food, how would that change your life and what would that do to you?" His answer was "The bank would foreclose on our house, my family would be hungry and homeless, and we'd have to move in with my brother-in-law."

I explained to Neil what I explained earlier. He began to understand how the bank foreclosing on his house was (a) extremely unlikely to happen as a direct result of not making enough money this month to pay his mortgage and (b) more likely to happen simply because he feared it. The truth was that he was likely to be able to get a temporary loan from his family to pay his mortgage, even if he didn't find a full-time job for many months. And even if he didn't want to ask them for a loan, we were able to come up with a number of other short-term solutions for covering his house payment and getting enough food for his family. He began to understand how his fear was based on a lie, but this understanding had not yet reached his spiritual heart.

So I asked Neil next: "If what you fear actually happened, how would you feel?" He answered, "I'd be so ashamed—I'd feel like an utter failure to my wife, my kids, my wife's family, and myself." I explained to him that the same thing that's true for his answer for question 2 is true for question 3—it's not that this shame will happen in the future. Rather, this shame already existed in his spiritual heart as a human hard-drive virus and needed to be eliminated immediately, just like a computer virus, if he ever hoped to have the life that he wanted.

The good news is that this diagnostic identified a specific human hard-drive virus for Neil: shame. He was experiencing it constantly in his spiritual heart, and sooner or later it would have played itself out in his external circumstances, whether it would keep him from performing well during his job interviews and prevent him from getting a full-time job, or cause a significant health problem, or any number of possible negative symptoms. So we applied the Three Tools to his experience of shame in order to deprogram that fear and reprogram it as love. It didn't happen instantly—we would use one of the tools during a session, and Neil was usually able to rate his feeling of shame at a 1 or lower immediately afterward, but it would still be there a week later at the beginning of our next session.

At the same time, however, his internal stress was lifting, and he was finding himself more relaxed during his interviews. Soon he was hired for a full-time job that wasn't exactly in his field, but it provided a regular paycheck that would more than cover his family's basic expenses. His internal state and his external circumstances were showing evidence that the fear in his spiritual heart was being reprogrammed as love. And sure enough, during one of our scheduled phone check-ins, when I asked him again what he was most afraid of, he couldn't think of anything. The tools had completely removed the fear so that he was now afraid of nothing.

## USING THE THREE TOOLS WITH THE REVERSE GENIE DIAGNOSTIC

Just like Neil, to remove the fear and stress and to stop creating the external reality you most dread based on your internal state, you need the kind of internal healing that will allow your answer to question 1 to become *nothing*. If your life isn't in mortal danger this moment, the response of healthy, well-functioning internal programming is "I'm afraid of nothing right now." I promise you, it is possible. There are people all over the world who have gone through this process who now experience that reality. That's exactly what the Three Tools are for.

Now I want you to do this for yourself. I want to walk hand in hand with you to make sure that your answer to question 3 is not the long-term description of your life. Return to your earlier answer. Following the instructions outlined in the previous chapters, use the Three Tools on your answer to question 3, until your response to question 1 is "I'm not afraid of anything." You can use the tools one at a time, you can use the Energy Medicine tool and the Heart Screen tool together on your specific answer to question 3, or you can use the combination technique, allowing the Reprogramming Statements to diagnose and heal the core belief behind your answer to question 3. It may take a day, a week, a month, or sometimes (but not usually) a year. However long it takes is fine, and best for you. You will have the rest of your life to live in love, free from fear.

# DIAGNOSTIC 3: LIFE VOWS

So many people I've met over the years have felt stuck in one area or another. They've tried everything, but they just can't seem to move forward. They may even be exhibiting addictive behavior or bad habits in multiple areas. The reason why, almost invariably, is that they made a life vow.

A life vow is a promise we make, usually early in life and under extreme pressure and pain over time, to protect ourselves from ever experiencing that pain again. Consciously or unconsciously, we make a vow that says, "If I can just get (or avoid) this, I'll give up that." For example, perhaps your parents argued a lot when you were a child, and it often frightened you. One day, your subconscious mind may have made a promise, or a bargain, to provide some relief from the pain. Perhaps your mind said, "I'll do whatever it takes to just get away from Mom and Dad screaming." So as a child, you start doing anything that takes you away from the pain of the screaming: you hide under the house, you fantasize about an imaginary friend or an imaginary place—whatever it takes, regardless of the consequences. You've taken yourself away from the screaming by distancing yourself from them— and eventually, everyone else.

That life vow becomes lifelong programming. As an adult, an earlier vow may translate into something like "I may have to give up having the family life I'd like to have, but I'm absolutely not going to be in a place where everyone's screaming." It affects all your relationships, and you can't figure out why. It mandates that you constantly live in self-protection mode, which equals constant massive stress. A life vow is a viciously strong "I need this to survive" belief, even if you're thirty-five and you don't need that situation to survive at all. Life vows can also explain why people can seem to have everything on the outside but they can't enjoy it on the inside.

Self-destructive, cyclical patterns of behavior result from life vows. As an adult, if you're wondering *Why do I keep doing this? I can't seem to stop!*, you probably made a life vow as a kid. Its strength does not depend on any objective definition of trauma or on your conscious understanding as an adult. It depends on how much adrenaline and cortisol your stress response was pumping through your body at the time it was made. Life vows are typically made during the delta/theta brain wave state, when there's an excessive amount of adrenaline released. If you experienced that situation as extremely stressful as a child in that moment, that life vow can be running your life to this day—even if your adult mind would view the original experience as no big deal and you have no clue that life vow even exists. Internal experience, perception, and interpretation are everything when it comes to our spiritual heart.

## THE LIFE VOW DIAGNOSTIC IN ACTION: STACEY

Back when I was counseling full-time, I had one client, Stacey, with multiple addictions: chocolate, alcohol, sex, shopping, soap operas, and so on. She had been in therapy for years, and she knew she had multiple compulsive behaviors and desperately wanted them to stop, but she had not found anything that was able to help long term. Her words to me were "I don't feel like anything in my life is real." In fact, she was the face of apathy herself. If you were asked to describe her in one word, it would likely be "dull," in every sense of the word: the light seemed to have gone out in her eyes. Her many previous therapists were happy to have her paying her money to someone else—I talked to several of them, and they were stumped.

Because life vows typically result in addictive behaviors, I had a strong suspicion Stacey had made a life vow. I asked her questions and did several other diagnostics, but she couldn't remember anything significant. One day she came into to the office and the first thing she said was "I found it."

"You found what?" I asked blankly.

"I found the life vow." Apparently the previous night, as she was drifting off to sleep, she had a strong memory of lying in bed as a child, listening to her parents scream at each other, and her dad hitting her mother. Her dad was a violent alcoholic, and such abuse was common in her household. Yet until that moment, even though she knew objectively that her dad was an abusive alcoholic, she had never had any personal memories of her experience in that household. At that moment, she also remembered what she was thinking: *Whatever it takes, I am going to get out of this, and never go through it again.* She had indeed found her life vow.

And that's exactly what Stacey did. She made choices in her life from that moment on that would ensure she would not experience any conflict or anger—or any strong emotion, for that matter. She married a man who, frankly, had the personality and activity level of a telephone pole, but at least he wouldn't be screaming at her. Eventually she lived vicariously through her own various addictions because engaging the real world with her desires was just too risky.

Once we were able to identify her life vow, we could apply the Three Tools and deprogram that specific fear from her spiritual heart and reprogram it with love. When I heard from her most recently, Stacey was still working through one or two addictions—down from at least twelve we had specifically identified. But most important, her entire affect had changed: the light had returned to her eyes, and she had life in her. She had also started engaging with her husband, her children, her work, her friends—the real things in her life.

## USING THE THREE TOOLS WITH THE LIFE VOW DIAGNOSTIC

If you suspect you have also made a life vow, based on your current symptoms (and especially if you struggle with addictive behavior), you, too, can heal that programming. Here's how to diagnose any life vows that are functioning as human hard-drive viruses in your spiritual heart:

1. First, I suggest you "sit under your tree," as I call it, or pray and/or meditate in whatever way is natural for you. When your mind is in an open and relaxed state, ask yourself what behavior in your life seems to fit this self-destructive, cyclical pattern that is characteristic of a life vow. When you were young, were you in pain or under stress for a long period of time, or a short but extremely pressure-packed time? If so, can you recall a time when you consciously or subconsciously said to yourself, *If I can only do, have, or avoid _____, I will do or live without _____?*

2. If you can't find a memory like that, just focus on the repetitive behavior that is bothering you now and is working against your ability to live the life you truly want: living in love moment by moment.

3. Apply the Three Tools to this memory or to the repetitive behavior. Again, you can use each tool separately on your life vow, a combination of the Energy Medicine tool and the Heart Screen tool on your life vow, or the combination technique, simply allowing the Reprogramming Statements to diagnose and heal the core belief behind your life vow. You will know the deprogramming and reprogramming is complete when the symptoms, habits, or addictions disappear. Again, don't worry

about how long it takes. It may be several months or it may be in an instant—but the results will be worth it.

...

Remember how I said at the end of chapter 1 that you probably weren't able to live out the Love Code yet, even if you fully understood what to do? Well, now you should be able to, if you've done what I have suggested up to now. The core of the Love Code process includes the seven principles for the transformational *aha* (chapter 1), the Three Tools, and the Success Issues Finder test to diagnose your subconscious viruses and track your progress in healing them. But for those of you who would like a more detailed, step-by-step program, in chapter 11 you'll receive the Love Code 40-Day Success Blueprint to help you finally reach success in specific areas of your life—especially where it's been so elusive in the past.

# QUICK REFERENCE: THE LOVE CODE

## The Seven Principles of the Transformational *Aha*

1. It's not *ever* your fault.

2. The internal always creates the external—never the other way around.

3. What you really want most is never an external circumstance—it's always the internal state of love, joy, and peace.

4. WIIFM love (which is what most people call, and believe is, real love) often looks like love on the outside, but it is really an unhealthy attempt to control others and circumstances to get the external circumstances that you think will make you happy—but they never will, long term!

5. Your willpower, fueled by fear and faulty programming, has a one-in-a-million shot at making you happy and successful. Ninety-nine percent of the time, it will leave you stressed and frustrated.

6. The internal state of love, joy, and peace is a miraculous/divine power source for life and success that virtually always works.

7. Living in love for the next thirty minutes as best you can, giving up external and physical results and circumstances, will produce success and happiness beyond your wildest dreams—no matter what!

## The Combination Tool

You can use the combination tool in two ways: with the Reprogramming Statements, or with an issue that's bothering you right now. Follow the steps below, or visit www.thelovecodenow.com for a ten-minute audio that guides you through the process.

1. Begin by stating the first Reprogramming Statement to yourself: "I desire and pray/ask to believe the whole truth and only the truth about who and what I am, and who and what I'm not." Or, if you'd like to work on a particular issue, identify that issue clearly in your mind.

2. Consider how you feel about that statement, or about having your particular issue heal or improve. Do you feel any fear, stress, or resistance, whether in your thoughts, your emotions, or your body? If you do, that's a sign that you have a source memory with fear in it regarding the statement or issue, and this combination tool will help heal the source of that fear. If you don't, and you're working with the Reprogramming Statements, you can move on to the next Reprogramming Statement until you do feel some resistance to the statement.

3. Once you have noticed some specific resistance to a Reprogramming Statement or to the healing of the issue, ask yourself, *When have I felt this way before?* To get as close as you can to the source, try to think of the earliest memory you have of feeling this way.

4. Say a prayer from your heart that you will be able to see the images on your heart screen that will heal the issue you're experiencing. Note: As you go through the process below, remain open to whatever appears on your heart screen. Many people have experienced amazing images on their heart screen

that have resulted in far deeper healing than they had thought possible. So don't try to control the images that appear on your heart screen too much; simply allow the images to arise.

**5.** Now imagine on your heart screen the resistance or problem you're experiencing regarding the Reprogramming Statement or issue. If it's difficult to imagine that resistance on your heart screen, you may want to create a metaphorical image, such as an animal or a plant that needs nourishment or care. Or you can just imagine the feeling you're experiencing. For example, if it's fear or anxiety, imagine the word fear or anxiety on your heart screen. Again, don't work too hard at the imaging; just relax and let it happen. If you just have a feeling right now and can't visualize anything, that's fine, too.

**6.** Place both hands over your heart (the first position of the Energy Medicine tool).

**7.** Imagine the light and love (of God), the source of your life, filling your heart screen. You might see a gentle and powerful light flowing in, bringing warmth and comfort into your heart screen. Let that light and love saturate your entire heart screen, including any resistance. You may see the resistance image change as a result, but don't try to make it change. You might want to take a few deep breaths into your belly; continue to relax into the experience.

**8.** Now shift both hands to your forehead (the second position of the Energy Medicine tool).

**9.** Imagine someone who knows you and loves you unconditionally, such as God, Jesus, a family member, or anyone else you admire and feel 100 percent safe with. With their presence, they are bringing even more of this light and love, so that the entire atmosphere seems to be in perfect harmony. Your problem or your feelings about the problem may be shifting as well, but let those images shift and change on their own. Whatever shows up on the heart screen is fine. Just let it happen.

10. Finally, shift both hands to your crown (the third position of the Energy Medicine tool).

11. Imagine the opposite feelings of what you were feeling before start to fill the heart screen. If you were feeling grief and hopelessness before, imagine feelings of joy and hope filling your heart screen. Perhaps you see positive images, or you just feel positive feelings of love, joy, and peace, so that there is no more fear or impatience or frustration or anger. Allow that positive feeling or image to fill your heart screen, blending perfectly with the light and love surrounding you, and with the presence of your loved one, and your feeling of resistance.

12. Finally, place both hands back over your heart.

13. Imagine, amidst this light and love, a small child, perhaps six or nine years old. When you walk over to the child, you notice that the small child is you. You, as a child, are becoming aware of all this love and light surrounding you, and of God or your loved one right there. Perhaps before you were feeling alone, but you now see that there is love all around you. Now you notice another person coming onto the scene approaching the young child—and it's also you, now as an adult. The grown-up you kneels down before you as a child, embraces the child, and says, "I love you. It's all right now, I'm with you. You are not alone. It is not your fault. It's never been your fault." At that moment, you as a child realize you are loved deeply.

**14.** Continue to take everything in: the love and light (of God), the presence of God or your loved one, and you as an adult embracing and loving you as a child unconditionally are all blending together around you in perfect harmony. You know you are loved, and you know you are safe: you feel it in you and through you, deep in the core of your being. As you feel this love and embrace it, allow whatever images that arise on your heart screen to simply be there.

**15.** To conclude, take a deep breath from your belly, nice and slow. Smile. Gently open your eyes, and know that you are loved.

## The Success Issues Finder Test

You can use the free online Success Issues Finder test at www .thelovecodenow.com to diagnose the subconscious issues you need to deprogram and reprogram using the Three Tools (or the combination tool above), and to track your progress.

## chapter 11

# THE LOVE CODE 40-DAY
# SUCCESS BLUEPRINT

By now you know that true success is not merely achieving your desired external circumstances, no matter how impressive they may be. Living in love in the present moment, the direct antidote to stress and fear, is the only way that our conscious mind and body can possibly be aligned—at peace, healthy, and happy. Focusing on past or future expectations or trying to create what we want through willpower will by definition create stress and failure, physically and nonphysically.

Before we get into the steps of the Success Blueprint, I'd like you to know that I was a little conflicted about whether to put the Success Blueprint in the book at all, because it can make the process more complicated for some people. However, in my private practice, if I knew my client was process oriented and would benefit from a detailed, step-by-step program, I would almost always recommend this 40-Day Success Blueprint. I'd also like to take some more time to define what I mean by success. I believe that each of us has a personal destiny—or "a calling," as I like to put it. However, I do not believe that we are destined to end up in a single, particular place, no matter what. If this is true, and it's all prewritten and determined, then why try? Even though we may have a particular calling or destiny, we create this destiny by whether we live in fear or love. We are all called to love, as the law of love is written on our hearts through our conscience, providing a perfect guide for us in every circumstance. But it's still our choice whether we follow that calling or not—a hundred times a day, 365 days a year.

Whenever I live out of fear in any moment, I am moving away from my calling, or delaying it. Whenever I live out of love, by definition I am stepping into my ultimate and perfect calling for me, because if I live this way consistently over time, I will live my perfect life. Living in love is the best and perhaps only way we can create the perfect external circumstances that are the visible manifestation of our success. Yes, I learn from my mistakes when I act in fear; I need them, like a booster on a rocket, to show me that living in fear and selfishness won't work long term and takes me away from my calling, happiness, and health.

However, I don't need these mistakes once I am deprogrammed, reprogrammed, and living in the present in love. Once the rocket is in orbit, the booster is no longer needed, and it falls away—it's done its job. To retain it now would work against the mission.

Also, your "perfect calling" is not perfect for anyone but you. This is one reason why comparison has ruined so many good days for so many people. Comparison is worse than useless, most of the time. For many people, comparison is the root cause of their expectations. It is one of the biggest black holes for our spiritual energy on the planet. When we could make a comparison that causes us to be grateful or content, we often don't make that comparison. We dwell on what is *not* the way we want it. Yet the key to contentment is not wanting.

The way we reach our perfect calling is *not* to focus on an end result in the future, make a plan to get it, and use willpower to get it. Not only will that rarely work, you may very likely be "wrong" about what the perfect outcome is for you. The way to your perfect calling is to live in love *now*. This is not only the end result that is always perfect in the present, but also it will produce your perfect calling for the future— and is quite possibly the only way to ensure that. Focusing on what you "think" your perfect calling is like throwing darts in the dark and puts you in chronic stress. Conversely, doing what is best for you now (being and doing love), and giving up the future to God/source/love, creates your perfect future every time, even if it is something you would never have dreamed of. And it does it automatically and effortlessly.

No matter where you've been or what you've done, there is always a possible path to your perfect calling from where you are now. You can never "blow it" for life. Just start to live in love now—deprogram, reprogram, and give up the end result—and your path will start to transform, first internally, then externally.

If you believe that the Love Code is the best path for you, then it will be your ultimate guide in gaining the success that you've envisioned for yourself. In fact, I believe it would be impossible for you *not* to become successful if you live these principles, and I have thousands of people all over the world as proof.

If you will go sit under your tree (that is, pray and meditate) and discover your heart's desire, overlay a success goal onto that desire, deprogram and reprogram your spiritual heart, and walk it out moment by moment in love, I may just be getting a call or letter from you in the near future.

Also, for this 40-Day Success Blueprint, space is provided for you to write your answers down right in the book, to help you capitalize on any momentum and inspiration you have in the moment. But feel free to write down your answers in a designated notepad or journal, or create a new document on your computer, if you need more room to answer.

One last thing: If you start to get overwhelmed with the details of the Success Blueprint, take a break and use your favorite of the Three Tools (or the combination tool) on the anxiety and feeling of being overwhelmed before you continue. You can also feel free to come up with your own creative way to use the principles and the tools. Also, a continued sense of overwhelm may indicate that this step-by-step approach isn't for you.

Remember, you can either use the simpler Love Code process summarized beginning on page 208, or use this more detailed Success Blueprint. Either approach will work, depending on what process appeals to you most. In the end, whatever works for and feels best to you *is* best for you. Don't get stressed about doing it exactly the way I say. Experiment and do it the way it works for you.

Let's get started.

**1. Determine your ultimate success goal.**

You determined your ultimate success goal with the three-question exercise back in chapter 1. If you haven't completed that exercise, answer those questions now, so that you know the internal state you want most. Here they are again:

**1.** What do you want right now more than anything else?

**2.** If you got what you most wanted in question 1, what would that do for you and what would it change in your life?

**3.** If you got the things that were your answers to both questions 1 and 2, how would you feel?

**2. Determine one success desire that you would like to work toward and achieve in your life.**

What do you want to work toward achieving in your life right now? Begin by brainstorming end results you would like to achieve in different areas of your life, such as a particular kind of relationship, a career accomplishment, a specific achievement, increased finances, or improved health. At first, don't eliminate anything that occurs to you. Then choose the ones that "feel" the strongest to you. Which ones make you smile the most? Which ones make you feel the best deep down inside? Which ones create the most peace? Which ones fire your heart, stir your imagination, or serve a need? Which ones would make the most difference in your life right now?

Now put your three strongest desires through the basic filters of a success desire described in chapter 4: Are they based in truth, are they based in love, and are they in harmony with your ultimate success goal? If you think of something that is not possible given the objective facts of a situation, you either have to find a way to make it possible, or find a new success desire. We don't want you wasting months or years of your life on something unobtainable. At the same time, I believe *anything* is possible. If we look back in history, our greatest heroes have been those who have done what seemed impossible according to popular beliefs and even the so-called objective facts. If I asked the seventy-two-year-old from chapter 4 if his NFL desire was in truth and he said that he had prayed about it, researched it, prepared for it, and it was absolutely in truth for him, my response would be "Go for it!"

Second, ask yourself, is it based in love? Describe, so that anyone could understand it, why you want to achieve *this* desire, instead of some other success desire. Convince me that it is win/win/win with no losers and that it's not strictly for selfish reasons. Note: Doing something strictly for the money when you are in great need of money can absolutely be the loving thing to do, as long as there are no losers. You cannot love others until you love yourself, and we all have a need for shelter, clothing, food, the ability to pay our bills, and to otherwise meet our basic needs. There is a big difference between that and the contractor from chapter 4 who just wanted more and more toys.

Third, you'd ask yourself, is it in harmony with my ultimate success goal (step 1)? If the desire contributes to your ultimate success goal, it passes through this final filter as well.

**List your top three success desires here.**

1._____

2._____

3._____

Great! But we have to choose one of these to get started. (You will be able to address all three if you decide to, eventually.) What is the best one for you to work on now, based on the factors? If you think you know which one that is, and I always suggest going with your gut, then go with that one. You may need to do some research and talk to some people to have the information you need to make this decision. Go ahead and do that. If you have trouble picking one, then continue with two, or even all three, for the time being. One usually floats to the top as you go through the process. If applicable, write your top success desire below.

Your success desire: _____

_____

### 3. Envision that success desire actually coming to fruition.

Go ahead: close your eyes and experience the end result of achieving this success desire. Yes, I'm telling you to touch it, taste it, smell it, and wallow in it. (I know I criticized other success experts for doing this, but we're doing it here for a different reason.) Vividly visualize achieving it until the sentiment becomes very real to you, and you can see and feel it in significant detail. When you envision the success desire, try to envision all aspects, not just the positive ones, so your image maker can give you an accurate picture.

If your success desire was to start your own at-home business, here's what you might see: you would be able to pay all your bills without stressing, because you would always have plenty of money in the checking account; you'd be able to get the pool membership that the kids have always wanted; you wouldn't have to use your calculator during your grocery trips; you'd feel more self-confident when you told your friends and family you were a "business owner"; and you'd wake up each morning feeling both at peace about your ability to provide for your household and joyful about new daily challenges. You'd also have to navigate working at home amid the distractions of your family life, you'd have a steep learning curve to know how to start and run a small business, and you might have to give up your weekly lunches with your friends.

Now write down what you see. Describe the results of your success desire in enough detail so that if you were telling me about it, I could see what you see and feel what you feel.

**4. List the negative thoughts, feelings, or beliefs that arise from envisioning your success desire and rate them on a scale of 0 to 10.**

Now I want you to recall any negative feelings or beliefs that came up for you as you envisioned this particular success desire, or that come up for you now when prompted. In our example, even as you were thinking about all the good things that would result from achieving your success desire, you might have still noticed thoughts like *The economy's too bad. I don't have enough time to start a business with my current job. I don't know the first thing about starting a business at home—I'm never going to figure it out. I'm not really good at anything—I don't even know what kind of business to start.*

Write each one of the negatives down and rate them on a scale of 0–10 in terms of how much each one bothers you right now. It may also be helpful to note the emotion, thought, or belief that feels the most negative, but it's not necessary.

You've just identified your human hard-drive viruses that are specific to this desire and that are blocking you from success.

**5. Use the Three Tools to deprogram the negatives that came up for you.**

Just as you did in the Basic Diagnostics chapter, you can use one or more of the Three Tools one at a time, you can use the Energy Medicine tool and the Heart Screen tool together on the specific negative belief, or you can use the combination technique that allows the Reprogramming Statements to diagnose and heal the core belief behind the negative thought, emotion, or belief you're experiencing. Note: For the Reprogramming Statements, the only thing you need to change is the prayer before you begin to ask specifically for healing all the negative beliefs, thoughts, and feelings that are blocking your current success desire. Because this tool also works as a diagnostic, it will help you identify and heal your problem issues automatically.

Whichever tool you use, your unconscious will automatically be working with you and agreeing with you about eliminating all the fear and living in love, because you have that love compass, or law of love on your heart, that always wants that for you. How much resistance your fear-based programming is presenting may determine how long it takes to heal the blocks, but they *will heal eventually*. Love always wins over fear. However, I would encourage you to always include the Energy Medicine tool because, in my experience, it's so immediately effective. Use these tools on each negative emotion, thought, or belief, or use the combination technique to work through all the Reprogramming Statements, until you would rate them all at 0.

Let's use the negative belief "I don't have enough time to start a business" from the earlier example. You decide to start with a combination of the Energy Medicine tool and the Heart Screen tool. These are the steps you'd follow in this context:

- Picture a screen in your mind: a tablet screen, computer screen, TV screen, or movie screen—whatever most easily comes to mind. However, whatever screen you picture, make sure this screen is connected wirelessly to the Internet, just as your heart screen is connected wirelessly to everyone around the planet. Think of this screen with two parts: the conscious and the unconscious. Now picture a line across the screen about a third of the way down (because your unconscious is *much* bigger than your conscious) to signify the conscious and unconscious portions of the internal screen for your image maker. This is your heart screen.

- Focus on the negative thought, feeling, or belief you want to address—"I don't have enough time to start a business"— which you've already rated as a 7.

- Picture that experience of not having enough time on your heart screen in words, pictures, memories of past experiences, or however you want. Perhaps you see yourself panicked as you're trying to complete a task, or you can remember an incident where your mother was angry at you for being slow as a child. Or a clock appears, and you hear an alarm bell ringing.

- Once you see this image on your heart screen, ask that it no longer be on your heart screen, and that all its source memories be completely healed. You might say, "Let the light and love of God be on my heart screen, and nothing else." You might customize this to get specific about what you're feeling right now: "Let light and love *and patience* be on my heart screen, and nothing else, *including panic*." You might need a break from focusing on your problem and say, "Let light and love and patience be on the *unconscious* side of my heart screen, and nothing else, *including my problem of feeling time-crunched*." You won't stop thinking about being time-crunched, but eventually you won't think about being time-crunched with a feeling of panic anymore.

- Then picture light and love on your heart screen, however it is most vivid and evocative to you. You may see it as streaming light from a divine source, a beautiful sunset, a stunning vista, your pet, or any other image that represents pure light and love.

- Now introduce the Energy Medicine tool. While continuing to picture light and love on your heart screen, place your hands on your heart, your forehead, and your crown, for one to three minutes each.

- Continue to picture this light and love and repeat the three-position cycle for up to two or three times in one sitting, or until the discomfort in your mind and body are gone and you rate that negative thought, feeling, or belief below a 1, which means it doesn't bother you anymore. If you need to, you can add the Reprogramming Statements, either separately or with the combination technique, following the instructions in chapters 7 or 9.

- Continue to use these tools on each one of your negative beliefs until they all no longer bother you. It may take a day, a week, or three months. It's rare that it takes three months, but don't worry about how long it takes—you'll have the rest of your life to enjoy the success!

6. Once all your negatives are gone (below a 1 on a 10-point scale), use the same tools to create a supersuccess memory, or to reprogram the positive success desire you would like to achieve.

If the negative thoughts, feelings, and beliefs are the viruses in our human hard drive we need to deprogram, then we need to *reprogram* our human hard drive with what I call supersuccess memories, or the equivalent of the right software for your spiritual heart for your success goal. To reprogram your spiritual heart, you use the same tools you used to deprogram, but this time focus on the positive end result success picture.

- Return to what you envisioned in step 2, and imagine this end result actually happening, in all the detail you listed. Rate how you feel about the likelihood of this end result happening on a scale of 0–10, with 0 meaning "This is never going to happen for me" and 10 meaning "I know this is my future; I absolutely see this happening for me." Keeping with the same example, you would see yourself calmly paying all your bills ahead of schedule, knowing you had plenty of money in the checking account; you'd see yourself telling the kids you got them a membership to the neighborhood pool and the excited, surprised looks on their faces; you'd see yourself telling your acquaintances about your new business; you'd see yourself waking up each morning feeling joy and peace at the day ahead; and so on. As you imagine this scenario, you're feeling it's possible, but a little out of reach, so you rate it as a 4.

- Use the Energy Medicine tool, Reprogramming Statements, and Heart Screen tools, separately or in combination, on this positive picture until you can rate it as a 7 or higher, which is the positive feeling "I believe I can do this—let's get started!" (Remember, if you use the Reprogramming Statements, you simply need to customize the prayer at the beginning, asking for any blocks to be healed so you can achieve your positive success picture, and work through the statements as written.)

7. **Begin a forty-day period with the goal of keeping these scores at the same level: the negatives below a 1 and the positive above a 7.**
Once you reach the point where your negative thoughts, feelings,

and beliefs about your desire are below a 1 (i.e., not bothering you) and your positive sense about achieving your desire is at or above a 7, you immediately start a forty-day period. Remember, it may take you just a day to get started on the forty days, or it might take three months. When you begin the forty-day period, think of a caterpillar moving to the cocoon phase. Your goal during this forty-day period (and yes, this goal meets all four criteria!) is simply to keep your negatives below a 1 and your positive sense about your ability to achieve your desire above a 7 by repeating steps 4, 5, and 6. Here's what the forty-day period should look like:

- Begin each day with a morning check-in. (If afternoon or evening works better for you, that's fine, too.) First ask yourself how you would rate the strength of each specific negative belief you identified back in step 4. In our example of starting a small business, we listed the following negative beliefs: *The economy's too bad. I don't have enough time to start a business with my current job. I'm never going to figure it out. I'm not really good at anything.* You'd rate each belief, based on your physical and nonphysical subjective feelings, on a scale from 0 to 10. If any belief was at a 1 or above, you would repeat using the tools to work on each one until you could rate all your negative beliefs at below a 1, or they don't bother you right now (step 5).

- Now visualize achieving your desire, as you did in step 3. In our example, you would visualize successfully starting a small business at home that brings in $1,000 extra per month and consider how likely this result feels to you. If you would rate your positive sense of achieving it at below a 7, you would use the tools on the positive picture until you would rate it at a 7 or higher (step 6).

- Follow this procedure each day for forty days. When the negatives increase, follow step 5 to lower them as before; when the positive sense decreases, follow step 6 to increase it. If there's no change, do nothing; just monitor each day. Note: You do not start the forty days over when you need to use the tools to address the negative emotions/thoughts/beliefs or your positive success vision—you simply fix them, and continue with the forty days.

After this forty-day period, most people will be able to wake up each morning with their negatives below a 1 and their positive sense about achieving their success desire at a 7 or higher. When you reach this benchmark, you know you've been fully deprogrammed and reprogrammed regarding your particular success issue. Instead of your unconscious and subconscious mind blocking you from success, they will take you toward your success like a rudder on a ship. Your viruses related to this issue are gone, and you have powerful new success software.

If you still don't feel ready after forty days, start another forty-day period. Perhaps after forty days, you're still rating your negatives at a 1 or higher and/or your positive sense of achieving your desire at below a 7 at the beginning of your daily check-in. If so, that's fine. Start another forty-day period and follow the same procedure for a full forty days, or however long it takes until the negatives stay below a 1 and the positives stay above a 7. And if you still don't feel ready after that second forty days, do another forty days. (Personally, I've never seen anyone do more than three forty-day periods. But again, it doesn't matter how long it takes. The time it takes is the right time for you.)

You know when the deprogramming and the reprogramming are complete when in everyday life you feel that the negatives don't bother you any longer, and you have a strong, positive sense of "I can do this"—and you actually start doing it!

**8. Set your specific success goals using the Love Code.**

Now that you've been fully deprogrammed and reprogrammed about any issues blocking success for your desire, it's time to determine and put into action your success *goals*, or what you will do in each thirty-minute time segment as you walk in the direction of your desire. Remember, a success goal has four parts: it must be in truth, in love, and 100 percent under your control, and typically done in the present moment.

Let's start with the *truth* of your goal. You've already thought about the truth in broad terms when you were determining your desire. What are the objective, practical facts related to achieving your desire? Think about everything you need, everything you already have, and everything that has to be done. If you're starting a business at home to provide an extra $1,000 per month for your household, how much money do you need to start? Do you have the right space in your home? Who's going to do your website? What are you going to sell? Are you going to outsource customer service? What equipment do you need? When will you start? Where will you get customers? Write down everything you know it will take to make your desire a reality.

_____

_____

_____

_____

_____

You may still need some practical education on success related to a particular area, such as marketing, woodworking, or web design. I would seek out good, valid data from the many writers, thinkers, and teachers out there and integrate your new knowledge into your daily practice. In truth, integrating particular knowledge and skills will be very easy after being deprogrammed and reprogrammed. It is the underlying programming that makes those things difficult; your fear programming is what gets in the way of easily learning. I would have given anything to have been deprogrammed and reprogrammed before graduate school—statistics would have been a breeze then!

Take a moment to examine the list above, and reflect on whether the tasks are indeed in truth for your success desire. Do you need any further information to verify? For example, if you've written above, "Get Mike to do website," and upon reflection you're not sure Mike is the best one to do your website, rewrite as "Research top websites in my field" or "Find out who did Monica's website"—whatever the next logical step is in finding out the truth of what you need to do.

Now let's look at the *love* aspect. For each of the tasks, consider whether you can complete each one in love, so that its successful completion results in a win/win/win situation, with no losers. If not, you need to either strike that from your list, or find a way to do it in love. Write down all the tasks that can be completed in love, and specify how they need to be done to create a win-win-win situation for all involved parties.

_____

_____

_____

_____

Examine the list above, reflecting on whether each task is indeed based in love. Is your list realistic? For example, if you would like to hire freelancers as part of your business, and you've found the cheapest labor available but aren't sure they're asking fair professional wages, you may decide to change your task from "Hire freelancers from Company XYZ" to "Research fair freelance rates" for the job you need to outsource.

Third, is each task listed above 100 percent under your healthy control? In other words, can you complete each task successfully by doing whatever it is in truth and love, for the next thirty minutes? Or does the completion of each task depend on circumstances beyond your control or involve pursuing end-result expectations with your willpower?

This step is where the rubber meets the road, so let me walk you through it. To continue our previous example, let's say that to get your home business moving, one of the tasks you listed was to have a conversation with the phone company about adding a phone line and switching to a small business account. It seems to meet all the criteria of a success goal: it's in truth (you know you need a second phone line for your business, and this is the correct procedure to follow), it's in love (successfully completing this task does not inherently take anything away from anyone involved), and it's 100 percent under your control (you can look up the company's phone number and dial it).

But almost as soon as you dial the number, you get sucked into a quicksand of voice mail and mailboxes, with multiple redirects and requests to key in your supersecret customer code (which you've never heard of). After about twenty minutes, you couldn't be further from love, joy, and peace. If you're like most people, you're frustrated and irritated, and you want to throw the phone out the window and scream. Why? Because even though you may *think* your goal is to call the phone company about adding a phone line and switching to a business account, your anger is a surefire sign that your real, hidden goal is quite different. Your real goal is to achieve the end result of getting your business account and extra phone line quickly and easily. In other words, you became focused on the end result rather than on the process, and you're therefore shifting into unhealthy control. Now you're pursuing a stress goal, not a success goal!

Remember, your internal state reveals your real goals. You can identify a stress goal instantly, at any time, in yourself and everyone else, by the presence of anger, or any emotion in the anger family: irritation, frustration, resentment, bitterness, being overwhelmed, and so on. When you feel like screaming and throwing the phone out the window, you can take it to the bank: you have a stress goal related to the thing you're angry about.

So how can we change this specific stress goal into a success goal? Before you even call the phone company, you decide that your goal is *not* to get your new line and account as quickly and simply as possible—actually, you have *zero control* over that. Your specific success goal is to make that call in love, focusing on the present moment for the next thirty minutes. No joke.

So how would that look different? Before you even pick up the phone, you say to yourself, *This call is going to take however long it takes. I may have to go through long wait times or a voice-mail maze or my call may even get dropped. I can't control that. What I can control is making that call in love. When I actually get on the line with the phone company representative, my goal is not getting the phone line. My goal is making the call in love. My goal is that the rep will feel better having talked to me than he or she did before, or if the person had not talked to me at all.*

Let's say the phone company representative is a lady. She's just a person doing her job, right? She didn't set up the voice mail, she didn't make the phone company's rules, and she's probably got a husband who loves her and children who run to her and say "Mommy!" when she comes in the door. If I met her on the street, we might hit it off and become friends. If I'm angry at her, I'm hurting both her *and* me—that anger adversely affects virtually every aspect of my physiology, as you'll remember: it dumbs me down, causes an energy spike and then a crash, messes up my digestion, suppresses my immune system, and makes me negative about whatever I'm doing for the next part of my day. Most likely it does the same thing to her.

Would you call that success? Probably not. Yet almost everybody I know reacts this way in situations where the results are beyond their control. External expectations are a happiness killer every time. I do not want that for you anymore. I want you to live your life every moment of every day in happiness, health, love, joy, peace, financial abundance, rich and intimate relationship—in other words, I want you to experience outrageous success internally *and* externally! It truly can start this very moment, if you set success goals rather than stress goals.

Note: Shifting from stress goals to success goals is 100 percent under your healthy control *only* after you have been deprogrammed and reprogrammed. If you find that it's not under your control—in other words, you continue to experience uncontrollable anger, anxiety, or other negative emotions even after you try to shift to a success goal— then you need to do more deprogramming and reprogramming until you *do* have healthy control and can go through the next thirty minutes in love (perhaps not perfectly, but for the most part).

Now it's your turn to make sure your specific success goals are 100 percent under your healthy control. This principle holds true no matter what you're doing throughout the next thirty minutes, whether it's filing, paperwork, negotiations, meetings, writing, shopping, or research. The facts (the truth) you listed about your specific desire determine what you do in the moment. Love is the why. And the Love Code determines how you do it: in love for the next thirty minutes, out of an inward state of love, joy, and peace, viewing specific end results as a desire, not an expectation or a goal, all of which you are able to do because you have been deprogrammed and reprogrammed.

Doing whatever you do in love for every thirty-minute period for the rest of your life may seem very difficult now. But I promise that it will get easier as you continue to heal and change your underlying programming. With the right programming, it's as easy as sitting down at the keyboard and typing in basic commands. The difficult part becomes *not* acting in love and focusing on the present moment!

To finish out this step, write down on the following page how you actually see yourself doing and accomplishing the specific success goals you listed in the first set of blanks. What are you going to do? How are you going to do it in love as best you can? What mental preparation will you need to do on the way to your desired result?

**9. Find or develop an organizational system to get those tasks done in a way that's most efficient for you.**

It's time to return to a point I made back in the introduction. When living in love for the next thirty minutes is your practical goal, it doesn't mean you ignore all the details of getting things done. You will still address every detail that needs to be done to walk in the direction of your desire. In fact, you'll find that if you follow this Success Blueprint, you'll complete all the necessary details even better than you would have if you had focused on the external details, because your stress response is no longer sabotaging you.

So you need to examine your personality and work habits and determine how you work best, and find or develop an organizational system (such as Stephen R. Covey's *The 7 Habits of Highly Effective People*, David Allen's *Getting Things Done*, or any tried-and-true productivity method) that will help you keep track of all the details you need to manage in order to work responsibly and efficiently. For some of you that will include calendars and scheduling tasks, whether on paper or electronically. For others, rather than writing things down, it may just mean doing the things you know you need to do in the moment. For example, my wife, Hope, is extraordinarily detail oriented and always writes everything down ahead of time: she plans every event and task well in advance, keeps detailed checklists along the way, and checks and rechecks those checklists. I'm a go-with-the-flow guy—I just do whatever I know I need to do in the moment, and somehow everything manages to get done, eventually. (My wife marvels at how much I'm able to get done this way, and I marvel at her ability to track every detail.)

If you do some research and ask around, you'll find dozens of different ready-to-use systems "guaranteed" to increase productivity, but I've found the best way to do it is to come up with your own system that's simple and intuitive to you. The right system will support your productivity, rather than feel like an extra burdensome chore. The important thing is to find an organizational system that works for you, even if it takes some trial and error to find the right approach.

**10. Walk in the direction of your desire by completing the tasks for the next thirty minutes with two goals: completing your tasks in love, and making sure your tasks are in harmony with your ultimate success goal from step 1.**

Once you have been deprogrammed and reprogrammed regarding

your success issues and have followed the process, you have only two jobs to do: (1) Complete your tasks in harmony with love, always being open to change, new directions, and new people; and (2) Ensure your tasks are in harmony with your ultimate success goal. Note: I have never done this perfectly. No one has. If I have a day where I don't mess up five times, it's been an extraordinary day. This Success Blueprint is designed to help you walk in love—but beating yourself up is not based in love. It violates the system, causes you stress, and undermines the whole process. So don't do it!

Keep walking it out until the perfect *result* happens for you. Your actual end result may look just like the desire you envisioned, it may look nothing like the desire you envisioned, or it may be somewhere in between. For example, as you walk toward the desire of starting your own business, you may decide to start a graphic design service. You start small, doing free work for the nonprofit you volunteer for, and eventually through talking to a lot of people about your new business, you get your first paying project. Then you get another, and another. Eighteen months later, one of your very first clients, who had been very pleased with your work, tells you that her company is looking for a part-time marketing designer and she invites you to apply. You decide to send in your résumé and some sample work. After an interview, they offer you the job—and frankly, a job is a lot more appealing to you than the pressure of being self-employed. You decide to take the job.

Does that mean you failed at achieving your desire? No! Because you were focused on living in love in the moment, you were capable of building a positive relationship with a client who not only was impressed with your work, but also sensed that you'd be a positive team member. If you were head-down focused on starting your business as your primary goal, you may have been less attentive to this client, or simply thought the job opportunity wasn't for you because your goal was to start your own business. Instead, you kept your ultimate success goal in mind (peace), and the reasons behind why you had this desire to start a business in the first place (to increase monthly income). The part-time job opportunity ended up being an equal or even greater success for you because you kept your stress response turned off and you were open to changing direction.

**11. Once you begin to walk this desire out, and you feel ready, you can repeat steps 2–10 to work on another success issue.**

Be a little careful here. Working on multiple issues at once can become stressful in and of itself. Always do what feels peaceful. But if you feel ready, once you've established the habit of walking out your success desire, you can repeat the process and begin working on another success issue. If you're actively walking out the best success for you in starting a small business, you can return to step 1 and begin working on your marriage relationship, for instance. I have some clients who have achieved ten success desires, and they're currently working on five more, continuing to check in with me on a regular basis.

Also, in addition to using the Success Blueprint for long-term issues, you can also use it for short-term or maintenance issues. If you feel stress or discouragement or anger, or notice negative thoughts or beliefs such as *Why did I ever take this on? I don't know what I'm doing—I'm never going to be able to do this,* just use the same process and tools for that emotion or belief in the moment.

I want to reiterate what I said before: don't worry about following the Success Blueprint perfectly. As you begin to follow it, you will mess up, stumble, and fall from time to time. No big deal. The loving thing to do in that situation is to forgive yourself, then get back on track and go at it again. The longer you follow this blueprint, the better and better you'll do. And the better you do, the happier you will be. After you get pretty good at living in love in the present moment, don't be surprised if people start saying things like "What's going on with you?" or "What's happened to you?" What they're thinking is, *Wow, I want some of whatever you have!* Because this is what everybody really wants: to live in love every moment of every hour of every day. Success, happiness, health, and everything else we all want flow effortlessly out of love.

I believe with all my heart that success is waiting for you: *your perfect success*, unlike anyone else's. It may involve money or not, fame or not, achievement or not. But it will be just right for you, and you will know that in your bones when you get there. This success is not based on trying harder, world peace, a bull market economy, other people, or even the physiology of your body. No bone, blood, or tissue has to change, and where you are right now is the perfect place to start. In fact, where you are right now may be where you have been waiting all your life to start from, even if it's in the gutter. For you to have your ultimate success, nothing external or internal has to physically change. You now have the principles, process, and all the tools you need.

At the same time, I want to remind you of the paradox of the Love Code: giving up the expectation of external results is the *best* and maybe the *only* way you will get the best external results for you. The Love Code is truly how you can have it all: internal *and* external success, with happiness, contentment, and peace.

Remember, in the long term:

> *Love never fails!*
> *Fear never succeeds!*

What is *your* choice?

quick reference

# THE TEN STEPS OF THE LOVE CODE 40-DAY SUCCESS BLUEPRINT

**1.** Determine your ultimate success goal: the inward state such as love, joy, or peace that you want most.

**2.** Name a success desire that you would like to work toward and achieve in your life—one that is in truth, in love, and consistent with your ultimate success goal from step 1.

**3.** Envision that success desire actually coming to fruition.

**4.** List the negative feelings or beliefs that arise from envisioning your success desire and rate each on a scale of 0 to 10.

**5.** Use the Three Tools (the Energy Medicine tool, the Reprogramming Statements tool, and the Heart Screen tool) to deprogram the negatives from step 4. Use these tools until your negative beliefs no longer bother you (or you'd rate them below a 1 on a 10-point scale).

**6.** Once all your negatives are gone, use the same tools to reprogram a supersuccess memory for the positive success desire you envisioned in step 3. Use the tools until you have a positive sense of "I believe I can do this!" (or you'd rate your positive sense at a 7 or higher on a 10-point scale).

**7.** Begin a forty-day period with the goal of keeping these scores at the same level, with the negative beliefs about your desire below a 1 (i.e., "They don't bother me anymore") and the positive sense about achieving your desire above a 7 (i.e., "I believe I can do this!"). After forty days, most people are fully deprogrammed and reprogrammed about their success issue, with their negatives below a 1 and their positive sense at a 7 or higher without using the tools. If your negative beliefs are still bothering you and/or you still don't feel ready to start working toward your desire, start another forty-day period.

**8.** Set your specific success goals using the Love Code. They are based in truth, in love, 100 percent under your control, and able to be done in the present moment (once you have been reprogrammed).

**9.** Find or develop an organizational system to get your specific success goals done in a way that's most efficient for you.

**10.** Walk in the direction of your desire by completing your specific success goals in love, focusing on the present moment (or on the next thirty minutes).

# LOVE TRULY

---

I'd like to return to the promise I made at the beginning of this book: I believe that the Love Code is the key to success in every area of your life. It's not a matter of *whether* this will work for you. The only question is whether you will do it. If you do it, *it always works*. And now you have all the tools, and the full set of instructions, to live a life of happiness and success beyond your hopes and dreams.

As I said before, I believe that twenty years from now, practicing the Love Code (or something like it) will be the norm for counseling and therapy, peak performance in athletics and achievement, corporate training, and more. I have used it in all these contexts, with fabulous results. It provides what our current paradigms are missing but what is desperately needed: deprogramming our human hard-drive viruses, reprogramming for success, and then focusing on peak positive performance in the present moment.

The truth is, I could keep helping people find success in their lives, one person at a time, for a very long time. I have a personal client waiting list and do webinars and remote coaching. I've tried to multiply myself by training coaches who practice all over the world, and we've built the largest practice of its kind worldwide, with clients in all 50 states and 158 countries (and counting). But how many people can I help this way? Whatever that number is, it's not enough.

We need millions—*tens* of millions—of people throughout the world living in love. Love is the answer to all global conflict, all difficulties in race relations, all economic problems, and all environmental degradation. Love is the ancient solution to every problem we have. I wrote this book so that anyone and everyone could have access to this solution in the most simple and straightforward way possible, and so that sharing it wouldn't depend on the efforts of a select few.

So I am on a mission. My mission includes the Love Code and helping you live a life beyond willpower and expectations, but it is much bigger than that. My mission is to live according to the principles of nonreligious, practical spirituality and help others to do the same. It is to help one person at a time shift from living in fear, focused on the past and the future, to living in love, focused on the present moment. Any problem or crisis—your tumors, your relationships, terrorism, economic disasters—can be traced back to someone not running decisions through two primary filters, which are my two-point criteria for everything I do, think, feel, and believe:

1. Is this in harmony with my ultimate success goal, and the inward state I "really" want most?

2. Is this in harmony with living the next thirty minutes in love?

This two-part filter is the essence of nonreligious, practical spirituality. It determines my every decision and every action. My filter is not whether something makes money. It's not any particular achievement. The forty-day process is my desire, or what I'm hoping for, and sets the direction I walk in. But in terms of my daily goals and actions, if the action is not in truth or love, if it's fear based or falsehood based, I will not do it.

I'm calling this mission "Love Truly." Not "true love," which tends to signify finding something by accident, like a penny on the ground.

I'm talking about an active verb, not a noun. Loving truly is a feeling, belief, experience, and commitment of the heart that is beyond words, and a conscious intention to always act in the best interest of everyone in your life both physically in the external world and through your spiritual heart technology. You could also think of it as "defacto love," based on our definitions of placebo, nocebo, and defacto in chapter 3. To love truly is something you can choose every moment of every day, once you have been deprogrammed and reprogrammed either by the tools or the transformational *aha* and then plug into God/source/ love. If you love truly, it will change you on the inside, then change you on the outside, and then will transform your home, friends, work, finances, and so on. If, after deprogramming and reprogramming, you consciously and intentionally love (as an active verb) in the present moment, you will have love (the noun) come to you from all directions. However, this typically does not happen in reverse. If you are just trying to find love or have it fall out of the sky to you, it may never happen.

This Love Truly movement is nonjudgmental, and about loving truly regardless of one's circumstances or how others respond. I am looking for new spiritual brothers and sisters with whom to join hands, one by one, in this mission. Not brothers and sisters by blood, but by spirit (which is much more powerful and relevant).

So I have just two requests. First, apply this process to your own life. Remember, it's almost impossible for it not to work. No external circumstance or blood, bone, or tissue needs to change. This process depends only on what is (nonphysically) internal to you. I don't mean you won't mess up. That's part of it, too. Learning to live in love means forgiving yourself when you don't follow through, but getting back up and trying again.

I'd like to refer you back to the end of chapter 1, where I advised you to begin by asking for a transformational *aha*. I'd like to encourage you again to pray and meditate over these basic concepts and give yourself the chance to experience this transformation. In my experience, if you pray and meditate consistently and for long enough (i.e., the right time for you, individually), it often happens. Feel free to do this while you are also using the Three Tools. The two approaches do not have to be done separately. Again, it isn't about willpower—it's about allowing love to work through you.

Second, once you've completed the process and are truly living out all the positive effects, if you believe the Love Code really is the key to success in everything you've been struggling with, my second request is for you to share it. In fact, I'm on my knees, begging you to share it. Even more, I ask you to spread the word about living according to nonreligious, practical spirituality. This is exactly why I wrote this book in the first place. Don't misunderstand: I am not saying this to sell more books. You can loan your book to someone, or explain the principles and tools to a friend over a pizza. If you're living in love, and you have the antidote to what ails your family, your friends, and your neighbors, you're not going to be able to keep it to yourself. That's what love is!

If, after doing all this, you realize that you would like to be a part of this Love Truly mission, I invite you to turn to the epilogue that follows. You don't need the epilogue to put the Love Code into practice in any way; you already have everything you need in the preceding chapters. But if you have completed the deprogramming and reprogramming work and would like a glimpse of what it really means to live in love practically for the long term, keep reading.

If you'd like to share your experiences with the Love Code with me, I'd love to hear from you. Visit www.thelovecodenow.com.

My love goes out to you—continuously!

# PRACTICAL SPIRITUALITY

Imagine you're visiting a friend and, upon your arrival, as you approach the front door, you notice a junk car in his driveway. It's in terrible shape—the body is all rusted out, the hood's up, the engine's gone, and the upholstery's beyond repair. You look at that car, roll your eyes, and say, "There's no way that car's going to run again." The next time you visit, the car isn't there anymore. One year later, you visit again, and your friend has a new car in the driveway. Its body shines with glossy red paint and shiny chrome trim, its soft leather upholstery looks top of the line, and when your friend proudly lifts the hood, you see a brand-new 300-horsepower engine. "Wow, when'd you get this?" you ask your friend. "Oh, this is that junk car I've been working on," he replies. You're stunned. What a transformation!

That's how I feel whenever I see someone transform from living in fear to living in love. I don't have the words to describe it. The results are literally night and day. The Love Code offers exactly this kind of total restoration. It provides the tools you need to stitch yourself up and the antiseptic you need so you don't get infected in the process. But as miraculous and transformational as the Love Code is, it's only the beginning—just like it was only the beginning for the restored car. You wouldn't leave the new car just sitting in your driveway, would you? No—you'd want to drive it around everywhere you went! There's an entire world available to you far beyond what you've imagined.

In this epilogue, I'd like to leave a few bread crumbs toward a path that leads far beyond your personal success and up to the mountaintop of life. If you look ahead to where the bread crumbs lead, you will see before you an ancient door. It looks like it hasn't been opened for centuries, and you would have passed it right by if the bread crumbs hadn't led you to it. Now that you've noticed it, however, you feel strangely drawn to it. Above this ancient door something is written, although it is difficult to read. After some effort, you can make out the words *Practical Spirituality*. You then notice a very aged and discolored paper nailed to the door. In smudged calligraphy, the first line reads, "The Tenets of Practical Spirituality: The Way of Truth, Love, and Grace for All Who Seek to Enter."

This epilogue does not contain the full contents of the document attached to the door, but it will give you enough of a taste to decide if you want to open that door and walk through. I have spent my entire life praying, searching, traveling, studying, and testing various principles to arrive at this belief system. I would like to invite you to consider the following truths with an open mind. If they don't resonate with you, no problem—I thank you sincerely for considering them. If they do make sense to you, I would be honored to have you as a fellow traveler!

Of course, if you enter, you can decide to leave anytime. However, I have never seen anyone choose that. What I typically hear is something like "I can't imagine ever living any other way!"

...

Practical spirituality is all about results. You probably bought this book because you want success and happiness, and you want to overcome failure, health problems, and unhappiness. You want results. So which worldview, belief system, or paradigm gets you what you want, and which takes you where you don't want to go?

To answer that question, we begin at what may be a surprising place: the human body. As we learned in the previous chapters, we have no mechanisms in the body that produce unhappiness, negative emotions, or disease, only those that produce happiness and health. When we experience negative symptoms, physically or nonphysically, it is always the result of a malfunction of these success- and health-producing mechanisms. So what causes the body to malfunction?

You now know the answer to that question: fear. If we are not in a truly life-threatening emergency, fear in our unconscious, subconscious, and conscious mind always causes a malfunction (known as stress) that leads to darkness in the body's cells and energy systems, which over time leads to illness, disease, failure, and unhappiness.

On the other hand, love in our unconscious, subconscious, and conscious mind always eliminates the effects of fear and stress, which allows the body's healing systems to work the way they are designed, and success, happiness, and health follow. Love in the mind always manifests as light in the body's cells and energy systems, which leads to correct functioning and therefore health, success, and happiness. As the Harvard Grant Study confirmed, "Happiness is love. Full stop."[1]

What is true physically is also true spiritually. If your worldview is based in fear, or any version of the pain/pleasure principle, cause-and-effect principle, or Newton's third law of motion, it will produce illness, disease, failure, and unhappiness. No matter how long it's been practiced or who endorses it.

...

In our discussion of practical spirituality, let's begin with the term "spiritual." I believe there are four points of evidence for the existence of the spiritual, or love/source/God:

1. **The heart screen and the latest neurological research.** As we already know, the heart screen is the creative force from which everything we see was built, and yet science has not been able to find any evidence of a physical screen or mechanism for the imagination. I believe it's because the heart screen is in the spiritual realm. That's how Dr. Eben Alexander experienced his "proof of heaven" when all his neural mechanisms were nonfunctional.

   Remember, based on the latest neurological research, the number one factor that heals and prevents long-term problems in our brain is our connection to the spiritual, specifically through prayer and belief.[2] (The health of our brain also determines whether our failure mechanism is turned on, or our success mechanism is turned on.)[3] As we learned in chapter 3, the only kind of belief that really works long term is defacto belief, or believing the truth. So if believing in a spiritual reality produces reliable long-term results, this belief must indeed be true!

2. **The vast majority of people believe it (approximately 97 percent, based on statistics), yet it has the least empirical evidence.** We mentioned this point in chapter 3. Galileo was ostracized when he said that the earth revolves around the sun instead of the other way around, even though he was right. Ignaz Philipp Semmelweis, MD, was a laughingstock in the medical field because he insisted on washing his hands before surgery, believing there were invisible things called germs, and was eventually forced out of medicine altogether. Medical doctors

told us for years that nutritional supplements merely produced "expensive urine." Yet in each of these cases we now almost universally believe the opposite. Why? Now we can see the evidence! Historically, the majority belief has virtually always been with what is clearly and empirically observable and measurable. In this case it should mean that the vast majority believes that nothing exists beyond the physical, or what we can see and measure. Yet the opposite is true. I don't know if you could find a 97 percent level of universal agreement on any other issue—even if it's that the sky is blue! How can that happen? Because we have something inside us that tells us the spiritual is real. And that brings us to number 3.

3. **The existence of grace and love.** People whom we truly love we naturally and automatically treat with grace. Grace simply means unconditional love, acceptance, or offering forgiveness and kindness even when someone doesn't deserve it, and the power to do what cannot be done by willpower or the natural. People whom we don't love we tend to naturally treat according to karma or law (treating them exactly as they deserve according to a list of rules, or by WIIFM—what's in it for me). If we stop loving someone, we will tend to shift from grace to karma; if we start loving someone, we will tend to shift from karma to grace. Love comes from grace and leads back to it. As we'll discuss in more detail, grace is supernatural by definition, because it violates the natural law of everything in the physical universe—Newton's third law of motion, stimulus/response, cause/effect, you reap what you sow and get back what you give. In fact, most of the time, love defies basic human logic— just as the supernatural does. So love is the proof of grace, and grace is the proof of the supernatural, or spiritual.

**4. Personal experience.** This last piece of evidence is the one that means the most to me, but possibly the least to you. And that is the fact that I have experienced it. In fact, I am experiencing it right now. If you don't believe there can be no other evidence more convincing than our personal experience, try telling a person who is truly head over heels in love with someone that they are not in love with them, that it's just some chemical anomaly in their brain. Then try telling them that the other person doesn't love them either. Finally, tell them that love doesn't even exist. But do this very carefully, because they just might punch you in the nose. You see, it's not that big a deal if someone tells you that they don't like your car, or they disagree with Democrats, or they believe people in the northeastern United States are smarter than those in the South. Those opinions usually stimulate lively conversation, with points on both sides. Most times it even ends up friendly, with both sides agreeing to disagree. But when someone experiences the "real thing" way down deep, and then you tell them it's not real—well, "them's fighting words!" You cannot be convinced what you've experienced doesn't exist, because you *have* experienced it.

Now let's talk about the "practical" aspect of practical spirituality. Over the years, I have observed four distinct categories of spirituality.

**1. Religious.** The religious tend to make spirituality about rules and the judgment associated with adhering to rules, instead of love and freedom. Their credo is that you reap what you sow, and their focus is on external goals and expectations accomplished by willpower. Another name for this is karma, which is the natural law of the universe. Based on everything we have learned thus far, we know that this approach is fear based rather than love based. Sometimes the leaders of religious groups have commonalities with politicians, where power, control, and money reign—but not always.

2. **Nonspiritual.** Because those who deny the existence of the spiritual at all only believe in the natural laws, they are inherently relegated to the principle of cause and effect, or karma, and therefore also have a worldview based in fear. They fear the effect or result that they don't want, or of not getting an effect that they do want.

3. **Impractical spirituality.** This category includes those who talk about the spiritual, may call themselves "New Age," and typically follow the law of attraction, also known as the law of "likes." They may be among the closest to true spirituality, but their spirituality is impractical because it can rarely produce the results they want. They talk about living in love and nonjudgment (and mean it), yet their credo tends to be the law of attraction, yet another name for the cause-and-effect principle, and the inherent judgment based on that physical law. Fear, not love, comes from the physical law of cause and effect. Love comes from spiritual grace and violates the physical cause-and-effect laws—always. Also, the law of attraction says that I get what I put out. Like attracts like. If I put out good thoughts, feelings, beliefs, and actions, I get good back. If I put out positive energy, I get positive things in return. If I put out negative energy, I get negative things in return. But generating the positive energy is left up to my willpower, in order to secure positive future results. So if I have a problem, the solution is my own willpower focused on an expectation— which as we know cannot result in real love and lasting, perfect success. The word *manifesting* is common in impractical

spirituality, in statements such as "manifest anything now!" It actually manifests stress and malfunction now! This worldview tends to be fear masquerading as love.

All three of the above are focused on realizing a future expectation through willpower and, worse yet, trying to create the spiritual (love, joy, peace) through physical laws and mechanisms. Again, the principles of cause and effect, stimulus/response, "reap what you sow," karma, the law of "likes," and the law of attraction are all based on Newton's third law of motion: for every action, there is an equal and opposite reaction. A quick online search will reveal that the expert practitioners and standard teachings of these principles all say the same thing: you know what you're going to get, every time. But also by definition, these principles shift your mind and body into stress, which causes you to malfunction. How long do you malfunction? As long as you are living by those laws, which for most people is their whole life. It just won't work!

4. **Practical spirituality.** In contrast, practical spirituality is based on the principle of love. Love directly violates the universal physical laws of nature, and Newton's third law in particular. Why? Like doesn't always attract like. With love, you never know what you will get. Sometimes you get love back, but many times you don't. It is always an adventure. Think of the true nature of parenting, marriage, and friendships. There are no guarantees regarding end results. That's because love is not of the physical world, it is of the spiritual realm.

This "road less traveled" includes those few who genuinely plug into the supernatural and give up control. This means they give up external expectations (but not hope), and know they can't live in love with their willpower alone. By giving up control and plugging into

God/source/love, they automatically receive grace—the only truly love-based way to live, and the power to produce supernatural life results. Then they can live in the present moment in love, coming from an inward state of love, which produces their perfect external results constantly. This group includes Gandhi, Mother Teresa, Jesus, and many other less-than-famous peaceful spirits. I believe that if an open-minded person can understand the whole truth and be deprogrammed and reprogrammed by prayer, a transformational *aha*, or energy-based tools, they will inherently choose this path, with or without this book.

I believe that there are people on this "road less traveled" all over the world, in all the groups listed, and meeting in buildings with all types of names on them. Practical spirituality simply means living from a heart of love, plugged into the source of love. Those who follow practical spirituality live by the "law written on their hearts," no matter how they were raised, what their pain is, what they desire but do not have, or the name of their group.

In fact, it's virtually impossible to tell whether someone is living according to practical spirituality based on the group they associate with or even the words they use. There is only way to tell for sure—they will "love truly" and be at peace at virtually all times, regardless of their circumstances. There are at least two ways to tell when someone is *not* living in accordance with practical spirituality. The first is if they experience emotions in the anxiety or anger categories. Even if they constantly talk about love and light, or smile and hug easily and say they "love everyone," people with religious, nonspiritual, or impractical spiritual worldviews are pretty quick to experience anxiety, anger, irritation, frustration, or judgment (especially toward people in the other groups), and they are more likely to have health problems. As we learned in chapter 4, experiencing any emotion in the anger category is proof that you have a stress goal, or a fear-based goal focused on an external circumstance achieved through willpower. In other words, almost any expression of anxiety or anger (with the exception of "righteous" anger) indicates that individuals are living according to a system based on the law of cause and effect in their spiritual heart, even if they would never admit it or don't even realize it. For example, in my experience, nonspiritual people tend not to like people in spiritual or religious groups and sometimes may feel superior to them. *How can they be so gullible?* they think. The religious usually seem afraid of and/ or angry with those in the other groups and may even see them as the enemy. Those living according to impractical spirituality typically accept everyone except the religious and are often angered by their narrow-mindedness. The impractically spiritual will also tend to think they are living in practical spirituality, even though they feel/think/believe/act according to the principle of cause and effect, or fear-based law.

On the other hand, the proof of practical spirituality is experiencing close to 100 percent unconditional love and acceptance, nonjudgment, and the resulting internal love, joy, peace, health, happiness, patience, and understanding, regardless of your circumstances or whether the company you are in agrees or disagrees with you. In my experience, people living in practical spirituality truly love and respect people in all groups and religions. They see their job as not to judge or convert, but to love, with no strings attached.

The second indication you are not living in accordance with practical spirituality is unforgiveness. I have never seen a health issue without a forgiveness issue. My colleague Ben Johnson says he has never seen a cancer without a forgiveness issue. Unforgiveness is experienced on the path of fear, action/reaction, cause/effect, and law. Forgiveness is experienced on the path of grace and love. By "forgiveness," I mean forgiving yourself, forgiving others, forgiving *everyone*—without requiring them to "pay" for their mistakes. You know when you have truly forgiven someone when you 100 percent unconditionally accept them as a person without their having to "make it right."

Most who have trouble forgiving, or simply refuse to forgive, are living by law, not grace—and they may tend to apply this standard to themselves as well. They are living in an earthly hell, because no one can "do everything right"; we are all stumbling forward. According to the law of cause and effect, "doing things wrong" means getting the results we didn't want or were afraid of.

By the way, 100 percent acceptance of the person does *not* mean accepting the behavior. You can accept the person without accepting the behavior. What it does mean is that the behavior does not define that person, just as yours does not define you. If we are judged according to our behavior, we are all doomed.

• • •

Practical spirituality, or living in the present moment in love, is not intended to be based on willpower, or at least no more willpower than it takes to brush your teeth. One important way to reduce the amount of willpower it will take to love is, of course, to deprogram the inward state of fear and reprogram a state of internal love, so love becomes your default state and feels almost effortless. But there's another very important way, and that is to intentionally plug into the source of love itself.

As we said earlier in the book, every issue boils down to a relationship issue—which has to include our relationship with God/source/love. I'm not here to define that for you, but I do believe this is why virtually every civilization in history has believed in something beyond themselves, even if it's not logical to the natural mind. We inherently knew that we need and want love more than anything else— well before we had the scientific evidence that linked love to happiness and success. In the same way, we also inherently know that there is a God or a spiritual reality, even though it doesn't make logical sense (as far as what we can see and measure in the natural). We believe in

a spiritual reality and in love because we have a built-in mechanism
to seek God/source/love, which is the source of love and what we are
programmed internally for and need most. In other words, we need to
be plugged into the heart screen of God/source/love—that's our server.

Virtually everything that exists can be classified as *frequency*
(energy) and *amplitude* (power). Frequency is the specific thing, and
amplitude is how much of it there is, or how much power it has. So
to live in truth and love, you need the grace/love/truth frequency with
enough amplitude to eliminate the fear/falsehood programming. To
choose love, you simply need to plug into the source of love. If you
believe that *you* are the source of grace and love, so that you don't need
to "plug in" to the source, I would ask you to do this. Exert your power
and cause the things you want in your life to happen now—and cause
the things you don't want to be eliminated now. The clinical research on
this indicates that people who believe and try to do this are successful
approximately one time in a million. It is my position that if you really
are "the source" and you really are "the power," the percentage would
be significantly better—something like having what you want happen
97 percent of the time (the percentage of time I would claim the Love
Code is successful). Love does eliminate fear, and light does eliminate
darkness, but there has to be enough love and light for the amount of
fear and darkness. A penlight won't light up a stadium, but the stadium
lights will.

I have found that I don't have enough power to eliminate or
overcome my internal fear/falsehood, pain/pleasure programming.
However, I have also discovered that love/source/God is everywhere
and in everything. And love/source/God has more than enough of the
specific frequency and amplitude I need to eliminate my fear/falsehood
programming and live in light and love. Because love/source/God is all
and in all, I can plug into that spiritual Wi-Fi server anytime, anywhere,
and be connected to exactly what I need.

Every person is built and designed to live in love, joy, and peace. After all, if we don't, our mechanisms start to malfunction. The fear response is only supposed to kick in when we are in imminent danger, then immediately turn off when the danger has passed. We come preprogrammed with our own personal built-in spiritual homing beacon (what some people call the conscience, and what I call our love compass). However, unless we actively follow this homing beacon and seek the source of love and plug into it, we will not have enough of the love/light frequency and amplitude, and we will default to fear/darkness and cause-and-effect thinking, beliefs, actions, and physiology.

Practical spirituality lives in the present moment in real love and truth, regardless of the external circumstances or behavior of others, internally plugged into the source of love, constantly receiving grace. In contrast, impractical spirituality seeks to "earn and produce" love through the cause-and-effect law of attraction. The impractical try to get love by doing the right thing, or earning it. The religious also try to "achieve" love via the principle of "you reap what you sow" (i.e., karma or law)—you have to "be good enough." None of these perspectives are consistent with the nature of real love—agape, not eros. Real, agape love is "free" and cannot be earned—or lost. It has nothing to do with how good or bad you are.

Don't get me wrong. The law of cause and effect (or karma, or Newton's third law of motion) is absolutely real—it operates all day, every day, in the physical world, just like gravity. It is a natural law that exists now and has since the dawn of time. But in my opinion, grace is simply a higher law. It is, in fact, the exact opposite of the principles of action/reaction, stimulus/response, and reaping what you sow. It means receiving good from God/source/love, regardless of what I deserve. Grace is the only choice that love would ever make for the object of its love: forgiveness, mercy, the opportunity to start over with a clean slate and try again. Receiving grace requires *giving up* the focus on the physical, material world and achieving end results through willpower. It requires plugging into the source/love/God and giving up control in belief/hope/faith/trust, rather than trying to be your own source (which limits you to the strength of your willpower). Grace supersedes the natural cause-and-effect paradigm and is governed by and in harmony with spiritual love.

In a recent interview, Bono, the lead singer for the band U2, discussed this very issue. I have been a fan for years, so excitedly read his take. He said that given the choice, he doesn't want to get what he deserves based on karma or the law of attraction. He wants to get what he doesn't deserve—grace. Here's what he said about it:

> It's a mind-blowing concept that the God who created the universe might be looking for company, a real relationship with people, but the thing that keeps me on my knees is the difference between Grace and Karma. . . . I really believe we've moved out of the realm of Karma into one of Grace. . . . You see, at the center of all religions is the idea of Karma. You know, what you put out comes back to you: an eye for an eye, a tooth for a tooth, or in physics; in physical laws every action is met by an equal or an opposite one. It's clear to me that Karma is at the very heart of the universe. I'm absolutely sure of it. And yet, along comes this idea called Grace to upend all that "as you reap, so you will sow" stuff. Grace defies reason and logic. Love interrupts, if you like, the consequences of your actions, which in my case is very good news indeed, because I've done a lot of stupid stuff. . . . I'd be in big trouble if Karma was going to finally be my judge. I'd be in deep s—. It doesn't excuse my mistakes, but I'm holding out for Grace.[4]

Grace is a paradox, just like success is. You must give up wanting and striving for what you want in order to receive it. Karma is in harmony with the way everything in the physical universe works; it's right according to logic and reason, our legal system, our idea

of fairness and justice. Grace—receiving not only the good but the
absolute *best*, no matter what you do—would violate all these physical
and logical laws. It just doesn't make sense, and it seems impossible
to most people I explain it to. It's not natural! If grace exists, it would
be outside the natural workings of the universe. It would have to be
*super*natural. In other words, it would have to be a miracle.

Bingo! That's exactly right. Grace is a miracle—just as love is a
miracle! It's supernatural and evidence of the spiritual. Think about
it: Why would you ever logically choose to do many of the things that
love causes us to do? In the case of marriage and having children, for
example, love causes us pain that we would not experience otherwise,
costs us hundreds of thousands of dollars, and takes away our freedom
to do what we want when we want it. We would have to choose love for
a reason that is illogical, not according to the natural laws. And there is
a reason: we have an inherent, internal knowing beyond words that it is
the only thing that will give us what we want and need most at the core
of our being.

So this life is something of a test. Will you follow the natural
laws, or the spiritual laws? Will you choose love or fear? Will you live
according to action/reaction, or grace? The choice is ours, with a
hundred different opportunities to choose every day. We will never do it
perfectly, but we can be on the right path.

...

Understanding the practical, spiritual nature of love and fear
completely changes our understanding of freedom and bondage. If I
am living and acting completely in love and light, I can do *anything* I
want, and it will be right. If I am living in fear and darkness, *anything*
I do (out of fear and darkness) is likely to be wrong. Anything not
done in love will bring rotten results—never the results I "really" want.

Anything done in love will bring the perfect results in time, even if they are results I had never imagined. In fact, that's the only way I can have the perfect results for my life.

But when you choose any worldview based in fear, or the law of cause and effect, you are choosing bondage, because you are choosing to have to be a virtual perfectionist if you have any hope of getting peak results through that system. Worse than that, you have to be a successful perfectionist—and any psychologist or therapist will tell you that there are few things more internally damaging than perfectionism because of the massive stress it causes. Why? Not only are you focused on creating external circumstances with your willpower (which we know leads to failure), you have to do it perfectly, or there will be a result that is not okay with you! The next time you blow it may cause your cancer, or your failure. Talk about stress! We have billions of well-meaning, wonderful people who have unknowingly fallen "victim" to one of the oldest laws in the universe and are now innocently living in bondage to fear. I think this happened largely because people, like me, started to become fed up with fear-based religion, and so they threw it overboard and looked for a better way. However, their new paradigm ended up being another cause-and-effect principle, simply repackaged and painted pretty. But it still puts people in bondage to end results based on willpower, which ultimately ends in failure—similar to the fear-based religion they were determined to get away from.

True love and grace free us from end results. When we live according to the Love Code, we're focused internally on love in the present moment, not on end results. We don't have to do anything perfectly; we don't even have to do it well. We have an unlimited number of "get out of jail free" cards, because love forgives every mistake, every missing of the mark, every choice of fear over love—*even when it's intentional and we know we could have done better.* And the end results that do occur are not dependent on my willpower, but on supernatural power that can produce the perfect result, beyond my abilities. So I have no need to worry or be angry. I can relax and trust that everything will come out right for me in the end. That is true freedom.

I hope and pray that you will consider making the choice to live according to grace and love and practical spirituality! I did, and I would never, ever go back to law and karma.

...

There has been a fundamental shift happening for some years now, all over the world. I have been watching it keenly for the last twenty years. In reality it has been happening for centuries. However, it seems to be speeding up, rushing to an inevitable end. This fundamental shift I will call a polarization of light and darkness. Darkness in the world is becoming more dense and is spreading. But so is the light. Fear is growing by leaps and bounds, recruiting tens of thousands of new converts each month, but love is doing the same. Falsehood and judgmentalism have assumed attack mode more than ever in history, as have truth and nonjudgmental acceptance. Chances are you are more on one side of this polarity than the other. I see politics, religion, finance, race, color, and nationality being some of the main culprits and havens of darkness.

If you believe in love and acceptance, you cannot judge another for choosing fear and rejection. If you do, it means you are guilty of precisely what you are accusing others of. Judgment is *always* connected to comparison. And comparison is almost always based in insecurity or insignificance issues. Out of our insecurity and insignificance, we compare ourselves to others and experience superiority or inferiority. This causes us to worry over the results we need to be okay and attempt to manipulate events and people to create those results. All these actions are based on wanting, not peace—and remember, wanting is almost always fear based.

If the experience of our heart is secure and safe, we have no need to compare to pull others down, to try to convey a certain image, or to manipulate to get a certain end result. And in some instances, comparison can be helpful.

Typically we cannot rest, or experience peace, because we feel insignificant and insecure; we feel we're not "okay" at the core of ourselves, that something is missing. So we feel we must keep trying *externally* to become okay *internally*, which is the essence of living in want. But if we are okay internally (i.e., significant and secure), we can be at peace with any external circumstances, even if they're not what we would prefer. The only thing that can make us okay internally is becoming deprogrammed and reprogrammed from fear, plugging into God/source/love, and choosing the path of love and light in the present moment continually.

In my experience, only about 1 percent of us choose the path of love and light, while the other 99 percent choose the path of fear and darkness, often unconsciously. How do you know which path you have chosen? Again, you know you have chosen the 1 percent path if you experience peace and joy, and love and acceptance of all, regardless of your circumstances or the behavior of others (remember, you can unconditionally accept individuals and not accept their behavior or even spend time with them, if doing so is unhealthy). Your legacy will be the side you choose, not in the past, but from now on!

How do we know which side will win? Put another way, which side has the best results? Gandhi has already told us: "The way of truth and love has always won," and it will win this current war in the end as well. So, if you are unforgiving, less than 100 percent accepting, or judging, you have chosen to live under law and are the guilty one and are on the losing side, even if you are doing those things in the name of "light and love."

...

So if you resonate with these principles of practical spirituality, and choose to truly live in love/light/grace, what do you do next? Well, the first step is the Love Code. You need to have a transformational *aha*, or deprogram and reprogram, so that you are capable of living in love, and then you start living in the present moment in love, internally plugged into love/source/God continually.

But even after you decide to live in love in the present moment and become capable of doing so, plugged into the source, that doesn't mean choosing between the path of love and the path of fear is always easy. Every day, hundreds of different situations and choices will present themselves where the distinction between the path of love and fear may not be completely clear.

I know this from experience. In fact, for the past twenty-five years, I have prayerfully been documenting and finding solutions for hundreds of these types of practical daily events for the sake of my two sons, Harry and George. I knew that someday they would be adults, and if I wasn't around for some reason, I wanted them to have an owner's manual from me about how to live out this kind of practical spirituality in their lives. I call these the Spiritual Laws of Nature.

But that's a discussion for another time. For now, I pray love, light, and success for you, every day and in every way!

# FURTHER RESOURCES

To access the Success Issues Finder online test, a printable workbook, and other resources to help you apply the Love Code to your life, visit www.thelovecodenow.com. There you can also learn more about other tools developed by Dr. Alex Loyd, such as:

- **The Healing Codes**, which in large part saved Alex's wife, Hope, from severe clinical depression, are geared toward healing the source of health issues. You can also learn how to use the Healing Codes with Alex's book *The Healing Code* (Hachette, 2011), coauthored with Dr. Ben Johnson.

- **The Success Codes** program follows the same principles as explained in *The Love Code*, but with a completely different intervention and tool. It provides another bazooka-powered energy medicine technique to heal the underlying issues of success as described in this book.

- **The Master Key** also follows the principles of this book and has separate interventions for spirit, mind, and body, but in a literal push-button format: Put headphones on and press play. The Master Key fits hand in glove with *The Love Code*. It takes as little as ten minutes a day, and you can do it during the same time you spend on the Love Code.

Note: With the information in this book, most people won't need any other tool or process, but if you feel stuck, or want faster results, they are available. If the Love Code process is a fully equipped general toolbox, these other programs provide additional specialty tools.

# NOTES

## INTRODUCTION

1. Timothy D. Wilson, "Self-Help Books Could Ruin Your Life!," The Daily Mail online, August 15, 2011, www.dailymail.co.uk/femail/article-2026001/Self-help-books-ruin-life-They-promise-sell-millions.html#ixzz1ovSZDP2z.

2. For more about Hope's healing journey and a different set of tools that have healed a variety of physical and emotional symptoms at the subconscious source, see my bestselling book *The Healing Code* (Hachette, 2011), coauthored with Dr. Ben Johnson. For those of you familiar with the Healing Codes, you may be wondering why my wife did not use the Love Code to help heal her health problem. First of all, it wasn't quite ready yet. It took me several years to develop it enough to use it in my practice, and I was still in the process of discovering and developing two of the Three Tools described in this book. But perhaps, more important, I had tried so many things on her by the time I did develop the Love Code (and none had worked) that, quite understandably, she was trying to find her own way. Not long after that, the Healing Codes arrived.

3. Cort A. Pedersen, University of North Carolina–Chapel Hill; Kerstin Uvnas Moberg, *The Oxytocin Factor: Tapping the Hormone of Calm, Love, and Healing* (Pinter & Martin, 2011).

4. "75 Years in the Making: Harvard Just Released Its Epic Study on What Men Need to Live a Happy Life," FEELguide, April 29, 2013, http://www.feelguide.com/2013/04/29/75-years-in-the-making-harvard-just-released-its-epic-study-on-what-men-require-to-live-a-happy-life/. This article includes a synopsis of the study, but the full findings can be found in George Vaillant, *Triumphs of Experience: The Men of the Harvard Grant Study* (Belknap Press, 2012).

**5.** Anders Nygren, *Agape and Eros: The Christian Idea of Love,* trans. Philip S. Watson (Chicago: University of Chicago Press, 1982).

## CHAPTER I

**1.** Dan Gilbert, "Why Are We Happy? Why Aren't We Happy?," TED Talks (video), February 2004, https://www.youtube.com/watch?v=LTO_dZUvbJA#t=54.

**2.** Dan Gilbert, *Stumbling on Happiness* (Vintage, 2007).

**3.** Dan Gilbert, "Why Are We Happy? Why Aren't We Happy?," TED Talks (video), February 2004, https://www.youtube.com/watch?v=LTO_dZUvbJA#t=54.

**4.** Bruce Lipton, *The Biology of Belief* (Hay House, 2008), 98.

**5.** You may be thinking, *Who is he to tell me that what I really want is an inward state?* The reason I'm so certain is that I did my own personal ten-year study with every single client in my counseling practice, where I would ask each person, "What do you want most?" and then, "Why do you want that?" For every response, I would continue to ask them "Why?" until they ran out of answers. When they had, we had invariably reached an inward state.

**6.** Viktor E. Frankl, *Man's Search for Meaning* (Simon & Schuster, 1959).

**7.** If you struggle with the idea of prayer, I would highly advise Larry Dossey MD's wonderful book *Reinventing Medicine*, in which he reviews double-blind research studies where prayer yielded, as you might suspect, miraculous results—even when the people had no idea they were being prayed for. If you still have a problem with it, simply make a request of your heart rather than a higher source.

## CHAPTER 2

**1.** "Medical School Breakthrough," *Dallas Morning News,* September 12, 2004.

**2.** Sue Goetinck Ambrose, "A Cell Forgets," *The Dallas Morning News,* October 20, 2004, www.utsandiego.com/uniontrib/20041020/news_ z1c20cell.html.

**3.** Ibid.

**4.** Ibid.

**5.** Ibid.

**6.** Paul Pearsall, Gary E. Schwartz, and Linda G. Russek, "Organ Transplants and Cellular Memories," *Nexus* 12:3 (April–May 2005), www.paulpearsall.com/info/press/3.html. See also Claire Sylvia, *A Change of Heart* (Warner Books, 1997). For more anecdotes from organ transplant recipients and the connection to cellular memory, see Paul Pearsall, *The Heart's Code: Tapping the Wisdom and Power of Our Heart Energy* (Broadway Books, 1998).

**7.** Bruce Lipton, "The Biology of Perception" (video), 2005, www .youtube.com/watch?v=jjj0xVM4x1I.

**8.** Bruce Lipton, *The Biology of Belief: Unleashing the Power of Consciousness, Matter, & Miracles* (Hay House, 2007).

**9.** John E. Sarno, *Healing Back Pain: The Mind-Body Connection* (Grand Central Publishing, 1991), and *The Divided Mind: The Epidemic of Mindbody Disorders* (Harper Perennial, 2006).

**10.** Andrew Weil, *Health and Healing: The Philosophy of Integrative Medicine and Optimum Health* (Houghton Mifflin, 1983), 57.

**11.** Doris Rapp, *Is This Your Child?* (William Morrow, 1992), 62–63.

**12.** *Your Brain, A User's Guide: 100 Things You Never Knew, National Geographic,* special issue, 2012, p. 50.

**13.** This statement has been attributed to sources as diverse as the Talmud and Anaïs Nin, but regardless of its origin, this inspirational quote can now be viewed as a scientific fact.

**14.** Ibid.

**15.** As a side note, some people just need some information or instructions in order to take the next step toward success. Receiving counseling for information regarding career, relationships, and so on, is terrific— when individuals have no subconscious viruses regarding the issue, but just need more understanding.

**16.** Alexander Loyd with Ben Johnson, *The Healing Code* (Hachette, 2011), 123–124.

## CHAPTER 3

**1.** William Collinge, *Subtle Energy* (Warner Books, 1998), 2–3. Quoted in Donna Eden (with David Feinstein), *Energy Medicine* (Tarcher/ Penguin, 2008), 26.

**2.** "Cancer Cases Set to Rise by Half by 2030," Discovery News, February 4, 2014, http://news.discovery.com/human/health/cancer-cases-set-to-rise-by-half-by-2030-140204.htm.

**3.** 1 Corinthians 13.

**4.** Source: www.mahatmagandhionline.com/, accessed September 19, 2013.

**5.** Joanne V. Wood, W.Q. Elaine Perunovic, and John W. Lee, "Positive Self-Statements: Power for Some, Peril for Others," *Psychological Science* 20, 7 (2009): 860–866. Alex Loyd and Ben Jonson, *The Healing Code* (Hachette, 2011), 177.

**6.** According to Dr. Irving Kirsch of Harvard Medical School, "The difference between the effect of a placebo and the effect of an antidepressant is minimal for most people." He went on to clarify that it's not that antidepressants are ineffective, but their effectiveness comes from the placebo effect (the power of the belief in a positive untruth, that this pill will make me better), not the chemical ingredients in the drug. His research has also shown that the same is true for a number of other issues as well: irritable bowel syndrome, repetitive strain injury, ulcers, Parkinson's—even chronic knee pain. "Treating Depression: Is There a Placebo Effect?" *60 Minutes*, February 19, 2012, http://www.cbsnews.com/news/treating-depression-is-there-a-placebo-effect/.

**7.** Two double-blind studies out of Yale and the University of Colorado have indicated that "affirmations" can help close the gender and race gaps in academic achievement. If you state positive truths about yourself, it makes sense that your performance would improve, especially if you had been in a state of fear or stress previously. See Geoffrey L. Cohen et al., "Reducing the Racial Achievement Gap: A Social-Psychological Intervention," *Science* 313, 5791 (2006): 1307–1310; and A. Miyake et al., "Reducing the Gender Achievement Gap in College Science: A Classroom Study of Values Affirmation," *Science* 330, 6008 (2010): 1234–1237.

**8.** Caroline Leaf, *Who Switched Off My Brain? Controlling Toxic Thoughts and Emotions* (Thomas Nelson, 2009).

**9.** "About Lester," Lester Levenson website, www.lesterlevenson.org/about-lester.php. Levenson's student, Hale Dwoskin, developed a process called the Sedona Method. See his book *The Sedona Method: Your Key to Lasting Happiness, Success, Peace and Emotional Well-Being* (Sedona Press, 2007).

**10.** Eben Alexander, *Proof of Heaven: A Neurosurgeon's Journey into the Afterlife* (Simon & Schuster, 2012).

**11.** Diane Cameron, "Dose of 'Vitamin G' Can Keep You Healthy," *The Denver Post*, May 4, 2009, http://www.denverpost.com/search/ci_12281410. When I published my first book, *The Healing Code*, I received some criticism for connecting God and spirituality to health. Some assumed I had a religious agenda, which I don't. I do have another agenda, though—your health and happiness, and the health and happiness of everyone I can possibly help. I mention God in this context only because I have seen unmistakable evidence that a personal connection to God/source/love is the most powerful variable in our success and our health, and the scientific evidence proving that point is about to explode.

12. The conference was the Association for Comprehensive Energy Psychology. Paula E. Hartman-Stein, "Supporters Say Results Show Energy Psychology Works," *The National Psychologist*, July 24, 2013, http://nationalpsychologist.com/2013/07/supporters-say-results-show-energy-psychology-works/102138.html.

13. James Franklin on *The Dan Patrick Show*, January 14, 2014, http://www.danpatrick.com/dan-patrick-video/.

## CHAPTER 4

1. *Lombardi*, HBO Sports and NFL Films, originally aired on HBO, December 11, 2010.

## CHAPTER 5

1. It is also true that I believe prayer and being in a loving relationship with God/source/love are the most important things in my life. In my opinion, these supersede everything else I mention in this book. In fact, I believe they are the source of everything I've written in this book and everything of value I will learn in the future, which is why I always encourage everyone to give themselves the opportunity to receive the transformational *aha* before they try the Three Tools. That is not at all to say that you have to share my beliefs about God/source/love or prayer for these tools to work for you. You do not!

## CHAPTER 6

**1.** Donna Eden (with David Feinstein), *Energy Medicine* (Tarcher/Penguin, 2008), 23, 32, 76–78.

**2.** M. Andrew Holowchak, *Freud: From Individual Psychology to Group Psychology* (Rowman & Littlefield, 2012), chapter 2.

**3.** Dr. Mitsuo Hiramatsu, a scientist at the Central Research Laboratory at Hamamatsu Photonics in Japan, led a research team that discovered our hands emit more energy (in the form of light, or photons) than any other part of our body, as detected by a photon counter. In a study published in the *Journal of Photochemistry and Photobiology B: Biology*, they also noted that detectable photons are emitted by our foreheads and the bottoms of our feet. See Kimitsugu Nakamura and Mitsuo Hiramatsu, "Ultra-Weak Photon Emission from Human Hand: Influence of Temperature and Oxygen Concentration on Emission," *Journal of Photochemistry and Photobiology B: Biology* 80, 2 (August 1, 2005): 156–160; and Jennifer Viegas, Discovery News, September 6, 2005, www.abc.net.au/science/articles/2005/09/07/1455010.htm#.UaNAhLW1GCk.

## CHAPTER 7

**1.** Please forgive me. I have chosen to use the ungrammatical term "unforgiveness" throughout the book, rather than *Webster's* preferred "unforgivingness." Let the record show that my editors have properly advised me, but "unforgivingness" just didn't sound right to me.

**2.** Dan Gilbert, "Why Are We Happy? Why Aren't We Happy?" TED Talks (video), February 2004, https://www.youtube.com/watch?v=LTO_dZUvbJA#t=54.

## CHAPTER 8

**1.** Alexander Loyd with Ben Johnson, *The Healing Code* (Hachette, 2011), 63.

**2.** Ibid.

**3.** Rebecca Turner and Margaret Altemus, "Preliminary Research on Plasma Oxytocin in Normal Cycling Women: Investigating Emotion and Interpersonal Distress," *Psychiatry: Interpersonal and Biological Processes*, 62, 2 (July 1999): 97–113.

**4.** Sources: Cort A. Pedersen, University of North Carolina–Chapel Hill; Kerstin Uvnas Moberg, *The Oxytocin Factor: Tapping the Hormone of Calm, Love, and Healing* (Pinter & Martin, 2011).

## CHAPTER 10

**1.** "Facts and Statistics," Anxiety and Depression Association of America, www.adaa.org/about-adaa/press-room/facts-statistics.

**2.** For more about Dr. Peris's New England Centenarian Study, see www .bumc.bu.edu/centenarian.

**3.** Dan Gilbert, "The Surprising Science of Happiness," TED talk, April 26, 2012, www.youtube.com/watch?v=4q1dgn_C0AU.

## EPILOGUE

**1.** "75 Years in the Making: Harvard Just Released Its Epic Study on What Men Need to Live a Happy Life," FEELguide, April 29, 2013, http://www.feelguide.com/2013/04/29/75-years-in-the-making-harvard-just-released-its-epic-study-on-what-men-require-to-live-a-happy-life/. The full findings can be found in George Vaillant, *Triumphs of Experience: The Men of the Harvard Grant Study* (Belknap Press, 2012).

**2.** Diane Cameron, "Dose of 'Vitamin G' Can Keep You Healthy," *The Denver Post,* May 4, 2009, http://www.denverpost.com/search/ci_12281410. For more about neuroscientists Andrew Newberg and Mark Robert Waldman, and their book *How God Changes Your Brain,* see chapter 3.

**3.** For a list of all the effects of the failure/stress response (governed by the release of cortisol) and the success/love response (governed by the release of oxytocin), see the introduction and chapter 4.

**4.** Michka Assayas, *Bono: In Conversation with Michka Assayas* (Riverhead, 2005), 204–205.

# INDEX

## ABOUT THE AUTHOR

Alexander Loyd holds doctorates in psychology and naturopathic medicine. His private practice has become one of the largest of its kind in the world, with clients in 50 states and 158 countries (and counting), starting out of his basement with little money and no advertising. He believed that to truly resolve symptom issues in life, underlying spiritual issues had to be healed—and he developed a program to do that starting in 1988. Dr. Loyd has been interviewed live on ABC, NBC, CBS, Fox, and PBS news as an expert in healing the underlying source of success, relationship, and health problems. His first book, *The Healing Code*, is an international bestseller, currently in print in more than twenty-five languages.